BATTLE OF
THE GODS

BATTLE OF THE GODS

The Gathering Storm in Modern Evangelicalism

Dr. Robert A. Morey

Crown Publications
Southbridge, Massachusetts

Crown Publications, Inc.
P.O. Box 688
Southbridge, Massachusetts 01550

Printed in the United States of America.

Library of Congress Cataloging-in-Publication Data

Morey, Robert A., 1946-
    Battle of the gods.
    Bibliography: p.
1. God. 2. God — History of doctrines — 20th century. 3. Process theology — controversial literature. 4. Evangelicalism. I. Title.

ISBN 0-925703-00-1

ABOUT THE AUTHOR

D r. Morey is the author of nineteen books, some of which have been translated into Spanish, Italian, French, German, Finnish, and Chinese. He is the executive director of the Research and Education Foundation and has earned degrees in philosophy, theology, and cult apologetics. He is listed in *Contemporary Authors* and in the *International Authors And Writers Who's Who*. Some of his books include:

The New Atheism and the Erosion of Freedom

When Is It Right To Fight?

Death and the Afterlife

Horoscopes and the Christian

Reincarnation and Christianity

A Christian Handbook for Defending the Faith

How To Answer a Mormon

How To Answer a Jehovah's Witness

Worship Is All of Life

The Saving Work of Christ

The Bible and Drug Abuse

The Dooyeweerdian Concept of the Word of God

Is Sunday the Christian Sabbath?

To George Merisotis,
a man of grace,
a man of faith,
and a man of love

CONTENTS

PART IV: THE GOD OF CHRISTIAN THEOLOGY

ACKNOWLEDGMENTS

S pecial thanks to Helmus, Simon, Shenk, Pennay, and Blattenberger.

INTRODUCTION

One of the essential elements of the Christian Gospel is that the God of the prophets and the apostles is the *same* God in whom we believe today. What God was to Abraham, Isaiah, or Paul is *exactly* what He is to us today because He is the same yesterday, today, and forever in His being and attributes. His immutability is the very foundation of our confidence that God is forever our strength and our high tower.

But what if we took the view that God is constantly changing in His nature and attributes? What if He were too ignorant or impotent to help us? What if He were less than perfect and thus (or were) capable of making mistakes and even doing evil? What if God were only a finite god like Baal or Zeus? What if He were ignorant of the future and powerless before Luck or Chance? What if He were limited by space and time like us? Who could trust such a god!

There is a battle of the gods that rages all around us today in which the historic Christian conception of God is being challenged by new views of God. The most important issue of our times is the contest between the God who has revealed Himself in Scripture and modern gods that man has made in his own image. The battlelines are clearly drawn between those who accept the God revealed in Scripture and those who accept gods that man has made on the basis of his own reason, intuition, and feelings.

Some people might be tempted to think that the attributes of God have no bearing on daily life. But what we think about God is very important, because a direct relationship exists between what people think and how they live.

In Proverbs 23:7 we are told, "as [a man] thinks within himself, so he is." In other words, what we think directly affects what we do and say. Our understanding of God and His relationship to the world and to man has a direct bearing on our attitudes and actions.

This understanding is essential for a proper "self-image." The importance of a proper "self-image" is heralded on every radio/TV talk show and has fueled hundreds of pop-psychology books. But what is totally missed by the secularists is that no one can have a proper self-image unless he begins with a proper understanding of God. For example, if we view ourselves as "animals," we will live and die like them. But if we view ourselves as the image bearers of God, we will live differently. Wrong ideas about God will lead to wrong living just as surely as right ideas will lead to right living.

If someone believes that an infinite, all-knowing, and all-powerful God is holding him accountable for all his thoughts, words, and deeds, and that this God will sovereignly bring him into judgment one day, this will tend to curb his violent tendencies and dampen his lusts.

If, on the other hand, he believes that no ultimate accountability or judgment will occur because God does not exist, or that God is neither omniscient nor sovereign, or that we are all god or gods, then nothing really will curb his evil ways.

One of the main evidences of the Gospel is its power to transform sinners into saints. When someone begins to think about God as He has revealed Himself in Scripture, this will affect the way he thinks about himself and the world around him. This is "the truth that leads to godliness" (Titus 1:1).

Our understanding of God will inevitably determine how we view ourselves and how we treat others. But what we often fail to understand is that what is true on an individual level is frequently true on a corporate level. Units of people such as families, tribes, and nations will act according to what they think about God. Hitler's view of God, which he derived from Nietzsche (who authored the phrase "God is dead"), led the German nation to war and ruination. The slaughter of more than 150 million people by the Communists since 1914 is a direct result of their denial of the existence of God. The Muslim terrorist who blows up an airplane full of innocent people is simply acting out his wrong views of God. The self-centered egotism of New Agers is only an outworking of their claim that they are gods.

On the other hand, when a family, tribe, or nation adopts right views of God, the results are wonderful. Missionaries have witnessed "people movements" in which entire tribes have turned from cannibalism to Christ. In the past, entire nations have converted from paganism to Christianity. And, lest we think that such national conversions no longer happen, we need but point to South Korea, which will soon be the first Asian country to have a Christian majority.

The prosperity and standard of living of the West was elevated to unheard-of heights when it was Christianized. The liberation of slaves, the birth of modern science, the industrial revolution, and the rise of democratic forms of government all owe their origin to right views of God.

Indeed, the United States became great because the kind of God in which the Pilgrims believed supplied them with an infinite point of reference, by which they could judge right from wrong in an absolute way. Thus they could have absolute moral principles. They also believed that divine absolutes lay in every area of life. Science, history, the arts, economics, and politics were to be structured by the absolutes found in the Bible. This is why the Declaration of Independence traced human rights all the way back to the Creator who gave them. These absolutes in turn created the free market system, which has been the secret of America's prosperity.

While a special blessing has been bestowed upon those individuals, families, tribes, and nations whose God is the LORD (Psalm 33:12), the converse is also true. A special curse is upon those who forget God. In Psalm 9:17, we read,

> The wicked shall be turned into hell,
> and all the nations that forget God (NKJV).

The curse of God rests not only on apostate individuals but also on those families, tribes, and nations who turn away from the God who has revealed Himself in Scripture. As Paul warns us, "God is not mocked" (Galatians 6:7).

> How much sorer punishment, suppose ye, shall he be thought worthy, who hath trodden under foot the Son of God, and hath counted the blood of the covenant . . . an unholy thing, and hath done despite unto the Spirit of grace (Hebrews 10:29 KJV)?

This insight supplies us with the answer as to why Western culture is so radically evil today. In plain terms, the West has forgotten God and is on its way to hell. And with hell as its inspiration, Western culture's love affair with death cannot be described as anything less that a death wish. This is why it joyously embraces abortion, infanticide, mercy killing, euthanasia, and suicide.

The historic Christian conception of God supplied Western man with an Absolute rooted in an Infinite/Personal God who was both all-powerful and all-knowing. With God as an infinite absolute, it was possible to derive absolutes for every area of life. Thus man could judge in an absolute way right from wrong, good from evil, truth from falsehood, beauty from ugliness, and justice from tyranny. The Christian God supplied Western man with an Infinite reference point by which he could understand himself and the world around him.

When Western philosophers rejected the Christian conception of God, they automatically went on to deny the idea that anything or anyone was infinite. In that instant, they lost any sense of the Absolute. They viewed themselves as finite men living in a chance-caused finite universe. Nothing was infinite or absolute. Everything was relative. Truth was simply a lie not yet found out.

This explains why modern philosophy is suicidal. By stating no Truth is to be found and no Morals apply to life, it has effectively destroyed the only reason for its existence. The philosophy departments in most universities are headed by individuals who are radically antiphilosophy, antitruth, and antimorality. Existentialism with its situational ethics has produced nothing but despair and gloom.

Modern science has also received its kiss of death. When the Christian God was thrown out of science, the basis of science was also thrown out. Modern science now denies there is any scientific Truth to discover! Everything is relative, including science.

Physics is fast becoming an exercise in Eastern mysticism. Anthropology has become zoology as man has been reduced to a hairless ape. Biology has become so intertwined with the myth of evolution that no real science is possible.

Modern psychology is, for all practical purposes, virtually worthless. Studies reveal that people can solve their own problems more quickly without paying someone an hourly rate.

Historians no longer deal with historical evidences or objective facts but try to psychologize historical figures by telling us what someone *felt* when he did something. The attempt to "get inside" the heads of people long dead and to theorize about their hopes, fears, loves, and motives is not history but fiction passed off as history.

Modern art has become anti-art for the most part. In one New York City "art" exhibit, a reclining nude man was covered with pig entrails!

The ugliness of much of modern art is a reflection of modern views of God. Since no infinite God exists to serve as a reference point to distinguish beauty from ugliness, gross ugliness has become beauty.

What passes as music today would not have been recognized as such by our ancestors. The squeaks, squawks, hisses, and caterwauling that comprises much of modern music isn't even good enough to be played in an elevator!

Modern movies have turned morality upside down. Hollywood movies often have evil triumphing over good. The typical "hero" is as immoral and wicked as the "villain." In fact, both are antiheroes. The amount of blasphemy and profanity has reached new heights. Even G-rated movies that are supposed to be for children contain foul language.

The Saturday-morning cartoons are filled with wrong views of God. God is pictured as a finite deity such as He-Man, Isis, Thor, etc. Magic, witchcraft, satanism, and satanic rituals abound in them. They even picture such things as demon possession as a good thing! They indoctrinate more than entertain.

In politics, the Puritan vision of man's having been given inalienable rights by his Creator is no longer acknowledged. Justice cannot survive when it is not rooted in an infinitely just and holy God. Governments claim that they can either give or take away rights as they see best. Thus the Supreme Court ruled that millions of precious little boys and girls do not have even the right to life. The slaughter of the young, the old, the handicapped, and the unwanted is proclaimed as the "moral" thing to do by judges who view themselves as the origin of truth and morals.

All of this should not surprise us. Once God is rejected as the infinite origin of meaning, truth, justice, morality, and beauty, something or someone else has to take God's place. For many people today, the state has taken the place of God as the final judge of what is true or moral. Nothing is higher or greater than the government. Statism has thus become one of the greatest evils of our age.

In modern liberal, neo-orthodox, and neo-evangelical theology, the historic Christian conception of an infinite, all-knowing and all-powerful God has been replaced with a bumbling finite god who is ignorant of the future and powerless to do anything about evil. They view God as if He were a piece of putty that they can mold into whatever they want. God is reduced to an impersonal force, a finite god, or is multiplied into countless gods and goddesses.

The confusion among such theologians opened the Pandora's box of the cults and the occult. The rise of witchcraft, satanism, magic, astrology, and the New Age movement are all symptoms of the loss of the Infinite. With no infinite God to look up to, man must either look to the Devil, Mother Earth, ancient deities, or within himself for the answers to the riddles of life. But none of these things can provide a sufficient basis for truth or morals because they are in turn only finite particulars in search of an Infinite Absolute to explain them.

If we step back and look at Western culture as a whole, it is clearly drifting onto the shoals of destruction. Could it be that Western culture lost its Christian consensus when it cut itself loose from its moorings in the Christian conception of God? Is it possible that the paganism around us is simply a reflection of pagan views of God? Was it just a coincidence that after humanistic philosophy rejected the Christian conception of an infinite God who is all-knowing and all-powerful, the cancer of relativism began to destroy all of human knowledge? In short, could it be that the decadence and decay around us is a direct result of the loss of the historic Christian conception of God?

In order to answer these questions we must rediscover the the God who has revealed Himself in Scripture. Then we can judge truth from error in philosophy and science, what is moral and immoral in ethics, and what is justice and tyranny in politics. Only by understanding where and why Western culture lost its Christian base can we ever have any hope of rebuilding it.

PART ONE

THE GODS OF
THE HEATHEN

ONE

THE GATHERING STORM

Process theology is the most dangerous heresy presently threatening the Christian Faith. Process thought is a total capitulation to paganism.

Ronald Nash

One of the key elements of Biblical wisdom is the ability to foresee evil and to deliver yourself from it (Proverbs 27:12). Today's gathering storm of controversy over the nature and attributes of God will touch the lives of all who claim to be Christians.

This controversy involves Roman Catholics as well as Protestants, Fundamentalists as well as Charismatics, Evangelicals and Neo-evangelicals, Calvinists and Arminians. The nature of God is so utterly fundamental to everything else in life that anything that touches upon it must be viewed as having supreme importance.

Processianism

Process theology (or processianism) teaches that the infinite God of historic Christianity is a myth. In its place is erected a finite god who is incapable of knowing or controlling the future because he is not omniscient, omnipotent, perfect, immutable, or, in some cases, omnipresent.

The finite god of processianism is trapped in a chance-driven universe that is out of his control. He himself is caught up in an on-going process and is evolving in his nature toward an unknown future. Only time will tell what this god will end up being.

Some processians go so far as to say that this god can fail, make mistakes, and is even capable of doing evil. But we can't blame god for

9

failing because he is dealing with a recalcitrant universe and has to cope day by day with unforeseen developments. After all, he is only finite.

Now the reader may be thinking that only some far-out cultist would believe in such a god. In fact, this used to be the case. Beyond the secular philosophers, the Jehovah's Witnesses have been the most aggressive religious body to teach openly the concept that god does not know the future and thus he is not omniscient, omnipotent, or omnipresent.[1] The concept of a finite god or gods is also a part of Mormonism, Armstrongism, and frequently appears in New Age material.

What is little known is that since the turn of the century mainline liberal universities, colleges, and seminaries have been teaching a finite god. Alfred North Whitehead at Harvard (Unitarian) and John Brightman at Boston University (United Methodist) are examples of this.

Today, the concept of a finite god is standard fare at such liberal seminaries as Princeton, Union, Emory, etc. Some of the chief spokesmen are Charles Hartshorne, Schubert Ogden, David Griffin, Norman Pittenger, H. P. Owen, John Cobb, Jr., Nelson Pike, and Lewis Ford.

The Storm Begins

As long as finite godism remained within cultic, liberal, and neo-orthodox circles, it did not pose a threat to evangelical Christianity. But several things have happened to bring processianism into evangelical circles.

First, there has been a growing denial of the inerrancy and authority of the Bible in evangelical circles.[2] The history of theology reveals that whenever the authority of the Bible is denied, human reason takes its place. The end result is always some kind of rationalism. This always leads to finite godism because man becomes "the measure of all things" including God.

In contrast to this, the historic Christian conception of God, according to such processians as David Griffin,

> clearly presupposes an outdated conception of the Bible, seeing it in terms of inerrant inspiration and verbal revelation.[3]

Those who bow before the authority of the Bible have no difficulty in accepting the Biblical teaching that God knows everything, including the future. But those who exalt human reason as the final authority always end up reducing God to the finite span of the human mind. As we shall see in a later chapter, the chief spokesmen for finite godism in evangelical circles clearly reject the inerrancy and authority of Scripture.

Second, for the past twenty-five years processian theologians have been slowly infiltrating evangelical, charismatic, and Reformed colleges, seminaries, and mission societies. It is only recently that some of them have publicly denied the historic Christian conception of God and openly taught the concept of a struggling finite god who is ignorant of the future.[4]

The Neo-Evangelicals

Processianism is thus now being taught in many places once considered "evangelical." For example, Anderson College and the seminary of the Church of God (Anderson, Ind.) have both allowed processianism to be taught. Azusa Pacific University and McMaster Divinity College have had professors who deny the historic Christian conception of God and teach in its place some kind of finite deity.

Those who teach finite godism do not always agree with each other or with processianism in every detail. Some of them will claim that they are not really processians because they do not agree with this or that minor detail. But the core belief of processianism is the idea that God is limited in power and knowledge and thus *cannot* know or control the future. A low view of Scripture is also a common element.

One of the spokesmen for finite godism in evangelical circles is Clark Pinnock, who has clearly stated, "I stand against classical theism."[5]

Pinnock identifies himself with liberal processian theologians who have rejected the inerrancy and authority of the Bible.[6] As a committed rationalist, he is quite open about his denial of the omniscience, omnipotence, immutability, perfection, infinitude, and timelessness of God.[7] We shall look in depth at Pinnock's theology in Chapter 7.

In 1983, an evangelical publishing house released Stephen Davis's book, *Logic and the Nature of God*.[8] Davis clearly rejects the inerrancy and authority of Scripture and is a committed rationalist.

Davis is more honest than most processians and is not afraid to shock the Christian public with such outlandish statements as,

- It is possible for God to do evil (p. 3)
- God is able to do evil (p. 86)

- God *can* sin (p. 88)

Davis goes on to argue that unless God is capable of committing such sins as lying, he is not worthy of our praise! (pp. 95f.) He concludes by saying,

- God has the ability to tell a lie (p. 96)
- God has the ability to break a promise (p. 96)

It doesn't take a Ph.D. in Greek to see that what Davis is saying is a flat contradiction of the Word of God, which states,

- God cannot lie (Titus 1:2)
- It is impossible for God to lie (Hebrews 6:18)
- God cannot be tempted by evil (James 1:13)

We will give a detailed treatment of Davis in a later chapter.

Moral Government Theology

Not only have the processians made inroads among evangelicals, but they have also become influencial in traditional Wesleyan Arminian circles. They are teaching a concept of god that would have been viewed as heresy by both Arminius and Wesley.[9]

In this new view, sometimes called "moral government," God is reduced to a finite deity who is neither omnipotent nor omniscient. God is limited like man in that He cannot control or know the future. It is claimed that if we reduce God to a finite deity, this will solve the problem of evil. As we shall see later, the problem of evil is always the bait on the hook of processianism.

Arminianism has traditionally taught that divine election is based on God's foreknowledge of man's faith.[10] The idea that God is ignorant of the future has been repeatedly rejected by the classic Arminian theologians.

Since the Arminian doctrine of election is based on God's foreknowledge, if that foreknowledge be denied, the entire system of Arminianism comes tumbling down like a house of cards. In this sense, "moral government" teachers are no more "Arminian" than Pinnock is "evangelical."

"Moral government" concepts have penetrated such mission-minded groups as Youth With a Mission, Bethany Fellowship, Men For Missions, Last Days' Ministries, Omaha Lutheran Bible School, and Agape Force, according to Alan Gomes, who is instructor of historical theology at Talbot School of Theology.[11]

Gomes fully documents that while "moral government" is not the "official" view of any of these groups, they have allowed the doctrine to be taught in their organizations. "Moral government" spokesmen are often involved in the training classes of such groups. Their books are sold in their bookstores and used as textbooks for various classes. Thus while "moral government" is nowhere put down on paper as the "official" view, it is clearly being taught to the young people who thought they were coming to an evangelical organization.

It is understood that these men do not agree with one another on every point and may disagree with process thought on certain points. It may be the case that some of them do not even understand the full doctrinal implications of what they are teaching. For example, the doctrine of the Trinity is not compatible with processianism. But the "camel's nose under the tent" is the idea that God *cannot* know the future. Once this is granted, all the attributes of God, including His triune nature, must be radically redefined.

Some of the "moral government" teachers who have been involved in Youth With a Mission are Winkie Pratney, Harry Conn, Howard Roy Elseth,[12] George Otis, Jr., and Gordon C. Olson.[13] An evangelical publisher has recently published a book by Seventh-Day Adventist Richard Rice, which clearly teaches processianism.[14] It can be found in Christian bookstores all over the world.

Alan Gomes is not alone in his concern over what is being taught in YWAM. Walter Martin's Christian Research Institute, the foremost cult-watch organization, has sounded the warning that YWAM is teaching,

> doctrinal aberrations concerning the nature and certain attributes of God and the Pelagian heresy.[15]

Clark Pinnock, one of the present champions of "moral government" teaching, also documents that Gordon Olson, Roy Elseth, and Richard Rice agree with his denial of the omnipotence, omniscience, immutability, and perfection of God.[16]

Gomes carefully documents that such YWAM leaders as Roy Elseth and Gordon Olson teach that God can sin; that God does not know or control the future; that God is not working out His plan in the world; that God does not have to keep His word or fulfill His promises.[17] Gomes goes on to document from their books and training manuals that they also deny the historic Christian doctrines of original sin, the necessity and the vicarious nature of the atonement, the imputation of Christ's righteousness in justification, and a host of other doctrines!

We acknowledge that some moral government people are no doubt sincere individuals who are "saved" and who "love the Lord." We have no desire to judge their hearts. But we must judge their theology in obedience to the command of Scripture (Titus 1:9-16). While we admire their sincerity and evangelistic zeal, they are doing much damage to the cause of God and truth. The faith of many young people has been devastated by the concept of a finite god who is ignorant and impotent in the face of evil.

This view of God is not a part of evangelical theology, whether Calvinistic or Arminian. It flows out of Alfred North Whitehead's process theology, which is sheer paganism. As we will later document, both Pinnock and Rice admit their dependence on Whitehead. There is sufficient cause to be alarmed.

The Charismatics and Processianism

Traditional charismatics have been shocked to find people in their circles teaching the idea that we are "little gods" who can speak our own worlds into being. As Dave Hunt put it,

> What seems most significant is the fact that only a few years ago Christians would have gotten up and walked out on anyone who tried to suggest to them that they were gods. This no longer seems to be the case.[18]

What has escaped most of the authors on the subject of the New Age Movement is that processianism is the philosophic basis of New Age thinking. Before a man can think of himself as a god, God has to be first thought of as a finite being. The idea of "god" as a finite being evolving toward divinity is the theoretical link between processianism, liberalism, New Thought, the New Age Movement, and charismatic godism.

When Hunt pointed out that such charismatic leaders as Casey Treat, Bill Volkman, Frederick Price, Robert Tilton, Kenneth Copeland, John Lake, Earl Paulk, and a host of other men were now teaching that man is a "god," he meant a *finite* god and not the Almighty Himself. Without the idea that god can be finite, no one can think of himself as a god.

Conclusion

The concept that God is a finite deity is slowly working its way into evangelical circles. Some pick up this concept through process philosophy. Others hear of the idea through "moral government." Some come into contact with it in the "positive confession" movement. Others pick it up in the New Age Movement. But the end result in each case is always the same. The god they believe in is no longer the infinite GOD of the Bible.

This then is the issue before us. Is the God who has revealed Himself in Scripture all-knowing, all-powerful, everywhere present, perfect, immutable, and sovereignly in control of history? Can any God less than that be worthy of the name GOD?

TWO

THE GOD-MAKERS

The Bible tells us that Satan is real and that he has been man's enemy from the very beginning. The Devil described in the Bible is a very shrewd and intelligent being. In fact, he is far too smart for man to defeat on his own. Satan's intellect is so vastly superior to our puny brains that he can outsmart us every time.

We are told in Scripture that he was originally created a beautiful angelic being named Lucifer (Isaiah 14:12-14). He was probably an archangel like Michael and Gabriel. But he fell into the sin of pride, according to the Apostle Paul in 1 Timothy 3:6.

Did God Make the Devil?

When someone asks the question "Why did God make the Devil?", he is assuming that Satan started out as an evil being. But God did not originally make an evil being called Satan or the Devil. God made a good angel named Lucifer who had the ability to obey Him. But Lucifer misused this ability and rebelled against God. Thus Lucifer made himself into the Devil.

In Isaiah 14:12-14 we are told that Satan boasted that he could become equal to God. He claimed that God was not any better or greater than he was. The qualitative and quantitative distinction between the Creator and the creature vanished the moment he claimed, "I will make myself like God."

The God of the Bible is "better" than the creature because He alone is divine in His being and attributes. And God is "greater" than the creature, for He alone is infinite in His being and attributes. When a creature claims equality with God, he is actually denying that God is better or greater than he.

In order for a finite creature to think of himself as equal to God one of two things must happen. The creature must think either that he is as infinite and perfect as God, or that God is as finite and imperfect as he. The creature must raise himself up to the infinite level of God, or God must be brought down to the finite level of the creature.

It is impossible for a finite being who is painfully reminded every day of his finite limitations and imperfections to convince himself that he is infinite, perfect, immutable, omniscient, omnipotent, omnipresent, and sovereign. The mere act of stubbing one's toe tends to dispel such delusions of grandeur.

In short, as long as God is viewed as infinite, the idea that a finite creature is or can become equal to God is impossible. But what if God is reduced to a finite, imperfect, fallible being? What if it is claimed that God is no different from any other finite, imperfect, fallible being, angelic or human? What if God is limited by the space-time universe in the same ways as all other finite creatures? The creature can then begin to entertain delusions of grandeur that he can be or is equal to God.

The Master Plan of Satan

This is the exact ploy used by Satan on Adam and Eve. An examination of the conversation between Satan and man in Genesis 3 reveals several things:

First, Satan began by denying that God was that infinite, immutable, sovereign, all-powerful, and all-knowing good God man had assumed Him to be. When the Devil posed the question, "Has God said . . . ?," he was actually attacking the infinite and perfect nature of God. In effect, Satan argued,

What's the real meaning behind what God said? I know what you've assumed, but I'm going to tell you what the real truth is. Now, God doesn't want you to know about this because He has been lying to you all along. Yes, God can lie! You must abandon any infinite and perfect views of God because an infinite God can tell you what to do and what not to do. He can even can punish you if you disobey Him. You would have to serve an infinite deity. You must be free of such a God. Instead, I want you to look upon God as your equal. He is not greater or better than you. God is only a finite being who is as mutable and limited in power and in knowledge as you. Once you see this, you will know that you can't trust God anymore because He is not immutably good or perfect. Who does this God think He is? Some omnipotent, omniscient, omnipresent being? Hogwash! God is simply a finite limited being just like you. Thus He has no right to push you around. The truth is that you can do whatever you want to do. You can know what you want to know. You can be whatever you want to be. Ignore this huffing and puffing deity who has delusions of grandeur. You can know, be, and do anything you want. You are your own god.

In Genesis 3, Satan began his temptation by raising doubts about God's nature and character. He began by whittling God down to the level of finite being. God was not immutably good or perfect, because He was keeping man from his full potential. God knew that if man ate from the forbidden tree man would become a god equal to Him. Thus God lied when He told man that he would die if he ate of the fruit. If God is not immutably good or perfect, then He cannot be infinite in knowledge. Thus God does not know the future. So, how could He know that man would die?

Freedom from God

Along with a finite view of God, the Devil introduced the classic humanistic concept of absolute freedom from God. Satan urged man to break free from God and His Law. He told man to do whatever *he* wanted to do. If God interfered in any way, then man was not "really" free. To Satan and his cronies, freedom only means one thing: freedom from the God who made them.

The issue of human freedom has perplexed the minds of philosophers since time immemorial. But the issue boils down to one central issue: Does man have *limited* or *absolute* freedom? Can the God who made man limit his freedom in any way? Is man limited by the Law of God? Does revelation limit man? Is he limited by his own nature? Does society and the world itself limit man?

The Christian turns to the Scriptures for an answer to these questions. And when we open the Bible we find that it begins with the doctrine that man has *limited* freedom. Nowhere in Scripture is man said to have the absolute freedom that humanistic philosophy teaches. Man is not "free" from God to be, do, or know whatever he wants to be, do, or know. The God who made man limits man by His own Law and Word. Man is limited by his own finite and fallen nature, human society, and the world around him.

In Genesis 2 and 3, the word "free" appears for the first time. Man is said to be "free" in a very limited sense. And when we examine all the passages of Scripture that use such words as "free," "freedom," "liberty," etc., we find the same meaning.

We are "liberated" and "freed" from sin unto obedience to God. There is no concept of being "freed" from God in the Bible.

- Freedom: John 8:32, 33, 36; Romans 6:7, 18-22; Galatians 5:1

- Liberty: Romans 8:21; 2 Corinthians 3:17; Galatians 2:4; 5:1, 13

This important insight can be used to judge whether an author is a humanist or a Christian. If the author is a Christian thinker, he will seek to answer such questions as the nature of human freedom by exegeting Scripture. The exegetical issues are these: Is God free? In what sense is He free? What about the angels and the saints in heaven? Are they free? What about man after the resurrection? In what sense will he be free? Where in the Bible is man's freedom spoken of? In what sense does the Bible speak of freedom? Is man limited by God, His Law, and His Word?

Instead of exegeting Scripture, *humanistic* thinkers begin by assuming that they can answer such questions on the basis of their own finite reason, experience, and intuition. In so doing, they have already assumed that man is "free" from God in an absolute sense. Thus man can be, do, and know whatever he wants. No one, not even God, can interfere or stop him. Man in effect becomes his own god.

The story of the Fall in the book of Genesis revolves around the issue of whether man's freedom is absolute or limited. Did God create man to be free from God? Or, was man limited by God's Truth and God's Law from the very beginning?

Limited Freedom

The Bible begins with the truth that man is not his own god. Thus man does not have the absolute freedom to be, do, or know whatever he wants. Man is a finite being created to glorify the God who made him. Thus he is not free to *be* anything other than what God wants him to be. He is not free to *do* anything other than what God commands him to do. He is not free to *know* anything other than what God wants him to know.

The Scriptural fact that God told man to dress and keep the garden means that man was limited to do what God wanted him to do. When God told him not to eat of the tree of the knowledge of good and evil, this meant that man was limited to know what God wanted him to know. The God who made man tells him what to do and what not to do. Thus from the very first chapters of the Bible we learn that man's freedom is *limited* by the God who made him.

> And the Lord God commanded the man, saying "From any tree of the garden *you are free* to eat; but from the tree of the knowledge of good and evil you shall not eat, for in the day that you eat from it you shall surely die" (Genesis 2:16-17, emphasis added).

When God told Adam, "You are *free*," the context cannot mean anything other than a freedom limited by God. Man was "free" to obey God but not to disobey God. He was "free" to eat only of those trees that God appointed. Man was told that he was not "free" to eat of the forbidden fruit.

A contrast between what God said in Genesis 2 and what Satan said in Genesis 3 is highly instructive (see Table 2.1 on next page).

The Master Plan

Satan attempted to accomplish two things when he tempted man in the Garden of Eden:

1. To bring God down to the level of man
2. To raise man up to the level of God

These two points in Satan's master plan are the foundational concepts of all pagan religions. It does not matter if we examine Eastern or Western paganism; in both cases God is lowered to the level of man and man is raised to the level of God.

The greatest barrier to Satan's master plan has been the Biblical concept that God is qualitatively and quantitatively distinct from the finite world He made out of nothing. There is only one infinite/personal and eternal God who is the immutable, perfect, omniscient, omnipotent, and holy Creator of the universe and judge of mankind.

Table 2.1: God's View of Freedom Verses Satan's	
God's View (Genesis 2)	**Satan's View (Genesis 3)**
Limited Freedom	*Absolute Freedom*
Man is at liberty to do what is right, just, and true. He may eat of any of the trees God set aside for him. But he is not free to do evil, or to disobey God. Man is not free to eat of any tree he wants in an absolute sense. It is not up to man to decide what fruit he may eat. The Creator has limited man by the nature He gave him in His Law/Word. Man's limited freedom is true freedom. Absolute freedom is a lie of Satan. To do evil is never freedom. It is not "liberty" but "license." It is not "freedom" but "slavery." True freedom is the ability to serve and glorify God. It is a gift of God's grace and a work of the Holy Spirit.	Man must have absolute freedom to do *whatever* he chooses, right or wrong, good or evil. God cannot restrain this absolute freedom in any way. When God denied man the freedom to eat of just one tree, absolute freedom to choose was denied. A limited freedom is only an illusion. God has no right to tell man what he may or may not do. By what right does God limit man's freedom of choice by limiting his options? Who says man can't eat of any tree he chooses to eat? Man is not limited by God, the world, human society, or his created or fallen nature. True freedom is independence from God: His power, knowledge, Law and Revelation. Man is absolutely free by nature or he is not free at all.

The Biblical idea of God forever spoils man's attempt to think of himself as a god. As long as people think of God as infinite and of themselves as finite, they cannot think of themselves as gods or parts of God.

This is why pagans have always been so anxious for people to think of God as a finite deity limited by time and space. Once God becomes a finite god, then the idea of finite man's being or becoming a finite god is not difficult. But if God is infinite, the idea of finite man's becoming an infinite God is ludicrous. The "omni" or infinite attributes of God stand in the way of all attempts to deify man.

We now face a coalition of pagan and occult groups and movements who all demand that Christians give up their concept of an infinite/personal God and adopt a finite god instead. Some of those who are calling for a finite and limited deity include liberal and neo-orthodox theologians, "God is dead" theologians; process thinkers; New Agers; witches; sorcerers; neo-pagans; Jehovah's Witnesses; Mormons; Armstrongites; Druids; Mother-Earth worshipers; yoga teachers; gurus; psychics; mediums; fortune tellers; radical feminists; human potential movements; and Eastern religions such as Zen-Buddhism, Hinduism, and Hare Krishna.

Now it is no surprise to us when cultists and pagans attack the infinite/personal God of Christianity. But we are shocked when we find the same pagan arguments against the Christian concept of God being taught in "evangelical" schools and mission societies. Evidently some "evangelicals" feel more comfortable with a finite pagan god than with the infinite God of historic and Biblical Christianity!

Since the confessional position of evangelical theology, be it Reformed, Lutheran, Arminian, or Anabaptist, is the historic Christian concept of an infinite God who knows all things including the future, anyone who teaches the concept of a finite god who is ignorant of the future has no right to call himself an "evangelical." The same is true for those who wish to be accepted as "evangelical," but who deny the inerrancy of Scripture.

While the names have changed, the same old heresies have resurfaced. What was known as "Gnosticism" in the first century, "Socinianism" in the sixteenth century, and "New Thought" in the nineteenth century is now called "process theology," "moral government," and "positive confession" in the twentieth century! Some Christians have foolishly accepted a "new" concept of god that in reality is nothing more an old heresy under a new label.

Idolatry

In order for idolatry to work, God's nature and attributes must be determined by *man's* nature and attributes. This is why humanistic theology always begins with man and then proceeds to God while the authors of Scripture always begin with God and then proceed to man (see Genesis 1:1).

The Bible clearly states that it is a grievous error to imagine that God is limited by what limits man. Psalm 50:21 says that it is wrong to imagine that God can be reduced to the level of man. Such an idea is deemed blasphemy by God Himself. We should not assume that God cannot be any greater or better than man. In Numbers 23:19 we are told not to assume that man is the measure of God. Just because man is capable of lying does not mean that God is likewise capable. Isaiah 55:8-9 declares that an infinite gulf lies between God and man. They are altogether different from each other in quality and quantity. Just because man's thoughts and ways are limited by space and time does not mean that God is likewise limited.

Once God is reduced to a finite being like man, there is no reason to assume that there is only one God. The belief in one God arose from the idea that since God was infinite, there was only enough room for one God in the universe. But if God is finite, then there is plenty of room for many gods. As we shall see, the finite god theory always ends in some kind of polytheism.

Since the gods were finite and limited like man, these gods were viewed as male and female deities. This led to the worship of male and female gods like Diana, Zeus, Jupiter, Isis, Thor, Adonis, Osiris, etc. Even political leaders such as the Pharaohs and the Caesars claimed divinity and demanded worship.

But man was not content to worship human gods. He descended the ladder of corruption and worshiped animals that were lower than man (Romans 1:23). The ancients worshiped such animals as bulls, goats, crocodiles, cats, dogs, storks, owls, and peacocks.

Then they sank even lower and worshiped insects, snakes, frogs, and turtles (Romans 1:23). The King James translation says "creeping things," and this refers to anything that crawls on the ground. Besides snakes, lizards, and turtles, this includes such insects as beetles, flies, and lice. It is interesting to note that the ten plagues of Egypt were attacks on the gods of the Egyptians, which included flies, frogs, and lice.

At last they sank to the bottom of the barrel of existence and worshiped impersonal things or principles such as Yin/Yang, positive/negative, male/female, the spark of life, universal energy, the Force, and cosmic energy. Man, who is a cognitive ego, a being who is self-conscious and can say, "I am," ends up worshiping an impersonal deity, an "it," that does not even know that "it" exists—an "it" that cannot know, feel, or love mankind! Such an "it" is inferior to man and thus is not worthy of the name or the worship of God. Surely the Apostle Paul was right to call this foolishness (Romans 1:21).

The Motives Behind Idolatry

Why does man engage in such absurdities? Why does he strive to be a god-maker and to be a god himself? What are the motives that fuel man's thinking?

First, the more God is limited, the more man is unlimited. God must be limited in order to give man unlimited power to be, do, and know whatever he wants. Thus the same groups that champion a finite god usually talk about the "infinite potential" of man. Having robbed God of His divinity, they have no hesitation in proclaiming the divinity of man!

Second, if God is no longer the sovereign Lawgiver, man is the creator of his own laws and rules.

Third, sinful man is threatened by an infinite Almighty God who is everywhere present and who knows all things. But there is nothing to fear from a finite god.

Fourth, the more we "lower" God, the "higher" we can raise man. We can have a better self-image if we dump the infinite God. We must reject the idea that we are sinners who will be judged one day.

Fifth, man can control the gods he makes. He can make this god do whatever he wants. This god will serve man instead of man serving God!

Sixth, man can fully comprehend and precisely explain the gods he makes. There is no need for mysteries and no need for faith. Finite gods are explainable and comprehensible for they are made by man. But the infinite triune God who is omniscient, omnipotent, omnipresent, eternal, immutable, and perfect in His being and attributes, cannot be fully comprehended by man's mind. The infinite God surpasses man's understanding. Therefore, He must go.

Seventh, man can instruct his homemade deities. These gods are ignorant and need the wisdom of *man*. Man can instruct his gods as to what is true, just, moral, or beautiful. Man can judge the gods and declare one good and another evil on the basis of standards dictated by man himself.

Eighth, man can be free from any rude interventions from manmade gods. While the Biblical God intervenes and interferes with man's plans by acts of sovereign judgment or mercy, manmade gods are impotent as well as ignorant. They await man's call into action. They do not take initiative or interfere with man, for man is Lord.

Ninth, these gods are assigned to only those tasks that man cannot perform at this point. But as soon as man evolves into a greater being, the gods will be limited and reduced until they have no function.

Tenth, no credit, glory, or thanks need be given to manmade gods. The good things in life are due to man's skill or blind luck. All the evil things are either the fault of the gods or blind luck.

Eleventh, we do not have to seek or obey God's will for our lives, for the gods created by man don't have a will, plan, or counsel for man's life. The gods themselves are controlled by blind chance. They must wait for the "roll of the dice" to see what tomorrow will bring.

Twelfth, history is not "His-story," following a predetermined plan of God with the victory of justice over evil guaranteed. History is controlled by luck, chance, and man. A finite god cannot control anything, not even His own destiny! The wicked may win in the end. There is no assurance of anything because there is no predetermined salvation or judgment.

How To Make a God

If we decide that we are no longer comfortable with the Christian concept of God, what are the steps we must follow in order to make a god that satisfies our personal tastes?

First, we must reject the inerrancy and authority of the Bible. After all, we cannot really be "free" if we allow God to limit us through His Word.

Second, we must set ourselves up as the "measure of all things," including God.

Third, we must create a god in our own image with all our limitations. After all, god cannot do what we cannot do. Thus god must be limited by our experience. Since we are limited by space-time and cannot predict or control the future, then neither can god. Whatever limits us must limit god.

Fourth, whatever god we make must "be in accord with human reason" and "meet the demands of reason." No infinite mysteries are allowable. Our mind must be capable of fully comprehending all there is to know about this god because he, she, or it is no greater than the finite span of our mind.

Fifth, our new god must also agree with our "intuitions" and "feelings." A manmade god must exist only to make us happy and never sad. We must not make a god who will turn around and judge us. An impersonal god is always a favorite among humanists because who fears an "it."

Sixth, we reserve the right to redesign our god when a need arises. We have to make god "relevant" to modern people. We must sand off the rough edges and streamline god by dumping any offensive attributes. If a skeptic doesn't like some aspect of god, we are free to omit the point of controversy. Anything goes when it comes to manmade deities.

Seventh, modern theologians have paved the way for us by changing god from:

- Infinite to finite
- Omniscient to ignorant
- Omnipotent to impotent
- Omnipresent to localized
- Immutable to mutable
- Perfect to imperfect
- One to many
- Good to evil
- Invisible to visible
- Male to female
- Personal to impersonal
- Living to dead
- Sovereign to slave

Just as General Motors puts out new car models every year, we can put out "new" gods. We can even claim that this new god is "newer" and hence "better" than the Christian God because it is in accord with the latest human reason, experience, and intuition.

Conclusion

As we face a multitude of man-made gods today, Christians must be resolute and uncompromising about idolatry. The finite god of processianism is not the God of the Bible (Jeremiah 10:1-16). Such gods are only the projections of the hopes and fears of a fallen humanity that is running from its Maker as fast as it can. The ultimate source of all idolatry is the Prince of Darkness, to whom all idolatrous worship is given (1 Corinthians 10:20). The choice is clear. Do we accept God as He has revealed Himself in Scripture, or do we construct some kind of god that conforms to our personal tastes and become idolators?

THREE

THE GODS OF
THE PEOPLE

Is there only one God or are there many? What do you say to someone who believes in many gods? How do you respond to those who claim that they are gods? What can you tell a Hindu, a Buddhist, or a Mormon that will lead him to give up his belief in many gods and accept the one true God revealed in Scriptures?

These questions are important today as there are now *millions* of polytheists in the West. For the first time since the Early Church, Christians must now *prove* that monotheism is better than polytheism. We can no longer assume that people believe in only one God. Christians today must learn how to refute polytheism.

This chapter is the first major effort in this direction since the time of the early Church. God has been pleased to use the material given here to cause Eastern pagans and Western cultists to turn from their idols and to worship and serve the one true God.

Let us begin by reviewing how the early Christians triumphed over the polytheism of their day.

First-century Polytheism

The ancient world was filled with a bewildering array of gods and goddesses. The early Greeks believed that the earth, air, fire, and water were actually deities. It was believed among the Germanic tribes that the gods lived in oak trees and one "knocked on wood" to ask them for good luck. Animals, insects, and even man were often elevated to divinity and worshiped.

As to how many gods existed, no one knew because as the old gods were dying off, new gods were being born. The hierarchy or order of the gods was just as uncertain, as the gods fought among themselves as to who was their chief.

At times, the gods were viewed as personal demons who could possess people. These spirits or demons were constantly on hand either to bless or vex one's life. Socrates, the greatest of the Greek philosophers, claimed to receive philosophic ideas from a demon who spoke to him during trances.

While the names of the gods and goddesses changed from nation to nation, they were basically the same. The *forces* of nature such as the seasons, wind, fire, and the thunder and lightning of storms were deified. Others were deifications of *parts* of nature such as the sun, moon, and the stars. Some aspect of the world was raised to the level of divinity and worshiped.

Some of the gods were obviously the deification of some *part* or *power* of man. Man's "reason" became the god "Nous" or Mind. His love became the gods Eros, Cupid, and Venus. His sexual procreative powers were turned into fertility religions, whose temples filled the ancient world. Human society was deified as the head of state became a deity. It was in this sense that a Pharoah, king, or Caesar would proclaim himself a god.

Polytheism and Christianity

The gods of Greece and Rome are of special interest to us as they form the cultural and religious background of the evangelism of the early Christians. In the midst of a raging sea of polytheism, the Church championed the concept of one eternal God existing in three equal persons.

To the average Greek or Roman, the Christian God was a barbaric concept that came from the Jews. It was not proper to go around putting down other people's religions and claiming that your God was the *only* true God.

In addition to this, belief in the Christian God was viewed as *atheism* for it denied the existence of the official gods of the state including the Emperor. When the Christians refused to worship the Emperor as a god, this was viewed as a civil crime punishable by death.

Yet, despite all the odds against the Christian Church, the Church triumphed over the ancient world and relegated the gods and goddesses to obscurity. Pagan temples were changed into Christian churches as the people turned from their idols to worship and serve the one true God (1 Thessalonians 1:9-10).

Why did the people give up the gods of their fathers and convert to a foreign religion? How did monotheism conquer polytheism? What were the fatal defects in the system of polytheism that led to its ultimate demise? What was *superior* about the Christian God that made Him *better* than the gods?

The average first century pagan was not bothered by abstract reasoning and abstruse arguments. He saw that Christianity was *superior* to his religion. The Gospel *worked* in a *superior* way. It was *better* than the dumb idols worshiped by his fathers. And, even though it might mean his death, he accepted the God who had revealed Himself in Scripture as the one true GOD.

The gods and goddesses fell into ruin because polytheism could not provide man with a sufficient basis for truth, justice, morals, beauty, order, meaning, dignity, or significance. The gods were not capable of giving man anything worthy of belief or obedience. Even the way the gods lived was worthy only of the utmost disgust and contempt. In short, the religion of the gods was unbelievable, unlivable, and unbearable. Gene Wolfe's novel, *Soldier of the Mist*,[1] gives a good picture of what it was like to live under the old paganism.

The Gods Were Finite

The main problem with the gods was that they were *finite* in power and knowledge. Thus they could not serve as an infinite reference point to give meaning to life. Because they were finite, they could not generate any moral absolutes or universals. Since the gods were many, they could not give *one* law or *one* truth for *all* mankind. Each god had his or her own idea of what was true, just, or moral. Thus the gods were in a constant state of chaos, confusion, and conflict.

The failure of the gods to give a unified, coherent, consistent, and cohesive philosophy of life to man resulted in relativism and confusion among men as well as among the gods.

The early Christians challenged paganism with such questions as:

- Since the gods are *fallible*, how can they give *infallible* truth or morals?
- Seeing they are *imperfect*, how can they give man *perfect* laws to live by?
- Because they are *mutable*, who can trust them?

- Since they are not immutably *true*, how can they be trusted to tell man the *truth*?

- Since the gods are *immoral*, how then can they serve as the basis of *morality*?

- Because the gods are *unjust*, how can they establish *justice* for man?

- Since the society of the gods is in constant *chaos* and does not manifest *order*, how can they help man to *order* his own life, his family, and his society?

The early Christians triumphed over paganism because it was defective in the very areas where the God of Scripture was superior. Paganism lost out because it became clear to the average person that the gods and goddesses were simply deified men and women. In other words, they were manmade deities. As such, they were no deities at all. That this was true is seen from a comparison of human nature and society with the nature and society of the gods.

The Gods Were Human in Nature

1. *The gods were not self-existent.* They did not exist outside the world but were a part of its existence. They could not exist by themselves apart from the world. They were in the world because they were of the world.

2. *The gods were thus dependent beings and not independent beings.* They relied on something else for their own existence.

3. *The gods were not the creators of the world but they were creatures made by the world and earlier gods.* Thus the gods were born from divine parents who copulated to reproduce themselves.

4. *The gods were not sovereign over the world.* Indeed, they were subject to the same forces that controlled man. Since they did not make the world, they could not control it even if they wanted to. The lower gods were ultimately governed by higher gods such as the gods of "time" and "chance." The higher "up" you went on the the ladder of divinity, the more imperial you became.

5. *The gods were not eternal in the sense of timelessness.* "Time" was one of the ancient gods who ruled over the lives of both gods and man and was known as "Kronos" among the Greeks and "Aion" among the Persians. Since the world was eternal, time was not created but endless. Time was eternal because the world was. While Kronos was superior to

most of the other gods, he himself was under even still more ancient deities.

6. *The gods were not all-knowing, i.e., omniscient.* Their finiteness limited their knowledge as well as everything else about them. The future was unknown for the most part, because the gods of chance made the future uncertain. Gamblers still speak of "Lady Luck." She was the goddess of "chance" who ensured that the future was uncertain and insecure.

7. *The gods were limited by space as well as by time because they were finite.* They were not omnipresent. They could be only in one place at one time. Being part of the world, the gods were limited by space and time.

8. *The gods were not omnipotent, i.e., all powerful, because they were only creatures and not the Creator.* They were dependent in being and could not exist apart from the space-time universe.

9. *The gods were not perfect but were growing and maturing everyday in knowledge and experience.* Thus they could not have any "omni" attributes such as omniscience. Their finiteness limited them in their being and attributes.

10. *The gods were often capricious and fickle, for they were not immutable.* They changed their plans without the least hesitation or provocation. They sometimes abandoned a man or a game because they grew bored.

11. *The gods could change their natures.* They could do evil and become "devils" just as quickly as being "good" gods. They also were capable of death because they were not immutable. They grew old and died just like men. Their mutable nature made it impossible for them to be immutable in goodness. They *could* sin.

12. *The gods were not holy, just, or righteous.* Since the gods were not immutable even in goodness or benevolence, it is no surprise to find that the gods often did what was unholy, wicked, unjust, and unrighteous.

13. *The gods were not at all moral.* They engaged in every form of immorality known to man, such as fornication, adultery, homosexuality, incest, bestiality, prostitution, and child molestation. They raped each other, men and women, adults and children, and even animals!

14. *The gods had human bodies that were either male or female, or in some cases bisexual, having both male and female organs.* They were corporate or visible, whereas the Christian God was neither.

15. *The gods were neither immutably true nor faithful.* They lied to and deceived each other as well as men. They could not be trusted as to their motives, words, or deeds. They could break their word.

The gods of the pagans were finite and personal. Their finiteness proved to be their undoing, for it rendered them incapable of providing any infinite standards for man, his family, or his society. The chaos of the gods doomed them from the very beginning.

It is interesting to note that one of the elder gods was named "Chaos." He is usually referred to as one of the first gods to emerge and to be the origin of all things. It was also taught that since the universe began with "Chaos," it would eventually end in "chaos." One interesting question that comes to mind in this context is whether the theory of evolution is only a modern form of the pagan belief in "Chaos."

The early Christians accused the pagans of two things:

First, the pagans were guilty of *idolatry* because they worshipped and served the creature instead of the Creator. Their corrupt deities were but dumb idols.

Second, they were guilty of *atheism*. By their belief in many finite gods, they denied the existence of the one, true, infinite, eternal, immutable God who existed prior to, apart from, and independent of the space-time universe which He created out of nothing.

The gods were only a *part* of this universe. They did not exist apart from it. All the pagans really believed in, therefore, was the world. Thus all different forms of pantheism are nothing more than religious forms of atheism because they view God as being one with the world.

While the processians claim to be pan-en-theists and not pantheists, because they view the world as God's "body" and God as the "soul" of the world, the end result is still pantheism because God is not viewed as existing independent from or prior to the world. The world is just as essential to God as God is to the world. This is religious atheism pure and simple.

The Gods Were Human in Society

Not only did the gods reflect the sinful nature of man but also the society of the gods was a mirror image of human society. Each pagan religion reflected the culture of those who created the gods in their own images. Thus Greek gods reflected Greek society while Roman gods reflected Roman society.

Just as man is arranged in terms of families with husband/wife, parent/child relationships, even so the gods were arranged along family lines. In Bulfinch's *Myths of Greece and Rome*, the different families are identified for some of the major gods. This chart is reproduced here in order to show how the society of the gods was arranged (see Figure 3.1 on next page).

As Bulfinch points out, just as human families are desecrated and defiled by such moral evils as adultery or incest, even so the gods defiled their own marriages. Jupiter was involved in adultery, homosexuality, incest, and bestiality. Pluto raped Proserpine, who was the illicit fruit of Jupiter's adulterous affair with Denetes. Diana of Ephesus, mentioned in the book of Acts, was the child of Jupiter and Latana, a particularly nasty goddess.

In their society, the gods were afflicted with many moral evils. They were constantly fighting each other and vying for glory or power. The gods committed every evil known and suffered every ill imaginable.

As to their relationship to man, since they were not man's creators, the gods had no special concern or love for man. They could rape or kill people at will without the least amount of compassion. Man was only a plaything of the gods. They would hold games in which people were used as the pawns.

That the gods amused themselves by frustrating men's lives did not speak well of them. They showed either contempt for man or a mildly amusing attitude toward man. But nowhere did the gods reach out to save man or to help man. One can think of the suffering, pain, and death connected with the adventures of Ulysses, which was actually a game played by the gods using human beings as game pieces.

Since the morality of the gods was not any "higher" than man's and was usually "lower" than that of most people, how could the gods provide any standards to live by?

No wonder the early Christians triumphed over the society of the gods! Since the gods could not provide order, beauty, truth, justice, or morals in their own society, how could they provide such things for human society?

When the Greeks and the Romans looked at the gods, they only saw a mirror reflection of themselves with all their ills and evils. Nothing in the gods elevated man above his own filth and depravity. The gods were in need of salvation and forgiveness as much as man! They needed some One greater than themselves to give them moral absolutes and truth.

THE DESCENT OF THE GODS

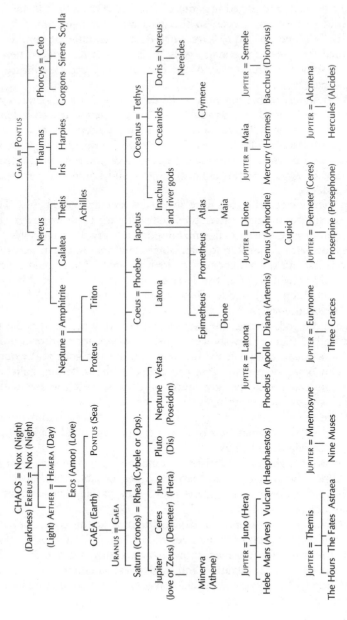

The worship of the gods thus failed man at every crucial turn. But this should be expected because whatever man makes, be it gods or ethical standards, it will always be as finite and relative as he is. A finite can never make an infinite, for it is impossible to make the jump from relative to absolute no matter how many relatives are piled up. Any god that man makes will always bear his limited and finite image.

If the yearnings of man for truth, justice, morals, and beauty were to be satisfied, he must turn to One God—not many; to an infinite/personal God—not finite/impersonal gods; to a God who is infinite in all aspects—not limited like man.

In short, only one God can provide a sufficient basis for truth, justice, morals, beauty, significance, dignity, worth, and meaning. This one God is the Christian God, who has spoken in Scripture and revealed Himself in Christ. This is why the common people turned away from their finite gods, who did not know or control the future, to worship the only, one, true, eternal, infinite, and personal Triune God of Father, Son, and Holy Spirit.

The Situation Today

While most Christians assume that the worship of the gods and goddesses of the ancient world has disappeared in the West, in reality, countless millions of Western people worship gods and goddesses. As a matter of fact, the number of "pagans" in the West is actually increasing, not decreasing.

The Roman Catholic Saints

The largest group of people worshipping gods and goddesses are the millions of misguided Roman Catholics who pray to and worship Mary and the saints. Despite the official teaching of the Church of Rome that Mary and the saints are only to be "venerated" and not worshipped, millions of Catholics do not see the fine distinction and go right on worshiping Mary and the saints the same way they do God.

The saints took over the functions of the "local" pagan deities in popular religion. The old pantheon of gods and goddesses were simply baptized with Christian names. For example, the devotees of "Venus" worshiped Mary as "the Queen of Heaven." She was no longer the simple, humble Jewish girl who had the privilege of giving birth to the Messiah. But she could now hear the prayers of anyone, at any time,

anywhere, and answer them from her throne in Heaven. Her divinity
outshone her humanity. She was no longer viewed as a sinner in need
of God's salvation, as she claimed in Luke 1:47, but she was viewed by
millions as a sinless goddess who did not need a saviour.[2]

The local gods and goddesses became the saints to whom prayer,
allegiance, and worship is given. Each local deity had his or her special
province or trade to bless. Thus in the ancient world were gods of the
sea, gods of the air, gods of fertility, gods of good fortune, gods of farm-
ing, and gods of all the various labors of man. The saints took over
these pagan functions. This is the historical origin of all "patron" saints
of fishers, farmers, bakers, soldiers, masons, gamblers, travelers, the sick,
etc.

That the Roman Catholic world is filled with polytheistic saint
worship is admitted and condemned by modern Catholic theologians.
The problem of "paganism in Catholic dress" in such places as South
America has been a special concern to the Vatican. Various directives
have been released to confront this problem, an example being the re-
duction of the number of the saints. But we have seen no visible sign of
change in the situation.

The Latter-day Saints (Mormons)

The second largest group of people who worship gods and goddesses
are the Latter-day Saints, or the Mormons, who now have over five
million members. Instead of Mt. Olympus being the birth place and
home of the gods, the planet Kolob takes on this position in Mormon
theology. There the gods and goddesses marry in polygamous unions
and through sexual intercourse produce other gods or goddesses called
"spirit children." Every faithful Mormon can become a god or goddess
by various Temple rites and obedience to the Mormon church.[3]

The gods and goddesses of Mormonism are deities inhabiting male
and female bodies. As such they are not infinite but finite. They are not
omnipotent, omniscient, omnipresent, or eternal. The pantheon of the
gods that is found in Mormonism is but a modern form of the gods and
goddesses of ancient Greece and Rome and is thus not "Christian" in
any sense. Even the liberals in charge of such ecumenical groups as the
World Council of Churches and the National Council of Churches
know that Christianity is monotheistic and Mormonism is polytheistic.
The conflict is irreconcilable.

Other Cults

The third group of polytheists is comprised of such cultic organizations as the Worldwide Church of God, the Unification Church, Elizabeth Clare Prophet, Theosophy, Unity, Science of the Mind, Scientology, Religious Science, and Christian Science. They all believe in the "divinity" of man although they disagree among themselves as to what that exactly means.

The New Age Movement

The fourth polytheistic movement in our day is "The New Age Movement," which is a growing and dangerous coalition of occult groups who believe in the divinity of man, reincarnation, ESP, psychic powers such as healing, astrology, pantheism, Yoga, and T.M.

The New Age Movement is promoted by media stars such as Shirley MacLaine, John Denver, Norman Lear, and Oprah Winfrey. Its principle writers include Alice Bailey, George Gurdjieff, and Marilyn Ferguson. It has been introduced to the American public by such movies as *Star Wars*, *Poltergeist*, and *E.T.* It is also taught in such "self-help" groups as EST, Silva Mind Control, and Life Spring.

The New Agers have joined forces with radical feminists in promoting the worship of finite female deities, with processians in calling for a rejection of the historic Christian God, with charismatic godism in proclaiming that we are gods, with "positive thinking" evangelicals in preaching "mind over matter," and with leftist neo-evangelicals in promoting "one world" social and political programs.[4]

Despite all the books on the New Age Movement that sound the alarm that the New Age Movement is out to destroy Christianity, the average Christian has yet to wake up to what is really going on around him.

Pagan Religions

The fifth polytheistic force in the West results from the growing immigration from heathen Third World countries such as India and China. Be it Hindus or Buddhists, the West is becoming pagan at an alarming rate due to a mass immigration of pagans who are bringing their heathen religions with them. The very survival of the culture, government, and religious values of the West is at stake today as the West is engulfed by a virtual tidal wave of foreign values and religions.

We must remember that the Judeo-Christian religion gave birth to the forms of government, economics, social structures, and law found in the West. The basis of these freedoms is being undercut by foreign religions hostile to the very principles that give them the freedom to voice their opinions.

The answer is to befriend those who have come to the West seeking freedom and a better life. Show them the love of Christ and share with them the glory of the Christian gospel. Be prepared to answer their questions as to why you worship only one God (1 Peter 3:15). Win them to the Christ you love and serve.

Conclusion

With all the paganism around us today, now is not the time to water down the Gospel or to deny the historic Christian concept of God. The Christian Church must arise and put her armor on and be strong in the strength that God supplies by His Word and Spirit. She must use the sword of the Spirit, which is the Word of God, to destroy human philosophy. She must take up the shield of faith to quench all the fiery darts of doubt. And she must go forth to conquer the forces of darkness in Jesus' name. To do this, the Christian Church needs truth—not error; courage—not cowardice; doctrinal vigilance—not sentimentality; sacrifice—not sacrilege; faithfulness—not betrayal; and strength—not weakness. The gates of hell cannot prevent the Church from gaining the victory.

FOUR

THE GODS OF
THE PHILOSOPHERS

W hile we may be tempted to dismiss the polytheism of the Greeks as gross ignorance and superstition, we cannot so treat the philosophers of Greece. Their beliefs were supposedly based on human reason and experience, and they prided themselves on being rational in all things.

Even more importantly, however, the philosophic ideas and issues that were developed by the Greek philosophers are still with us today. Zeller, one of the more astute humanists of our day, states in his standard work on the pre-Socratic philosophers,

> From Greek Philosophy, however, the whole of European philosophy has descended. For the ideas which the Romans express in their philosophic literature were not original, but were taken from the Greeks, clothed in the Latin language and passed on to the medieval and modern world.[1]

Some modern philosophers such as Alfred Whitehead not only admit their indebtedness to Greek philosophy but actually boast about it. On numerous occasions Whitehead proudly proclaimed that his process philosophy "only repeats Plato"! He assumed that the closer we get to Greek philosophy and the farther we depart from Christianity, the better off we will be philosophically and morally.

Greek Philosophy and Secular Humanism

Greek philosophy is also important because it represents secular humanism in full bloom. The Greeks attempted to explain the existence and form of the universe and the uniqueness of man solely on the basis of human reason, intuition, and experience. They developed their philosophies from themselves, by themselves, and upon themselves without any reliance on divine revelation. Again, Zeller comments,

> It was the Greeks who won for man freedom and independence of philosophic thought, who proclaimed the autonomy of reason.[2]

Zeller goes on to define what he meant when he said "freedom" and "independence." He meant "freedom" and "independence" *from* God. It did not matter if one is considering the being, attributes, sovereignty, salvation, works, law, or revelation of God, man must be "free" of God or he is not "really" free.

First, Zeller states, the Greek philosopher was free "to live life as he pleased" because he was "free" from "ethics founded on religious authority."[3] This has always been the great goal of man since his Fall into sin and rebellion in the Garden. Man must be "free" to be his own law-giver and judge. God and His Law must go if man is to be free.

Second, the Greek philosopher was free "to behave as he pleased" because he was "free" from "a religion based on revelation."[4] If man is to be a truth-maker, law-maker, and god-maker, he cannot be limited by the Bible or any other divine revelation. Truth, justice, morals, and beauty must be decided by what *man* thinks or feels about it. The concept of a God who reveals absolute truth or morals is clearly repugnant to Zeller.

Religion by reason and not by revelation was the basis of Greek thought and is still the basis of all apostate thought. "Freedom" to apostate man always means freedom *from* the God who made him. If man is not free in this absolute sense, he is not "really" free.

When Zeller spoke of "the autonomy of reason," he meant that the Greeks did not think that they were dependent on God for their existence, knowledge, or ethics. They assumed that they could "go it alone" *without* God because they were "autonomous," i.e., independent *from* God. They did not need God or His grace or revelation. The philosophic doctrine of human autonomy is the very soul and substance of all humanistic thought.

But can man really "go it alone" by relying solely on his own finite and corrupt reason, intuition, and experience? Is truth or morality possible if man begins by rejecting God and His revelation and relying only on himself?

Let us examine the Greeks and their philosophies to see if they were able to produce anything. After all, if man's reason, intuition, and experience are *really* sufficient, then *surely* the Greeks or some other humanistic thinker will have come up with a philosophy that is both believable and livable.

But if it must be admitted that after thousands of years in which humanistic thinkers have had all the time and resources needed to produce something, they have in reality produced nothing—then evidently man's reason, intuition, and experience are not really sufficient after all. Evidently God's revelation in Scripture is needed if we are to get anywhere philosophically or morally.

If, after all the exaggerated claims about human reason, intuition, and experience, man fails to "go it alone," then this calls for a radical change in the way that truth, justice, morals, and beauty are established. Perhaps the Bible *does* have the answers!

To trace Greek philosophy from the pre-Socratic period to Aristotle requires us to examine their development of the three main divisions of philosophy:

1. *Metaphysics*: What really exists? What is "reality"? What lies behind or beneath reality?
2. *Epistemology*: Can we know what exists? How can we know it? Is it possible to "know" anything?
3. *Ethics*: What is "good" and "evil"? Can we tell good from evil? How do we do this? Are there moral absolutes or is everything relative?

Metaphysics

The Pre-Socratics

With the appearance of a leisure class in Greek society, men acquired the opportunity to address themselves to some of the great questions of life. Where did we come from? How did we get here? Why are we here? What are we to do? Where are we going?

Thales is considered to be the earliest of the Greek philosophers. The main question to which Thales addressed himself was, "What is ultimate reality?," i.e., "What is it composed of or made of?"

Thales assumed that "reality" was ultimately "One," not "Many." This is the doctrine of monism, which states that there is no *qualitative* distinction between gods, men, animals or things. They all belong to the existence of the world. They are all part of "what is." They are all "One."

This is in stark contrast to the Biblical idea that God is distinct *qualitatively* and *quantitatively* from the universe He created out of nothing. The Biblical doctrine of creation means that God and the creation are *two* different things. They are *not* "One." We are not a part of God or one with God. While the Greeks, Hindus, Buddhists, and all monists believe that "all is One," the Bible teaches that all is "Two" not "One."

Since Thales assumed that everything was eventually and ultimately "One," he wanted to know the identity and nature of this "One" thing that composed all of reality. This "One" made up the existence of the world.

Thales assumed that whatever this "One" thing was:

1. It was a material substance,

2. It could be perceived by the five senses of man, and

3. It was as eternal as the world of space and time.

In other words, the "One" substance which made up everything was something man could touch, taste, see, feel, or hear. Thales chose WATER as the "One" ultimate eternal substance which made up all of reality. Ultimate reality was "One" and this "One" was WATER.

After Thales had asked the question as to the identity and nature of the "One" basis of reality, other philosophers put forth their own answers. At first, they assumed along with Thales that this "One" was a material substance perceivable by the senses.

Heraclitus chose FIRE as ultimate reality. Anaximenes proposed that AIR was the "One." And Empedocles topped them all by stating that reality was composed of a combination of EARTH, AIR, FIRE, and WATER!

Once the philosophers had exhausted all the substances open to sense perception which they thought qualified to be the "One," they decided that the "One" must be a material substance which was *not* perceivable by the senses. This substance lay "behind" or "below" earth, air, fire, and water. It could not be seen, touched, heard, tasted, or smelled.

Anaximander was first to propose this step toward abstract ideas. He stated that "APEIRON" underlay all of reality. It is difficult to translate this word, but it seems to refer to a material substance lying behind all things as a "ground of being."

Pythagoras believed that a material substance could not be the basis of reality, regardless of whether it could be perceived by the senses or not. Reality was actually "Number." This step in philosophy opened the door to Idealism, which holds that "ideas" or "numbers" are more real than material substances. This led to the classic contrast between "mind" and "matter" in Greek thought.

The Greeks finally came to the conclusion that the "One" of ultimate reality was *not* a material substance open to sense perception. It was an "idea" or a "number" that could be perceived only by the mind apart from the senses.

This led them to consider further questions concerning the "One" that made up reality. Was this "One" one or many in *quality* or *number*? Was this "One" at *rest* in an *unmovable* and *static* sense or was it in *constant flux* or *motion*?

Democrates put forth the idea that reality was "One" in quality but "many" in number, while Empedocles stated that the "One" was many in quality but one in number! Parmenides felt that reality was "One" in both quality and number. The "One" was ultimate. All else was illusion. This idea is the basis of such eastern religions as Hinduism.

Thus from the Greeks came the conflict between the monists and pluralists. Yet, they both assumed that reality was "One" and that it was eternal. No real distinction lay between things in this life. They all existed as part of "One" world and man could discover the nature of the "One" by reason alone.

Another conflict that arose centered in the debate between Parmenides and Heraclitus. Was the "One" that composed all of reality in a state of *being* or was it in the process of *becoming*?

Heraclitus championed the position that there is no "being," but all is "becoming" in a dynamic process of constant change. "No one steps in the same river twice" was Heraclitus' slogan. Everything was in flux. Thus perfect knowledge or morals were impossible for everything was constantly changing. What seemed "permanent" was illusory. Nothing is fixed, perfect, or immutable, not even the gods.

Parmenides taught that there is no "becoming" but that all is "being." Thus everything is static, fixed, and immutable in the sense of immovable. His disciple Zeno tried to demonstrate by several famous paradoxes that motion is an illusion. What is "real" is permanent. Change and movement are illusory.

The pre-Socratic period ended in a classic stalemate between Heraclitus' "becoming" and Parmenides' "being." They could not solve the contradictions between the two.

Plato

Plato was the first philosopher to attempt a compromise synthesis between the two systems of Parmenides and Heraclitus. He began by assuming with them that ultimate reality was "One," that it was eternal, and that man could discover its identity on the basis of his reason alone.

The Platonic solution was to place "being" and "becoming" alongside of each other. Plato's "World of Ideas" with its "Idea of the Good" took on all the attributes of Parmenides' being. It was eternal, static, immutable, and transcendent. Heraclitus' world of flux became the "World of Matter" which Plato defined as "non-being." It had all the attributes of Heraclitus' "becoming."

But merely laying them side by side did not bring them into contact with each other. No knowledge of this world was possible as long as "matter" and "mind" remained isolated from each other.

In order to overcome this problem, Plato invented the concept of a finite god who exists between the World of Ideas and the World of Matter. This "Demiurge" was not omnipotent, omniscient, or sovereign. The Demiurge molded formless matter according to the patterns he saw in the World of Ideas without any idea of what he was making or what the future of it would be. Thus Plato's god was not infinite in knowledge or power. He did not exist prior to or independent of reality. He was a finite part of a finite world. As such, he could not know the future of what he made.

But even with a Demiurge, Plato never solved the problem that what was knowable and what was real belonged only to the World of Ideas. The World of Matter remained unknowable and only reflected the ideas or patterns that molded it.

The Platonic system only satisfied philosophers for a brief time. Skeptics eventually took over Plato's Academy and ended up teaching *skepticism*, i.e., no true knowledge of anything is possible, and *relativism*, i.e., no absolute morals are possible. This is the logical conclusion of all philosophic systems that begin with the assumption of human autonomy. When man begins only with himself, he will always end in skepticism and relativism.

Aristotle

Even though he had been a disciple of Plato, Aristotle saw that Plato had not really solved the problems of meaning and knowledge. As a matter of fact, he had merely recast them. For example, instead of explaining the meaning of the chair in front of him, Plato pointed up to the idea of "chairness," which resided in the "World of Ideas." But merely shuffling the chair from "here" to "there" hardly constitutes an explanation!

In his *Metaphysics* Aristotle put forth fourteen arguments that refuted Plato's system. Plato was too idealistic and rationalistic in that he did not explain matter, he merely defined it away! Rearranging Parmenides' "being" and Heraclitus' "becoming" did not resolve anything.

But like all the philosophers before him, Aristotle assumed monism and human autonomy. Instead of Plato's dual world, Aristotle had one world composed of a mixture of "form and matter," "mind and matter," or "essence and matter."

"Matter" was pure potential and "mind" was pure actuality. An Ultimate Cause unto which all things were being attracted produced the motion involved in moving from potential to actual. In this way, Aristotle hoped to blend together Parmenides' "being" with Plato's "mind" and Heraclitus' "becoming" with Plato's "matter."

The fatal flaw in Aristotle's reasoning was that the "form" of something did not have to be consistent with its "essence." Thus the knowledge of particulars becomes impossible. Only universals were knowable in the last analysis. Once again no knowledge of this world is really possible.

Aristotle believed in many finite gods who were neither omniscient nor omnipotent and were only a part of the process of potentiality becoming actuality. These gods did not know the future. Since Aristotle's gods could only know universals, they could not know particulars.

Epistemology

The Pre-Socratics

The early philosophers were empiricists in that they restricted knowledge to what came into man by way of his senses. When this went nowhere, they turned to rationalism that relied only on the ideas produced in the mind. Further refinements such as idealism, materialism, realism, etc., flowed out of the basic conflict between Parmenides and Heraclitus.

The radical problem was that they all assumed that man could "go it alone" when it came to developing truth, justice, morals, and beauty. The doctrine of human autonomy doomed all their philosophies to ultimate relativism and skepticism.

Plato

Since Plato was a rationalist, he did not believe that all knowledge came from the senses. Man actually knew everything, for he had pre-existed in the World of Ideas. He had "fallen" into a body. This was a bad thing, because it made man forget all he knew. But as man reasoned, he could "remember" or "recollect" the ideas which exist in the "World of Ideas." While the Demiurge god was not omniscient, Plato felt that man was!

Aristotle

Aristotle championed empiricism against the rationalism of Plato. But like Plato, he still assumed monism and human autonomy.

In his theory of knowledge, Aristotle taught that we can "abstract" or "grasp" the "essence" or meaning of an object logically. Thus Aristotle placed knowledge not in things "as they are" but in their "essence" or "form." Matter was still unknowable.

Aristotle's system as well as Plato's was eventually refuted and abandoned. It gave way to skepticism and relativism, which always ultimately devour humanistic thought.

Ethics

The Pre-Socratics

Not having any authority higher than their own finite and corrupt reason or experience, the pre-Socratic philosophers could not generate any ethical absolutes that were infinite or universal.

Plato

Socrates and Plato tried to create absolutes on the basis of their own subjective and personal conceptions of the "idea of the Good."

Anything in conformity to their idea of "Good" was good. Anything in contradiction was "evil."

The main problem with this line of reasoning was this: How could Plato or Socrates prove that his own personal and finite idea of what was "good" was *better* than someone else's idea of what "good" is? Socrates never could refute Thrasymachus's argument that "Might Makes Right." Socrates' and Plato's own finiteness relativized any absolutes they tried to make.

Aristotle

Aristotle abandoned Plato's attempt to generate absolutes by an arbitrary concept of "the idea of the Good." In its place he taught that ethics was a matter of degree of pleasure and pain and not an issue of absolutes. What was "good" would be attracted to the Ultimate Cause to which all things were moving. But this attempt to have "relative" and "mutable" morals failed.

In the end, each philosopher was contradicted by the philosophers who followed him. Nothing was ever permanently established as certain or absolute. The Greeks failed to produce a philosophy or world and life view that was believable or livable.

We should not be surprised by this fact. Humanistic thought always fails in the end, for its foundational commitment to human autonomy renders it incapable of success. When finite man starts only with his own reason, feelings, or experience, he will always end in skepticism (no knowledge is possible) and relativism (no morals are possible). After all the exaggerated claims of man's independence from divine revelation, when the "rubber meets the road," human reason, intuition, and experience cannot take man anywhere.

The Gods of the Philosophers

The finite/personal gods that the philosophers invented were not worthy of worship or prayer. This is why the philosophers usually "meditated" instead of prayed. No god was omniscient or omnipotent enough to give meaning to prayer. If their god was an infinite/impersonal "it" such as "Apeiron," why pray to "it"? If god was a finite Demiurge, why bother praying to him? Either he knows what to do but doesn't have the power or, although he has the power, he doesn't know what to do!

When liberal theologian Paul Tillich was interviewed on television shortly before his death, he was asked, "Dr. Tillich, do you pray?" He responded, "No, I meditate." Tillich's god, which he called the "ground of being," was simply a modern restatement of Greek philosophy. Thus he could not pray. A god not quite omniscient or not quite omnipotent is a bridge broken at either end. No prayer is possible.

The gods of the philosophers were "time-bound" because they were "world-bound." Whatever limits this world limits everything contained in the world, the gods included.

To the Greeks, the world was "eternal" in the sense of "endless time" and "endless space." They had no concept of creation *ex nihilo*. The world and its limitations of space and time had no "beginning." Thus neither gods nor men could know the future infallibly. They could make some good guesses, but being limited by the world of which they were only a part, the future was unknown to them.

The God of Scripture

In this light, we can see how radically different the Biblical God is from the Greek gods. He existed prior to, independent of, and apart from the space-time world, for He created it out of nothing. Thus the world of space and time had a *beginning*. There is no "eternal time," any more than "eternal space." "Eternal matter" does not exist. God *alone* is eternal.

Since it was God who created the world with its space-time limitation, He Himself is not limited by space or time, but *greater* than both. Since He made the space-time universe, it does not make or control God. To say that the creation is greater than the Creator is absurd.

This is why Christians have always said that God is eternal in the sense of "timelessness" not "endless time." To say that God exists in "endless time" is to make time ultimate over God. It would make God depend on time for His own existence. This would make Time a higher god than God!

Just as Christians do not subject God to the limitations of space and say that He is decaying because of the Second Law of Thermodynamics, neither do they subject God to the limitation of time and say that He cannot know the future.

But processian philosophers have no difficulty in applying the law of decay to their finite god. On his walks, Pierre Teilhard de Chardin, a Roman Catholic processian theologian, used to collect bits and pieces of things and place them on a shelf above his desk. They were a part of "God" to him as "all was God and God was all." Yet, one day he noticed that the pieces of tin and other metals were rusting. This led him to the startling conclusion that "God" was rusting!

How different are the thoughts of the Psalmist in Psalm 102:25-27.

> Of old Thou didst found the earth;
>> and the heavens are the work of thy hands.
> Even they will perish,
>> but Thou dost endure;
> And all of them will wear out like a garment;
>> like clothing Thou wilt change them,
>> and they will be changed.
> But Thou art the same,
>> and Thy years will not come to an end.

When a philosopher or theologian claims that the idea of a "timeless God" is "incoherent" or "unthinkable," what he really means is that if one assumes that god and the world are "One," then god cannot be any more "timeless" than the world. Such a god can only exist in "endless time" since the space-time world is eternal. But this god cannot be "timeless" because he or it is only a finite part of this space-time world.

Dichotomies

Not only do humanistic thinkers assume the doctrines of monism and human autonomy, but they also assume that the issues and options open to man are in certain "either-or" categories, or dichotomies. Whatever man with his finite mind cannot reconcile is assumed to be incapable of reconciliation even by the finite gods or god he has made in his own image.

First, in terms of "Ultimate Reality," they assume the following absolute either-or dichotomies: Reality is either

- One or Many
- Being or Becoming
- Static or Dynamic
- At Rest or In Motion
- Transcendent or Immanent
- Infinite or Personal

Second, since they assume that god or the gods are only a part of the world, they assume that the gods are either:

- One or Many
- Being or Becoming
- Static or Dynamic
- At Rest or In Motion
- Transcendent or Immanent
- Infinite or Personal

Third, in terms of man, secular humanists assume that man is either:

- Autonomous or Nothing
- Knows Everything or Knows Nothing
- Absolutely Free or Not Free at All
- Responsible or Fatalistically Determined

The Christian must be careful to understand the arguments of the heathen at this point. They do not *prove* that God cannot be *both* one *and* many or that God cannot be *both* transcendent *and* immanent. They arbitrarily assume that if God is personal, He *cannot* be infinite. Why God cannot be *both* infinite *and* personal is never stated, defended, or proven. It is only assumed.

Humanistic philosophers and theologians always set up the issues and questions in the Greek "either-or" dichotomies. This means that they have already rigged the question to exclude the Christian answer from the outset. For example, when someone asks, "Is man really free? Then how can the sovereignty of God be true?" The question is constructed with the following assumptions:

1. Either God is sovereign or man is responsible.
2. Either man's freedom is absolute or illusory.
3. No concept of limited freedom is possible.

The humanist is assuming what he has yet to prove. Why is it assumed that the Greek view of "freedom," i.e., human autonomy, is the *only* possible definition of "freedom?" Can't man's freedom be limited but still be true freedom? The Bible teaches that God is sovereign *and* man responsible. Why can't we accept the Biblical idea of man's freedom, which includes *both* divine sovereignty and human responsibility?

Processian Assumptions

When processians argue against the Christian concept of God, they begin with certain assumptions that they have never established and which contradict the Bible. They usually argue,

- If God is infinite, then He cannot be personal.
- An infinite God would be perfect, immutable, infallible, transcendent, and static. Instead of this, we need a dynamic God who is in the process of becoming, i.e., growing and learning everyday. This finite God is imperfect, mutable, fallible, immanent and dynamic.

This line of thought assumes all the "either-or" dichotomies of the Greeks. It assumes that if God is infinite in His nature and attributes (i.e., God is omniscient, omnipotent, omnipresent, immutable, infallible, and perfect), then He cannot be personal.

In reality, the theologians who argue for a "dynamic" god assume that the attributes of Parmenides' One make up the historic Christian conception of God. Then they adopt the attributes of Heraclitus' "becoming" as the definition of their god!

Whenever someone labels the Christian God as "static" and goes on to propose a new "dynamic" god that comes from their reason or intuition, we know he is simply repeating Greek philosophy and not Biblical teaching. Christians must become sensitive enough to the issues that they don't allow themselves to be drawn into discussions that are rigged against the Christian God from the outset. Neither Parmenides nor Heraclitus wrote the Bible! The Trinity is neither "static" nor "dynamic" in the Greek sense.

We must also emphasize at this point that the God revealed in Scripture was not created on the spur of the moment by the early Church to fill in the blank spaces felt by Greek philosophy. The Christian God does not fit into the Greek mold at all. Indeed, He doesn't have to. Let their gods be ruled by Greek "either-or" categories. But let God be GOD as He has revealed Himself in Scripture!

Neither did the Church simply pick up some Greek god and make it into the Christian God. No Greek philosopher ever spoke of an infinite/personal God who existed prior to, independent of, and apart from the space-time world which He created out of nothing. The concept of a self-sufficient God who does not *need* the world for His own existence never crossed their minds. Creation *ex nihilo* was unheard of among the Greeks.

The God proclaimed in the Christian Gospel was thus neither made for nor made from Greek deities. If we keep close to the Scriptures, we will escape from the false gods of the philosophers.

Conclusion

The Greeks believed in gods who were only a part of a world, which was eternal. These gods were limited by space, time, and chance. If they spoke of an "infinite" god it was always an impersonal "it" that did not know that it existed and that could not know or care about man. The gods of the philosophers were neither omnipotent nor omniscient, being limited by the world that contained them. They could not know the future because they were limited by time as well as by space.

How different is the God of Scripture from the gods of the heathen! Their gods are not worthy of our worship. They cannot motivate us to love them. A god that is neither omnipotent nor omniscient is too weak and ignorant to trust. Why pray to such a feeble, tottering idol?

As we move into an age when the old gods of Greece and Rome are resurrected and represented as something "new," let us remember that these "new" gods are simply the old idols of the heathen world of whom the Scripture says, "Thou shalt not have any other gods before me."

THE FINITE GOD
TRADITION

FIVE

THE ORIGIN OF
THE FINITE GOD

One of the important matters to be considered when dealing with the idea that god cannot know or control the future is the history of this notion. Who in secular and church history has championed this idea? What religious bodies have made a finite god part of their creed or confession? What philosophers have defended it? Were they known for their love of Christ and His Gospel? Did they place their trust in the Scriptures as God's infallible Word, or were they known for their rejection of Scripture? Were they the enemies or the friends of Christianity? Does this idea reflect the best Christian thinking down through the ages? Is it part of the Christian tradition or part of the humanistic tradition? Was this belief ever a part of the Christian concept of God, or is it outside of orthodox doctrine?

These kinds of questions are warranted by such Scriptures as Jude 3, which states that the Faith, i.e., the body of doctrine comprising the Christian system, was once and for all of time delivered unto the Church of the first century. If a doctrine is not part of historic Christian teaching, it is not part of the "Faith." We have an obligation to ask two questions concerning any doctrine:

First, where is it explicitly stated in Scripture? Clear exegetical evidence must depend on more than one verse and not exclusively on passages that are highly figurative or symbolic in nature.

Second, where is this doctrine found in Church history? Can it be traced back to the early Church? If not, when, where, and by whom did it originate? What churches have taught it? What theologians have defended it?

When someone comes up with a *new* "doctrine," "insight," "revelation," or practice that cannot be found in Scripture and has no Apostolic or historic Christian pedigree, we have the right and the duty to be highly suspicious of its validity. The same holds for doctrines which are part of heretical or humanistic traditions.

We are aware of those in our day who do not care if what they believe can be historically or exegetically established. They choose doctrines on the basis of what feels "comfortable" to them. It does not matter to them if what they believe contradicts what the Christian Church has taught for two thousand years. They assume that they can believe whatever they want and that we should accept their beliefs as "Christian." But we cannot do this in good conscience. Those who deny the historic faith of the Church have placed themselves outside orthodoxy.

Where did the idea that God is finite in power and limited in knowledge originate? Who in history taught that God does not know the future?

The Ancient World

The Old Testament

The Old Testament condemned the pagan gods as "false gods" because they were limited in their power and knowledge (see Psalm 135). This is always seen in *contrast* to the God of Israel, who was not limited in power or knowledge.

Indeed, the only people pictured as believing that God is limited in His knowledge are the wicked (Psalm 73:11)! The Old Testament never states that God's power or knowledge are limited. The authors of the Old Testament clearly view with horror the idea that God is limited in His knowledge. The thrust of such passages as Psalm 73:11 can only mean one thing: It is a great *wickedness* to say, "How does God know the future? Is there infinite knowledge with the Most High?"

Instead, the authors of the Old Testament tell us that God "is infinite" (Psalm 147:5) and that He can "do all things and that no purpose of [His] can be thwarted" (Job 42:2). In terms of knowing the future, this is stated as being the main difference between the finite gods of the heathen and the infinite God of Israel (Isaiah 41:21-29).

Intertestamental Judaism

The idea that God is limited or finite in his power or knowledge cannot be found in the literature which arose between the Old and the New Testaments. The Apocrypha, Pseudepigrapha, Apocalyptic, Midrash, Mishnah, and Dead Sea Scrolls teach that God knows and guides the future.

Donald Carson demonstrates this in his definitive work, *Divine Sovereignty and Human Responsibility*. He states that in the intertestamental literature, "no limitation is placed on God's knowledge or power."[1] The great Rabbi Akiba stated, "All is foreseen (by God)."[2] Even Adam's fall into sin and judgment was foreseen by God.[3]

The rabbis taught that God both knew and controlled the future. The history of the world was following a plan preordained by the Creator. History was truly "His Story." The Messiah would come at the time appointed to usher in the kingdom. The righteous would ultimately triumph over the wicked because God had decreed it.

The New Testament

Not once are we told in the New Testament that God is ignorant or impotent concerning the future. Not once is it ever stated that God does *not* know everything. On the other hand, we are told that He "knows all things" (1 John 3:20).

Just because man does not know or control the future does not mean that God cannot know or control the future. Thus the apostolic watchword was "God knoweth!"—not "God is ignorant!" (2 Corinthians 11:11; 12:2-3).

The New Testament speaks of the future as something that is *secure* because it is both known and ordained by the sovereign Lord of the universe (James 4:13-15). The book of Revelation contains a description of the end times and what the future holds for the righteous and the wicked. It would have been a shock to the Apostles to hear that God does not know the future.

Fathers and Heretics

The Apostolic and Ante-Nicene Fathers were not ignorant of the finite god theory. As a matter of historical record, most of the early creeds were deliberately written as a refutation of the finite god theory.

To the Fathers, anyone who believed that God did not know and control the future was an atheist, for he had denied the existence of the infinite/personal God of the Bible. The idea that God is limited by time or anything else that He has made was viewed as heretical. (See the documentation set forth in Chapters 24 and 25.)

Thus, the finite god theory was alien to Biblical religion in the ancient world. We have already demonstrated that the idea of a finite god has its origin in pagan philosophy. In pagan tradition, god was limited by the world in the same ways that man was limited. Just as man could not know or determine the future, neither could the gods do these things. This was the kind of god in which Zoroaster, Cicero, and Plato believed. Their gods were only a finite part of this world and thus were subject to space and time like any other fragment of the world.

When we turn to the early centuries of the Christian Church we find that the only thinkers who championed the finite god theory were pagan-influenced individuals who were branded as "heretics" and "apostates" by the Christian Church, East and West. They were condemned by all the early creeds.

The Gnostics and the Valentinians

The early Church faced one its greatest challenges in keeping Gnosticism out of the Church. The Gnostics believed in a myriad of finite gods and they were willing to add a finite Christian god to the list if it would make the Christians happy. In this way, they tried to absorb the Church.

The basis of the Gnostic heresy was its monism. The Gnostics denied the doctrine of creation. They rejected the inspiration and authority of Scripture. They denied man's sinful nature. They depended on "reason," "intuition," "insight," and "visions" for their doctrines. Because the gods were only a part of "Being," they did not know or control the future. Man was "divine" because he was a "god-in-the-making." Some of the leaders such as Valentinus were worshiped as gods! No wonder the Ante-Nicene Fathers viewed Gnosticism with horror.

In addition to such Gnostic leaders as Valentinus, we can also mention Mani who tried to mix Christianity with Zoroastrianism. His followers, the Manichaeans, claimed that God had to be limited in power and knowledge, in order to solve the problem of evil. Mani claimed that God could not know the future if man was to be really free.

Marcion

Although Marcion was excommunicated and branded as a heretic in A.D. 144, his teachings continued to trouble the Church for centuries. He believed that the Old Testament god was different from the god of the New Testament. Both of these gods were finite and did not know or ordain the future. He denied the inspiration and authority of Scripture as well as its unity. He also denied the doctrines of creation, the Trinity, the infinite/personal nature of God, and the atonement. Marcion was a rationalist who depended solely on human reason for truth.

The great historic creeds of the early Church were written to refute such pagan ideas as a finite god. Due to the clarity and force of these creeds, the finite god theory disappeared until the time of the Renaissance, when there was a revival of Greek philosophy.

The Renaissance

During the Renaissance, the West witnessed the return of such pagan philosophies as rationalism and empiricism. Along with this was also a revival of the pagan concept of monism and its finite god or gods. Human "reason" was now placed above Scripture and was seen as being "against" such doctrines as an infinite/personal God, the Trinity, Creation, the Fall, and Redemption.

So opposed were these thinkers to the authority of Scripture that they labeled all of Church history as "The Dark Ages," contending that man had only the "darkness" of Scripture to go by. But now man was entering "The Age of Enlightenment," wherein he would be free to think and do as he pleased simply on the basis of his own reason and experience.

Paganism in its theological form did not take long to revive the finite god theory. Why should the Christian God be infinite when all the other gods of man were finite? Why should He be any different from the gods of India, Egypt, Rome, or Greece?

This was the period in which the so-called science of "comparative religion" originated. It was assumed that all religions were manmade. Thus the gods were made by man in his own image and they were all basically the same. All religions could be "compared" because they were all the same. They all worshiped the same thing (i.e., man) under different names. Later, the theories of evolution and Freudian psychology were used to explain how and why man made gods in his own image.

The only problem with "comparative religion" was that the Christian God simply did not "fit in" with the finite gods of all the other religions. The Christians believed that God was infinite and personal. They believed in creation *ex nihilo*. The world was neither eternal nor divine. They rejected monism, which formed the basis of all other religions. They believed in one God in Trinity, a doctrine that went "beyond" reason. Their belief in the Fall of man and his resulting depravity was not found in any other religion. In short, the unique beliefs of biblical Christianity stood in the way of the reductionism of "comparative religion."

The humanistic answer was to dump those doctrines of Christianity which could not be reduced to pagan ideas. In this way Christianity was stripped of its belief in an infinite/personal Triune God, Creation, the Fall, and Redemption. The Scriptures were reduced to the level of the fables of India and Greece. And all of this was done in the name of "Reason."

The Socinians

During the time of the Reformation, the Socinians were the first to use "reason" as the basis for rejecting the infinite/personal Triune God, Creation, the Fall, and Redemption.

Faustus Socinus (1539-1604) was a rationalist who chose his doctrinal beliefs on the basis of whether they seemed "rational" to him. He assumed, of course, that whatever was "irrational" to him would be "irrational" to any truly intelligent person. The Bible would be accepted to the degree it was in accord with human reason. Reason was "above" revelation.

In Latourette's A *History of Christianity*, we find that Faustus was much influenced by his uncle Laelius Socinus, who stood, "in the humanist tradition" because "he brought reason to bear on questions of faith."[4] Socinus's doctrines were "chiefly of humanistic origin."[5] His doctrines were based on a "humanism" which "with its emphasis on the competence of human reason, tended to rule out all that seemed to it irrational."[6]

In *The New Schaff-Herzog Encyclopedia of Religious Knowledge* we read that Socinianism tried to be "a rationalist faith."[7] All doctrines had to be in "accord with reason."[8]

With rationalism as their basis, the Socinians rejected the inspiration and authority of Scripture. Once they were no longer hindered by the Bible, they went on to reject the infinite/personal Triune God of the Bible, Creation, the Fall, Redemption, the deity of Christ and of the Holy Spirit, and nearly all orthodox doctrines. It is no surprise to find that modern day Unitarians and Jehovah's Witnesses trace their roots back to the Socinians.

The Socinians were particularly interested in reviving the Greek concept of man's absolute free will. They echoed the Greek philosopher Epictetus who boasted that his "free will" was more powerful than that of any of the finite gods. He claimed,

Not even Zeus himself can get the better of my free will.[9]

Who can any longer restrain or compel me, contrary to my own opinion? No more than Zeus.[10]

The Socinians did not like the biblical teaching that man was a "fallen creature" and that his will and his reason were tainted by sin. They wanted man to be "free" from sin as well as "free" from God.

Indeed, in order for rationalism to work, one *must* deny the Fall of man into sin and condemnation and man's subsequent depravity. If man really fell in the Garden, then his "reason" could not be the *final* judge of truth and morals. Man would become dependent upon God and His revelation for truth and morals.

The Greeks had taught that in order for man to be "really" and "genuinely" free, he must be free not only from the control of the gods but also free from their knowledge. After all, the idea that god or the gods know *everything* about us can be disturbing. We don't *want* God to know too much about us. Omniscient knowledge would be constricting, suffocating, and, worst of all, judgmental. Also, it would not be "fair" for God to know what we are going to do in the future, since this would make Him "greater" than man. Man is limited to remembering the past and experiencing the present; therefore, so must any gods that exist.

Socinus realized that in order for man to have absolute freedom, God had to be whittled down to size. In order for man to get "bigger," God had to become "smaller." God had to become a finite god in order for humanist man to be his own god. As *The New Schaff-Herzog Encyclopedia* states,

> Socinus was occupied mainly with . . . that of omniscience. God's foreknowledge is limited . . . otherwise there could be no human freedom.[11]

The Socinians were smart enough to avoid openly denying the omniscience of God. They used the familiar trick of *redefining* a term so that it would end up meaning the *exact opposite* of what it had historically and theologically meant.

The term "omniscience" has always meant that God knows *everything, including the future*. It does not matter what the subject is, God knows all there is to know about it. Be it the future or the life span of a sparrow, God knows it *all*.

The Socinians redefined "omniscience" to mean that God knows all that is "knowable." But what is "knowable" is to be determined by reason alone. In this case, "reason" declares that the future is intrinsically "unknowable." Thus God *cannot* know it. Of course, the fact that no Biblical passage that says that the future is "unknowable" can be cited meant nothing to these rationalists. Socinian theology, according to the *Cyclopedia of Biblical, Theological, and Ecclesiastical Literature*,

> denies that God foresees the actions of his creatures, or knows anything about them until they come to pass. . . . That they may not seem to derogate from God's omniscience, they admit that God knows all things that are knowable; but they contend that contingent events are unknowable, even by an infinite being.[12]

The Socinian methodology of redefining orthodox terms to fit heretical concepts has been followed by humanistic thinkers ever since.

Now, it must be admitted Socinus was right in that the *kind* of freedom that he wanted man to have was incompatible with an infinite/personal God. The Greek view of absolute freedom was developed in the context of monism, which did not have any concept of creation or its Creator. In such a system of thought, man could be "free" from the knowledge and control of finite gods, for they were as limited as man.

But if there were an infinite/personal God who created the space/time world out of nothing and made man for His glory, then man could not be "absolutely" free of such a God. This God could reveal truth and demand belief. He could reveal morals and demand obedience. Such a God could interfere in man's affairs either to save or to judge. Such a

God could stop the world and judge all of mankind by laws He Himself set up!

The kind of freedom that the Greeks and the Socinians wanted was actually atheistic. They did not want an all-seeing Judge. They did not want a God to whom they were accountable. They wanted to be accountable only to themselves. They did not *need* revelation. Their reason, intuition, and experience were sufficient. Man could "go it alone."

The Fathers and the Reformers had no problem in saying that man was "free" and that God was infinite because they believed in a *different* kind of freedom from that found in pagan philosophy. To them, "freedom" never meant "free *from* God"; it always meant "free *from* sin" in order to get "back *to* God." Man needs to be "set free" from sin (John 8:34-36). True "freedom" is a work of the Holy Spirit (2 Corinthians 3:17). Thus "freedom" always had a *moral* significance in Scripture and Christian theology. This was never the case with pagan definitions of freedom.

One of the most frequent errors in the entire controversy over God's "free will" versus man's "free will" is the failure to recognize:

1. The necessity of defining one's terms clearly. There are many different ideas of what it means to be "free."

2. That many definitions are simply incompatible with the authority of Scripture, the existence of God, Creation, the Fall, Redemption, moral absolutes, a Day of Judgment, hell, etc. For example, the demand of ethical relativists that man be "free" from God's Law so he can make up his own laws is incompatible with the concept of the Biblical God who is both Law-giver and Judge.

3. The Christian's need to base his definition of "freedom" on a careful exegesis of Scripture and not on pagan appeals to human reason, intuition, or experience.

The Socinians were the first religious body to place the theory of a finite god in a confession of faith. John Biddle, the father of English Socinianism, published a "Socinian Catechism," with the most important edition appearing in 1652. In the first chapter he openly denied the inspiration and authority of Scripture and exalted the place of human reason.

The Scriptures, according to Biddle, have,

contradictions in them; many things are or may be changed and altered in them; some of the books of the Old Testament are lost; those that remain are not of any necessity to Christians; all their assertions [must be submitted] to the last judgment of reason.[13]

In the second chapter of his Catechism, Biddle gives the Socinian definition of god. Notice that he is careful to state that his god does not know the future. God is:

finite, limited to a certain place, mutable, comprehensible, and obnoxious to turbulent passions, *not knowing the things that are future and which shall be done by the sons of men*; whom none can love with all his heart, if he believe him to be "one in three distinct persons."[14]

The key to the Socinian definition of God is found in their demand that God must be "comprehensible." The denial of the incomprehensibility of God always lies behind the finite gods of the heathen. The only god they will accept is one that is "understandable," "coherent," "comprehensible," "rational," or "thinkable" *to them*. Any concept of God that goes *beyond* their capacity to comprehend is dismissed with a wave of the hand as "unthinkable."

The problem with the Socinian doctrine of the comprehensible god is that it is self-destructive. Any god that can be fully understood and explained is *less* than man. Such gods are obviously manmade. A god who can be reduced to the finite limits of human reason can never be GOD. The God who made this world cannot be reduced to the span of the human mind.

Biddle dismisses those concepts of the Christian God that are not reducible to his "reason" and "comprehension."

1. The Trinity must go because "One in three persons" is not "coherent" or "rational." Never mind what the Bible or the Church has taught. The Trinity must go.

2. Since the concept of "invisibility" is "incoherent," god must be a visible being just like man. After all, who can coherently explain what it means to be "invisible"?

3. Like man, god has a body. This brings us back to the worship of the gods and goddesses of old.

4. Like man, god is finite. If he is personal, he must be finite. If god were infinite we could not pray to him or love him.

5. Like man, god can only be in one place. Doesn't the Bible use spatial language about God? God is said to go from "here" to "there." He goes "up" and "down." A finite god cannot be everywhere at once. God is not omnipresent.

6. As a finite god, he is mutable like man. He is not perfect but imperfect. He is not immutable. He can change. Like man, he can learn new things.

7. God is comprehensible by man in the same way that one man understands another man.

8. Like man, god does not have any "turbulent passions" such as wrath and judgment.[15] There is no hell, for this finite god is too good to judge man and man is too good to be judged.

9. Like man, this god is ignorant of the future. He has to wait and see what tomorrow will bring. Doesn't the Bible use temporal language about God? God "spoke" and "did" things in the past. He "does" things now in the present. God is not omniscient.

10. The only god that man can truly love is a finite god. He cannot love a God that is beyond his understanding. A God who is infinite is too impersonal and cold.

Socinus and his followers were at least consistent in their commitment to rationalism. They were not afraid of rejecting any doctrine if it was not capable of being reduced to what they felt was "coherence." That all the Protestant Reformers condemned the Socinian heresy speaks well of their commitment to Scripture.

The problem we face today in evangelical circles is that there are multitudes of halfway Socinians who don't have the courage to carry out their rationalism to the bitter end. They are not honest or bold enough to admit openly that they do, in fact, reject most of Christian theology. In order to keep their jobs in an evangelical seminary or college, many modern Socinians pay lip service to such doctrines as the Trinity, while "behind closed doors" they actually reject all such doctrines as "incoherent." The Church is always better off when dealing with honest atheists than with dishonest theologians and hypocritical clergyman.

The Jehovah's Witnesses

The most aggressive religious body since the Socinians to deny that God is infinite is the Watch Tower Bible and Tract Society or, as they are commonly known, Jehovah's Witnesses. They teach that god does not know all the details of the future. They also deny that god is omnipresent, immutable, perfect, and triune because such doctrines are not in accord with reason.

To support their contention that God cannot know or control the future, the argument is given in *Aid to Bible Understanding* (pp. 594f.) that God is *selective* in His knowledge of the future. Thus God does not *choose* to know *all* the details of the future. God's omniscience is optional, i.e., He can choose not to be omniscient.

The reason given for limiting God's foreknowledge is that if man is to be "really free," then God cannot know the future absolutely. Thus He chooses not to know what men will do in the future.

The main problem with this argument is that in order for God to choose what future events He wants to know and what events He does not want to know, He has to know *everything* at the beginning. For example, given that events A-Z will happen in the future, how can God choose to know A, F, K, J, L, P, R, O and choose not to know B, C, D, E, G, I, M, N, etc., if He does not know *why* not to know them?

The only other alternative is to think that God "rolls the dice" in some kind of gigantic cosmic crap game and lets chance decide what He should and should not know!

The attempt to solve the problem of evil by claiming that God chooses not to know all the details of the future solves nothing. Who would argue that someone who turned on his car, put it into gear, then jumped out with the doors and window locked, letting it run down the road until it ran over and killed thirty people, is "innocent" because he did not know all the details of what would happen and was powerless to do anything about it even if he knew? The Watch Tower's argument is worse than no answer at all.

Conclusion

The idea that God cannot know or control the future is foreign not only to the Bible but also to the Jews and the Christians. The only ones to champion such ideas have always been humanistic in their approach to religion. Instead of submitting to the authority of the Bible, they appeal to human reason, emotion, and experience. In their attempt to whittle God down to a manageable size, they have ended up with no God at all.

THE FINITE GOD OF
SECULAR PHILOSOPHY

The Socinian doctrine of a finite god who does not know the future received its greatest acceptance among secular philosophers who did not have to bother with Church sanctions. The philosophers we shall discuss in this chapter are the leading spokesmen for finite godism in secular philosophy.

It will be important to observe the attitude of these philosophers toward Scripture; their belief in monism; their rejection of Creation, Fall, and Redemption; their belief in a finite god or gods; and their trust in "reason" as the origin of truth, justice, and morals.

It will also become abundantly clear that the idea of a finite god is part of a pagan tradition that stands *outside* Christianity. The champions of finite godism are usually the bitterest enemies of the Gospel.

David Hume (1711-1776) and the Problem of Evil

This Scottish philosopher is known as the "Father of modern empiricism." Following the epistemology of Heraclitus, Hume limited knowledge to what the five senses could perceive. This position is self-refuting in that it itself is not perceived through the senses. It is a metaphysical view.

Although his argument against miracles was based on the logical fallacy of circular reasoning, his refutation of miracles is still read in most introductory courses on philosophy.[1]

Hume argues through the use of dialogue that one possible way to solve the problem of evil is to reduce God from infinite to finite. In this way, God cannot be blamed for the rise, existence, or power of evil. God cannot be allowed to be infinite if he is to be "justified" from evil.

An interesting observation can be raised at this point. Why do the heathen always focus on God when the problem of evil is addressed? Why do they demand that God has to "justify" Himself before the tribunal of *their* reason? Why is there never any discussion of *man* and *his* role in evil?

In contrast, the Bible never attempts to "justify" God before man or any one else. Instead, the Scriptures point to *man* as the one who is needs to be justified before God (Job 9:2). Sin, misery, and death entered the world through *man*, not God (Genesis 3; Romans 5). While the pagan points to God as being responsible for evil, the Bible points to man. God is never the author of evil, any more than man is ever the author of good (James 1:13-17).

This brings up another interesting point. Why do pagan philosophers always speak of "the problem of *evil*" instead of "the problem of *sin*"? They never speak of the "the problem of sin" because they don't believe that "sin" exists. They assume that nothing is wrong with man. They do not view themselves as *sinners* in need of God's grace. They know that if the word *sin* is allowed in the discussion, it will lead straight to the subject of *man's* moral accountability and responsibility to his Maker and the coming Judgment Day when the problem of both sin and evil will be taken care of by God.

Thus Christians should understand that the word *evil* is actually a "red herring." It is used to create a false trail that leads the discussion away from man's accountability for the evil he has brought on himself by his own sin and rebellion against God and His holy Law.

Whenever we are asked to discuss "the problem of evil," we should immediately turn the focus to man's sin. God does not even enter the picture until we begin discussing the *solution* to evil. While man is the *problem*, God is the *solution*. It seems quite clear that the humanists want to switch the focus from man to God in order to escape the fact of their own sinfulness.

We must also state that we are either part of the problem of evil or part of its solution. God has solved the problem of the evil of sin by sending His Son to atone for the sins of His people and to bring judgment on the wicked. Salvation and damnation are God's final solutions to the problem of all the evil that man's sin has created.

Pagans must also be reminded that God is not accountable to them and their perverse ideas of right and wrong. They are accountable to

Him. If they think that they can sit in judgment on God Almighty, they have a big surprise coming on the real Day of Judgment.

The authors of Scripture do not bother to answer the demand of rebel sinners that God "justify" Himself before them. When the wicked demand,

> Is God just? If so, why does He find fault with us? For who can resist His Will?

The Christian answers,

> On the contrary, who do you think you are, O man, that you can question God? A created object has no right to question its Creator for like a potter, the Creator has the moral right to do whatever He wants with what He has made. Therefore you have no right to question God.

The authors of Scripture turned the tables on the humanists of their day and insisted that *they* were the ones who needed justification (Romans 9:9, 19-23). The theist is actually under no obligation to justify the ways of God to anyone. And, given man's record of injustice, he is hardly qualified to sit in judgment on God.

Hume begins his argument with the assumption that the misery of the world around him must be blamed not on man and his depravity but on God. This is the hidden assumption behind every humanistic discussion of the problem of evil.

> His power we allow infinite: whatever he wills is executed: but neither man nor any other animal is happy: therefore he does not will their happiness. His wisdom is infinite: he is never mistaken in choosing the means to any end: but the course of nature tends not to human or animal felicity: therefore it is not established for that purpose. Through the whole compass of human knowledge, there are no inferences more certain and infallible than these. In what respect, then, do his benevolence and mercy resemble the benevolence and mercy of men? Epicurus's old questions are yet unanswered. Is he willing to prevent evil, but not able? then is he impotent. Is he able, but not willing? then is he malevolent. Is he both able and willing? whence then is evil?[2]

Notice that Hume assumes that human "happiness" is the goal of life and that Creation and Providence must serve man's "felicity" or be judged defective. He clearly rejected the doctrine that God created all things for *His* glory and that man exists to serve God. God is "judged" by Hume on the sole basis of whether He makes people "happy," when the real issue is whether God is glorified. It comes as no surprise to find that the "Humanist Manifesto" will later dogmatically state that "happiness" is the goal of life and the standard of morality.

Notice also that Hume assumes that God *owes* man happiness, as if He exists to serve man. This is, of course, "putting the cart before the horse," for man exists to serve his Maker. The Scriptures tell us in such places as Romans 4:1-5 that God does not "owe" us anything. Instead, we owe God our faith, love, and obedience because He is our Creator, Sustainer, Redeemer, and Judge.

Hume now offers a way to "save" God from his judgment.

> I scruple not to allow, said Cleanthes, that I have been apt to suspect the frequent repetition of the word, *infinite*, which we meet with in all theological writers, to savor more of panegyric than of philosophy, and that any purposes of reasoning, and even of religion, would be better served, were we to rest contented with more accurate and more moderate expressions. The terms, *admirable, excellent, superlatively great, wise*, and *holy*; these sufficiently fill the imaginations of men; and anything beyond, besides that it leads into absurdities, has no influence on your affections or sentiments. . . . But supposing the Author of Nature to be finitely perfect, though far exceeding mankind; a satisfactory account may then be given of natural and moral evil, and every untoward phenomenon be explained and adjusted . . . benevolence, regulated by wisdom, and limited by necessity, may produce just such a world as the present.[3]

Hume's solution is to make God finite. But does this really "let God off the hook" and absolve Him from being evil? No! The entire discussion of Hume is based on the assumption that God *is* guilty. This is a foregone conclusion. God is responsible for all the unhappiness that people experience. The only real issue for Hume is whether he will "forgive" and "excuse" God. If God will become a finite creature like man, "limited by necessity," then God can be judged "guilty but forgiven" for He did not know any better and did have the power to do otherwise.

The idea that God can be judged "guilty but forgiven" because He is finite is based on the assumption that *man* is to be absolved from all his sins because *he* is finite. Humanistic thinking has always assumed that man's chief problem is his finiteness. The only reason people "sin" is because they do not know any better and do not have the power to do otherwise. Thus man sins because he is finite.

The Scriptures clearly teach that man's finiteness is not a problem or an evil which man needs to overcome. God made man finite at the beginning and declared him good (Genesis 1-2). Man's problem is not metaphysical but moral. He sins because he is depraved, not because he is finite.

We must conclude that any attempt to "rescue" God from Hume's argument by making God finite does not solve anything because metaphysical finiteness cannot absolve anyone from moral evil.

Hume's Cleanthes admits that he "would measure everything by a human rule and standard" and that he is following the teachings of "the greatest libertines and infidels." When the Christian responds by pointing to the,

> infirmity of reason, the absolute incomprehensibility of the Divine Nature, the great and universal misery and still greater wickedness of men, Cleanthes dismisses it by calling it "stupidity," "ignorance," and "superstition."[4]

The Christian position is not *refuted*. It is simply *ridiculed* and then dismissed. This is another standard trick of pagan philosophers and theologians. They ridicule what they cannot refute.

John Stuart Mill (1806-1873) and the "Problem" of God

This English philosopher is known as the "Father of Utilitarianism," which is a revival of Greek Hedonism. This view of ethics has come down to us in the popular statement, "If it feels good, do it!"

Mill always spoke of God in the context of "the problem of God." He approached the Bible and theology in the same way. This is the typical humanistic approach, which views God, His revelation, and Christian theology as the "problem" that man must overcome. They never speak of the "problem" of man's rebellion against God or of the "problem" of man's finite, fallible, and sinful reason.

Theists must become aware of this hidden assumption and state that on the contrary the "problem" is man. Given the wickedness of man, it is *man's* existence that needs justification, not God's.

Mill begins with the idea that many finite gods are preferable to one infinite God.

> Though I have defined the problem of Natural Theology to be that of the existence of God or of a God, rather than of Gods, there is the amplest historical evidence that the belief in Gods is immeasurably more natural to the human than this more elevated belief if, compared with the former, an artificial product, requiring (except when impressed by early education) a considerable amount of intellectual culture before it can be reached. For a long time, the supposition appeared forced and unnatural that the diversity we see in the operations of nature can all be the work of a single will. To the untaught mind, and to all minds in pre-scientific times, the phenomena of nature seem to be the result of forces altogether heterogenous, each taking its course quite independently of the others; and though to attribute them to conscious wills is eminently natural, the natural tendency is to suppose as many such independent wills as there are distinguishable forces of sufficient importance and interest to have been remarked and named. There is no tendency in polytheism as such to transform itself spontaneously into monotheism. . . . Every God normally rules his particular department though there may be a still stronger God whose power when he chooses to exert it can frustrate the purposes of the inferior divinity. There could be no real belief in one Creator and Governor.[5]

In Mill's day, the myth was put forth that whatever was "natural" to man was deemed both good and true. The idea of "the noble savage" came into prominence. The evil man saw around him was caused by Christianity. The "natives" of heathen lands were innocent, fun-loving people who were corrupted by wicked missionaries' teaching them the Gospel.

But we must ask what is "natural" and what is "unnatural." On what grounds could these philosophers boldly state that Christianity was "unnatural" and polytheism "natural"? Each philosopher labeled whatever *he* believed in or whatever *he* wanted to do as "natural." It was totally arbitrary.

It is also interesting to note that monogamy as well as monotheism was condemned as "unnatural." These male philosophers claimed that men were much happier with many different gods and many different sexual partners. And since happiness was the goal of life, both monotheism and monogamy had to go.

Having dismissed monotheism by merely calling it "unnatural," Mill is quite willing to accept Plato's finite god. The world did not need an infinite God to explain its existence.

> The skill of the Demiourgos was sufficient to produce what we see; but we cannot tell that this skill reached the extreme limit of perfection compatible with the material it employed and the forces it had to work with. I know not how we can even satisfy ourselves on the grounds of natural theology, that the Creator foresees all the future; that he foreknows all the effects that will issue from his own contrivances. There may be great wisdom without the power of foreseeing and calculating everything. . . . he may have little power of foreseeing the agencies of another kind which may modify or counteract the operation of the machinery he has made. . . . we must rest content with a Creator less than Almighty; the question presents itself, of what nature is the limitation of his power? Does the obstacle at which the power of the Creator stops, which says to it: Thus far shalt thou go and no further, lie in the power of other Intelligent Beings; or in the insufficiency and refractoriness of the materials of the universe; or must we resign ourselves to admitting the hypothesis that the author of the Kosmos, though wise and knowing, was not all-wise and all-knowing, and may not always have done the best that was possible under the conditions of the problem?[6]

Mill can now refer to his god as an "it" because it is only one finite being among many others. This god is "guilty but forgiven" for "not always doing the best under the conditions" because a "still stronger god" or a stubborn universe may have frustrated his plans. He, like man, is not really accountable for his sins and failures because they arise out of his finiteness.

William James (1842-1910) and the "Freedom" of Man

James is remembered as the "Father of Pragmatism," which is a view of ethics that basically teaches, "If it works, it's good!" With this "pragmatic" approach to truth and ethics, James became deeply involved with the occult.

While the Holy Spirit did not interest James in the least, the "spirits" involved in witchcraft, satanism, and all the other elements of the world of the occult fascinated him. As a member of the Society for Psychical Research, he assumed that if the occult "worked," it was good. This was based on the idea that the result was all that mattered. Whether it came from God or the devil did not really matter. Results were the only issue.

James failed to see that an "experience" requires not only an explanation but also a moral judgment. Something can be "real" but evil. Just because someone has a "real" experience with Satan does not make that experience "good." Just because a witch or a psychic can pull off what looks like a supernatural feat does not mean it is good.

It must also be pointed out that something can "work" but be wrong. We must never forget that if pragmatism is true, then Hitler's ovens were "good" because they "worked"! The "final solution" succeeded in removing millions of "undesirables." But this hardly makes it "right." What is may not be what is right.

James begins his argument by appealing to the necessity of maintaining "freedom" for man. This "freedom" was the old Greek idea of pure "chance."

> But the word "chance" with its singular negativity, is just the word for this purpose. Whoever uses it instead of the word "freedom," squarely and resolutely gives up all pretence to control the things he says are free. For *him*, he confesses that they are no better than mere chance would be. It is a word of *impotence*, and is therefore the only sincere word we can use, if, in granting freedom to certain things, we grant it honestly, and really risk the game. . . . Any other word permits of quibbling, and let us after the fashion of the soft determinists, make a pretence of restoring the caged bird to liberty with one hand, while with the other we anxiously tie a string to its leg to make sure it does not get beyond our sight.[7]

When James uses the word "freedom," he is speaking of pure chance or luck. This means that he is not speaking of human responsibility, for *"chance" destroys any responsibility or moral accountability.* Who is deemed morally "guilty" for what happens "by chance"? When a plate drops "by chance," no one is to blame for such an "accident." No moral judgments can be made against things that happen "by chance."

What James is actually saying is that man is *not* responsible or accountable for his "sins" because they happened "by chance." If man is "really free," then he is "impotent" before chance. When people "sin," it is just an accident that happened by bad luck.

Christians must understand that the more we attribute the actions of man to chance, the less accountability he will have before God. Those Christians who have ignorantly thought that the pagan idea of "chance" and "contingency" will in some way support human responsibility must look elsewhere. Maybe they should try the Scriptures for a change.

James now continues his argument:

> But you will bring up your final doubt. Does not the admission of such an unguaranteed chance or freedom preclude utterly the notion of a Providence governing the world? Does it not leave the fate of the universe at the mercy of the chance-possibilities, and so far insecure? Does it not, in short, deny the craving of our nature for an ultimate peace behind all tempests, for a blue zenith above the clouds?[8]

James is not dumb. He knows the consequences of rejecting the biblical God. If God is not sovereign, then chance is. If chance is sovereign, then there is no guarantee that good will win in the end. If chance rules, then the universe is *not* secure. The devil may win in the end. Only time will tell the tale.

But there is a small amount of limited hope for the future. A finite god could work extra hard and might pull it off in the end. But it will be "touch and go" because this god does not know the future.

> The belief in free-will is not in the least incompatible with the belief in . . . Providence . . . if you allow him to provide possibilites as well as actualities to the universe and to carry on his own thinking in those two categories just as we do ours, chances may be there, uncontrolled even by him, and the course of the universe be really ambiguous . . . he cannot foresee exactly what any one actual move of his adversary may be. He knows, however, the *possible* moves of the latter; and he knows in advance how to meet each of them by a move of his own which leads in the direction of victory.[9]

James's finite god does not know the future because he thinks "just like us." The way to establish this god is to reject the doctrine of the timelessness or eternity of God.

> A mind to whom all time is simultaneously present must see all things under the form of actuality, or under some form to us unknown. If he thinks certain moments as ambiguous in their content while future, he must simultaneously know how the ambiguity will have been decided when they are past. So that none of his mental judgments can possibly be called hypothetical, and his world is one from which chance is excluded. Is not, however, the notion of eternity being given at a stroke to omniscience only just another way of whacking upon us the block-universe, and of denying that possibilities exist?[10]

To James the choice is clear. We must choose either God or chance. If we choose God, then man must be limited. If we choose chance, then God must be limited. He continues,

> The creator's plan of the universe would thus be left blank as to many of its actual details, but all possibilities would be marked down. The realization of some of these would be left absolutely to chance; that is, would be determined when the moment of realization came . . . the creator himself would not need to know *all* the details of actuality until they came; and at any time his own view of the world would be a view partly of facts and partly of possibilities, exactly as ours is now. . . . The great point is that the possibilities are *here*. . . . *That* is what gives the palpitating reality to our moral life and makes it tingle.[11]

Once God's knowledge of the world is reduced to "just like ours," then He cannot know the future. Indeed, He does not even know if He or the devil will win in the end.

The basis of James's finite god is his commitment to monism, in which God and the world are merged into one Being. Like the Greeks, he denies the existence of the infinite/personal God who existed prior to the world that He created out of nothing. Christian dualism is rejected and in its place James puts forth his brand of pantheism.

> God as intimate soul and reason of the universe has always seemed to some people a more worthy conception than God as external creator.

So conceived, he appeared to unify the world more perfectly, he made it less finite and mechanical, and in comparison with such a God an external creator seemed more like the product of a childish fancy.[12]

After calling the God of the Bible "a childish fancy," James proceeds to label the doctrine of creation "puerile" and Christianity an "outlandish savage religion," "obsolete," "adolescent," and "old-fashioned."[13] He continues.

The only opinions quite worthy of arresting our attention will fall within the general scope of what may roughly be called the pantheistic field of vision, the vision of God as the indwelling divine rather than the external creator, and of human life as part and parcel of that deep reality.[14]

God is an essentially finite being *in* the cosmos, not with the cosmos in him.[15]

There is a God, but he is finite, either in power or in knowledge, or in both at once.[16]

Having pronounced God finite, James now tells us that there are probably more gods than one. He believed in what he called "superhuman consciousness."

It may be polytheistically or it may be monotheistically conceived of. Fechner, with his distinct earth-soul functions as our guardian angel, seems to me clearly polytheistic; but the word "polytheism" usually gives offence. So perhaps it is better not to use it. Only one thing is certain, and that is the result of our criticism of the absolute: the only way to escape . . . from all this is to be frankly pluralistic and assume that the superhuman consciousness, however vast it may be, has itself an external environment and consequently is finite.[17]

Thus does foreignness get banished from our world, and far more so when we take the system of it pluralistically. . . . We are indeed parts of God and not external creation, on any reading of the panpsychic system. Yet because God is not the absolute, but is himself a part when the system is conceived pluralistically, his functions can be taken as not wholly dissimilar to those of the other smaller parts—as similar to our functions consequently. Having an environment, being in time, and working out a history just like ourselves, he escapes from the foreignness [and] from all that is human, of the static timeless perfect absolute.[18]

James's involvement with the occult is revealed in his use of such terms as "earth-soul functions," "superhuman consciousness," and the "reading of the panpsychic system." His thinking is filled with the vocabulary of spiritism.

It is also important to point out that James reduces God's knowledge and experience of the world until it is "similar to ours" and "just like ourselves." The "foreignness" which James is so desperate to remove the very thing which separates God from man. James's reductionism did not stop until nothing of the Christian God remained. The only thing left was man. But this is not surprising seeing that as a humanist he began with man.

William James rejoiced to see a religious movement in his own day which was based on a finite god. James referred to it as the "mind-cure religion or new thought."[19]

This was a reference to Spiritualism, Christian Science, Theosophy, Unity, and all the other gnostic cults that arose in the latter part of nineteenth century. They taught that the human "mind" determined all things including the health of the body. Man could "think," "pray," "project," "confess," and "image" his way to wealth and health because he was a god.

James even predicted that evangelicals would get involved with this new religion. Sad to say, he was right. The same teachings today can be found in the occult, the New Age Movement, positive confession, "name it-claim it" doctrines, and charismatic godism.

John Fiske (1842-1901) and the Ontological Fallacy

Although he was raised in a Christian home, Fiske became a vicious skeptic and infidel. He was an assistant librarian and lecturer at Harvard University and was noted for his evangelistic zeal in spreading the theory of evolution and fighting against the doctrine of Creation.

Fiske wanted to remold religion into an evolutionary scheme. The infinite/personal God of Scripture who was the Creator could not "fit" into evolution, so Fiske championed the idea that god was finite and limited in power and knowledge. God did not know the future since evolution, no god, controlled that. God was reduced to what he called "the Unknown," which was only a finite part of an evolving world.

The basis of his rejection of the Christian God was his acceptance of the Greek "either-or" dichotomy between infinite and personal.

> . . . the ideas of Personality and infinity are unthinkable in combination.[20]

We will hear this argument over and over again as if the mere repetition of it somehow makes it true. The humanist will arbitrarily label some aspect of God that he does not like as "unthinkable." He does not go on to demonstrate that it *is* unthinkable. He merely states that it is and goes on with his argument.

Fiske is a good example of the fallacy of "ontological thinking," which is the assumption that reality must conform to what I "think" it is. What is "thinkable" to me exists and what is "unthinkable" to me cannot exist. It does not matter if other people find it "thinkable." If it is "unthinkable" to me, then it is not true and it does not exist. The logical fallacy involved is the attempt to universalize one's subjective, personal thoughts and experiences. The same game is played with such words as "coherent" and "understandable." The humanist will reject a Christian doctrine on the sole basis that it is "unthinkable," "incoherent," and "not understandable" to *him*.

In reality, we must point out that the infinite/personal God of Scripture is "unthinkable" to humanists because they have false assumptions or presuppositions, which are incompatible with the Christian God. Since they begin by assuming that personality and infinity *cannot* be joined in one being, then the Christian God cannot exist. But their whole argument rests on the rather gratuitous assumption that has yet to be proven. Until they can *prove* that personality and infinity cannot exist in one being, their argument is just another example of circular reasoning.

Henri Bergson (1859-1941) and the Evolving God

Known as a "spiritualistic metaphysician," this French philosopher revived the Heraclitian concept that "all is flux." Everything was constantly changing and evolving toward an unknown future. Nothing in the universe, not even God, was infinite, immutable, perfect, all-knowing, or all-powerful. All is "One" and "One" is all.

Bergson reduced God to what he called "the life force." This god was finite and did not know its own future or man's future. It was evolving along with the rest of us into the Unknown. This "life force" is in man. Thus man is divine. God and man are viewed as "one."

> Let us put it more clearly: however close the union with God may be, it could be final only if it were total. Gone, doubtless, is the distance between the thought and the object of the thought, since the problems which measured and indeed constituted the gap have disappeared. . . . Gone the radical separation between him who loves and him who is beloved.[21]

Pantheistic thinkers have always argued that God is more "intimate" and "personal" if "it" is a nonpersonal god such as "life," or "mind," or "the force." We saw this argument in William James and now in Bergson.

The fallacy in this whole line of reasoning is that it takes *two separate persons* to have an "intimate" relationship. How can someone have an "intimate" relationship with a nonpersonal "it"? The pantheist denys that there is any divine "person" out there. Pantheists actually destroy any hope for an "intimate" relationship with God when they deny His personhood.

Also, we must remember that a cognitive ego who is self-conscious and conscious of the world around him, is qualitatively superior to a nonpersonal god. In other words, an "I am" is always and intrinsically better than an "it." For example, while we may crush, grind, melt, and use an "it" such as iron ore, we would hardly do this to human beings who are cognitive egos.

This being the case, man is *superior* to any pantheistic deity. Why then would we worship what is *inferior* to us? To worship an "it" who does not know that it exists or that we are worshiping it, does not bring any "intimacy" to man. It leaves him alone in a world devoid of a personal God.

Bergson's ultimate goal is to proclaim "the divinity of all men."[22] Man can clothe himself with divinity only by stripping God of His divinity. When God is reduced to finite being, we always find that man is elevated to infinite potentiality. Man is "free" only to the degree that God is "bound."

Bergson goes on to describe god as a "struggling god" who "suffers like us" by having to "grow toward knowledge" every day. The Christian God is described as static, cold, and unfeeling.

The concept of a "struggling" and "suffering" finite god will now become a permanent part of the finite god tradition. The Christian God will be vilified by *ad hominem* arguments. How the God who loved us so much that He sent His only Son to die for our sins is "cold" or "static" is never demonstrated. The pagan thinker simply mocks God with a few derogatory names or slurs and then rudely dismisses Him to oblivion.

Ehrlich gives us a good summary of Bergson's god.

> This persistently creative life, of which every individual and every species is an experiment, is what Bergson means by God. God and life are one. But, and this is important, God is finite, not infinite and omnipotent. God is limited by matter, overcomes inertia painfully, step by step by groping gradually towards knowledge and consciousness. God, thus defined, is not ready made. God is unceasing life, action, and freedom. . . . Our struggles and sufferings are the voice and current of the *elan vital* in us; it is the vital urge which makes us grow and transforms us and the earth into an unending creation.[23]

Bergson, following Spenser and Hegel, saw god as an evolving part of the world. This god came to life in man as he evolved upward and onward toward his ultimate divinity.

Samuel Alexander (1859-1938) and the Emergent God

Alexander was the first Jew to be a fellow at Oxford and Cambridge. This Scottish thinker built upon the work of William James and Bergson. He was the first to use the buzz word "emergent" and apply it to evolution and to God. He believed in a finite god who did not make the world but "emerges" from it. The biblical doctrine of Creation was rejected and "emergent evolution" took its place. God was the soul of the world just as the world was god's body. In the end, the heavens and the earth will create god.

> God's body, being the whole universe of Space-Time, is the source of the categories. . . . Since his deity is realised in a portion only of the universe, it might be thought that deity at any rate, which is equiva-

lent to some complex of mind, might be subject to the categories, and be a true individual substance. It is not however an individual, for an individual is the union of particular and universal. And realised deity is not universal. . . . The actual reality which has deity is the world of empiricals filling up all Space-Time and tending towards a higher quality. Deity is a nisus and not an accomplishment.[24]

Alexander believed that god is in the process of emerging. This theme will become very important to modern pagan philosophers. God is now seen as being helplessly swept along in the same chance-directed current of evolution that grips man and takes both of them into an unknown future.

Alexander now takes up the issue of polytheism.

Two different questions accordingly may be asked as to the existence of deity, to which different answers must be given. The first is, Do finite beings exist with deity or are there finite gods? The answer is we do not know. If Time has by now actually brought them forth, they do exist; if not, their existence belongs to the future.[25]

While Alexander's universe is "open" to the existence of many finite gods, it is "closed" to the existence of the one true infinite God of Scripture. Pagan philosophers will always plead for an "open" universe, that is, "open" to everything *except* the infinite God of Scripture. An "open" universe is always "closed" to God. In reality, they attempt to shut God out of His own Creation!

Notice also that "Time" has now taken the place of the Creator. This is only logical as the two choices open to us are whether God creates time or Time creates god. We can't have it both ways.

Alexander now deals with the concept of an infinite God.

The other question admits an answer. Does infinite deity exist? The answer is that the world in its infinity tends towards infinite deity, or is pregnant with it, but that infinite deity does not exist; . . . there is no existent infinite mind, only many finite minds. Deity is subject to the same law as other empirical qualities, and is but the next member of the series. . . . God as an actual existent is always becoming deity but never attains it. He is the ideal God in embryo. The ideal when fulfilled ceases to be God.[26]

Alexander's god is "in embryo." Time and chance have not finished creating him. But when god finally emerges, there will be a new race of gods.

When a philosopher says that time is "ultimate" even "over" god, this means that his god did not create time but that Time is eternal. Since Time is an eternal "given" that a finite god must obey, this god cannot know the future as to his own nature or the future acts of man. This god must bow before the Greek god Kronos.

The Mutable God of Andrew Pringle-Pattison (1856-1931)

Another Scottish philosopher, Pringle-Pattison argued for a finite god conceived along the lines of what James, Bergson, and Alexander taught. He began by stating, "The traditional idea of God must be profoundly transformed."[27] He went on to reject Creation and to put evolution in its place.[28] He freely admitted that Bergson and others were only reviving the Greek philosophy of Heraclitus.[29] His god could not know the future.

It should be pointed out at this point that once we believe that "change" or "flux" is ultimate, then god himself must be seen as "growing" and "changing" in his nature and knowledge. The implications of a mutable god are very serious. Just as Heraclitus argued that we can never step in the same river twice, neither can we pray to the same god twice! Prayer becomes a sham if the god we address is not only ignorant and impotent about the future but constantly changing in his nature.

Francis Bradley (1846-1924) and Plato's God

This British philosopher spent his life trying to revive the god of Plato. His attacks on the infinite/personal God of Christianity were often caustic and bitter.

> For myself, when I am offered the idea of a moral creator who tries to divest himself by some ludicrous subterfuge of his own moral responsibility, or the idea of a non-moral potter who seems to think it a fine thing to fall out with his pots—when, I say, I am offered these decrepit idols as a full and evident satisfaction of the highest claims of the human conscience, I am led to wonder if the writer and myself, when we use the same words, can possibly mean the same thing. It is

even a relief to turn back to the old view that the Deity is a person limited like ourselves, a person face to face with mere possibility and with chance and change, and in truth, like ourselves, in part ignorant and in part ineffectual. . . . I would in the end leave the limited Deity together and along with ourselves in a Universe, the nature and sense and final upshot of which would in the end be unknown.[30]

At least Bradley was honest! To him the biblical God was a "decrepit idol." Chance and change were the same for god as for man. God did not know the future because his own future was yet to be seen. God is "just like us" in that he is "ignorant" and "ineffectual." We need to turn back to the pagan gods of old. They will give us the "relief" we seek from the Triune Jehovah who created all things and will judge all men. A finite god cannot judge anyone for he makes as many "mistakes" as man does.

The Contracted God of Edgar Brightman (1884-1953)

Brightman was one of the chief spokesmen for what has come to be known as "Boston Personalism." A professor at Boston University, he was responsible for introducing the concept of a finite god into The United Methodist Church.

In a work entitled, *The Problem of God*, Brightman tried to solve the problem of evil by limiting the power and knowledge of God. This is attempted in Chapter 2, which is appropriately entitled "The Contraction of God."[31] "God is limited," says Brightman.[32] He is limited in his nature and in his attributes. Brightman argues for God's "contraction" by asserting that God is:

- either infinite or personal;
- either transcendent or immanent;
- either omnipotent or good;
- either omniscient or man is not "really" free.

Brightman simply repeated the dichotomies of Greek philosophy as if they were self-evident truths. He never understood that God has revealed Himself in Scripture as infinite *and* personal, transcendent *and* immanent, omnipotent *and* good, omniscient *and* man free in the biblical sense.

As a committed monist, he states,

> Nature, on this immanentist hypothesis, is in God. . . . To speak religiously, the universe consists of God and his family. Nature is divine experience.[33]

He is just as committed to Heraclitus' philosophy of "all is flux" as was Alexander. Everything, including his finite god, is ever changing.

Brightman begins by denying that God is "above" time. He agreed with Bowne that the "timeless" God of the Bible is "too hard to grasp," i.e., incomprehensible. Then he states that the Christian doctrine of the incomprehensibility of God is "a scandal to reason."[34] On this basis he concludes that the "expansion of God above reason contracts the reasonable basis for belief in his existence."[35]

> A known God must, therefore, be contracted within the limits of our reason.[36]

With this statement, Brightman lets the proverbial "cat out of the bag." He is a rationalist who wants a god that is *less* than his own reason. As with Socinus, the fundamental issues are:

- Divine revelation versus human reason.
- The incomprehensibility of God versus rationalism.

Brightman's views become even clearer in his work, A *Philosophy of Religion*. He uses the words "coherent" and "incoherent" on almost every page as the ultimate standard of truth. "Coherence" is even the judge of Revelation.

> If we are to know . . . God, coherent reason is the way of knowing most suited to the problem. In fact, coherence must be the arbiter of all the other ways of knowing. . . . Revelation claims must be judged by their coherence with our view of life.[37]

Brightman has set himself above Scripture. He will accept only what he subjectively labels "coherent" in terms of a previously chosen "view of life." He goes on to speak of his approach as the "rationalistic method."[38] His worldview is, based on . . . a complete and a rational account of all the experiences of man.[39]

The hypothesis of a finite God thus affords a coherent account of the structure of all experience; to deny it contradicts the implications of experience and makes God evil (or unknowable).[40]

It is, of course, the idea that God is evil if He is infinite that drives Brightman to a finite god. Only a finite god can give us a "coherent account" of evil.[41]

On the other hand, argues Brightman, if God were infinite, then He could make all our evils ultimately work for our good. But this absurd idea, says Brightman, is "cruel . . . irrational . . . unjust."[42] No, his god does not make good out of evil. Evil cannot be redeemed or turned into good. Romans 8:28 is an absurdity to him.

Brightman calls the biblical teaching that God overrules evil for good "cobweb" thinking.

The hypothesis that God is finite brushes aside these cobwebs, and shows that the whole difficulty arises from supposing that, if there is a God, he must be omnipotent and infinite in all respects. There is no evidence that power is infinite. All power is under limits; indeed, the mountain sometimes "labors and brings forth a mouse." If we suppose the power of God to be finite . . . we have a reasonable explanation of the place of absurd evil in the scheme of things.[43]

Brightman argues for a finite god from the problem of evil. But please notice that it is always the problem of *God's* evil. He never discusses *man's sin.* He assumes that God is the problem, not man.

He is not unaware that Christian theology has an answer to his demand for a "rational" and "coherent" explanation. But he dismisses the doctrine of the incomprehensibility of God as an "appeal to ignorance."[44]

In terms of the history of the finite god idea, Brightman is one of the few thinkers who had the honesty to admit that,

. . . theistic finitism began with . . . Plato.[45]

. . . there is no doubt that Plato held to the conception of a finite God.[46]

Plato had a well-reasoned view of a finite God.[47]

Plato, profoundly concerned about the problem of good and evil, puts into the mouth of Socrates the principle that "God is not the cause of all things, but only of the good things." This is explained more fully in the Timaeus, where divinity is represented, not as omnipotent creator of all, but simply as a good God who desires "that, so far as possible, all things should be good and nothing evil." So far as possible![48]

There is a fundamental reason why Plato should regard God as finite. In the Philebus he discusses at length the finite and the infinite. He holds that these two elements are to be found everywhere in the universe. But, contrary to our modern mood, he feels no awe before the infinite; it inspires in him only confusion. Goodness and beauty are not to be found in the in-finite, the un-limited; on the contrary, they exist only where the indefinite is made definite, the limitless is limited. . . . As Socrates puts it a little later, it is "the infinite bound by the finite" that creates "the victorious life." Thus, all meaning, goodness, and order are limitations on infinity by the finite.[49]

In terms of early Church history, Brightman is honest enough to admit that only the heretics taught the finite god theory. He refers to such Gnostics as Marcion who:

. . . concluded that the power for good in this world must be finite. . . . He wished to "justify the ways of God to man.")50

Brightman also points to Manichaeanism.

Another more erratic genius contributed to the history of thought about the finite God. He was named Mani (A.D. 215-276) or Manes, and his follwers were called Manichaeans. His doctrines were a mingling of Babylonian, Persian, Buddhist, Greek, and Christian ideas, but were closer to those of Zoroaster than anyone else.[51]

Brightman's survey of the history of a finite god turned up almost every rogue and heretic known in church history. While his "historical sketch began with Plato's conception of a finite God," he concludes with:

The greatest Anglo-American philosopher of the present time, Alfred
North Whitehead, is in a sense a modern Plato, who builds on the
Timaeus, and develops a modern version of the Platonic Demiurge. At
about the time of the appearance of Whitehead's *Process and Reality,*
there was a spontaneous outburst of thought favorable to a finite
God. . . . It may be said that philosophically-grounded belief in a finite God is more widespread in the present century than at any time
since Plato.[52]

Brightman uses the problem of evil as the excuse to limit the power
and knowledge of God. He first states:

All theistic finitists agree that there is something in the universe not
created by God and not a result of voluntary divine self-limitation,
which God finds as either obstacle or instrument to his will.[53]

Brightman's god is not the Creator of all things. Those things he
did not create, such as time, chance, evolution, etc., limit god. God
must "make do" with what is essentially beyond his power to create or
control.

God's will, then is in a definite sense finite. . . . the power of his will
is limited by the Given. . . . human freedom and the nature of the
Given probably limit his knowledge of the precise details of the future.[54]

Once we reduce God to a finite being struggling to cope with the
"Given," he sounds very much like man. Indeed, this is the hidden
agenda. God and man are made equals. God is not ultimately any "better" or "greater" than man.

But what of God's perfection? Surely God is a *perfect* being while
man is flawed. No, says Brightman, a finite god is *not* perfect. He is only
perfectable like man.

Along with the notion of a finite God goes a revised notion of perfection. . . . When . . . we substitute for perfection the ideal of inexhaustible perfectibility, we have a concept applicable to both God and man
and adequate to man's religious need . . . inexhaustible perfectibility
in everlasting time, these are the perspectives which are open for the

cosmos and for every enduring person in it if the empirical evidence for a finite God has guided us toward truth.[55]

God is not perfect now and he will never become perfect. In this way the universe is "open" and man "free" to pursue his own perfectibility.

Brightman's god does not have perfect, infallible, or immutable knowledge of himself or the world around him, for his knowledge is changing all the time. Given this starting point, it is no wonder this god does not know the future of men, seeing that he does not even know his own future!

The Christian idea of an infinite, eternal, perfect, infallible, all-wise, and all-knowing God is dismissed as "impersonal," hence "unthinkable." Brightman's god is part of the evolutionary flow of time itself. What god will ultimately become is left up to chance.

What never seemed to dawn on Brightman or his followers is that a finite god whose future nature is left up to blind chance could just as easily end up being *evil* as well as good. In other words, we may be worshiping a god who is the next Satan! Once the "fixed" and "perfect" nature of God is denied, who can guarantee that we won't end up worshiping the Devil?

The logic of this point cannot be dismissed simply because it is "unsettling." Arguments are not like taxicabs that you may get out of at any point. You must ride until you come to your final destination. It does not matter if you end up where you never planned to go. Perhaps the champions of a finite god never intended to open the door to Satan worship. But this is where the logic of their argument leads us.

Another problem that the processians do not deal with is the fact that when god is viewed as moving up the "scale of being" in the future, this means that he moves down the same scale in the past. In short, if god is becoming *more* godlike as he moves up the Gnostic scale of being, then he must be viewed as being *less* godlike as we go down the scale. If we say that god becomes *more* nearly perfect in the future, this means that he was *less* than perfect in the past. To say that god gets *bigger* as we go into the future is to say that he gets *smaller* as we go back into the past. To say that god reaches his ultimate *existence* in the future is to say that god must be reduced to *zero* or *non-existence* at some point in the past. To say that god becomes *more* knowledgeable in the future is to say he was *less* knowledgeable, i.e., *more* ignorant in the past. To say that god will be *greater* in the future, is to say that he was *lesser* in the past.

Another problem with the idea of god's *growing*, is that this opens the door to the idea of god's *beginning* at some point in history, *decaying* at some point, and *dying* in the end. A finite being who is capable of growth must also be capable of decay. This is where Teilhard de Chardin ended. He came to the conclusion that god rusts and decays!

Brightman ends up with a deity who is in all ways human. This divine "man" is the only one he will accept.

The Finite God of H. G. Wells (1866-1946)

Although he is best known for his science fiction novels, such as *The War of The Worlds* and *The Time Machine*, Wells tried his hand at writing history, theology, and philosophy. His popularity made his attacks on Christianity and his belief in a finite god highly controversial. He was a very bitter enemy of Christ and the Gospel.

One of the controversies that fueled the Fundamentalist-Liberal debates at the beginning of the twentieth century was the belief of Wells and religious liberals that god was a finite god who neither knew nor controlled the future. The literature of this period focused on Wells as the most vocal defender of a finite god.

In his book, *God: The Invisible King*, Wells begins by stating in his preface:

> This book sets out as forcibly and exactly as possible the religious belief of the writer. That belief is not orthodox Christianity; it is not, indeed, Christianity at all.[56]

Wells's forthright statement that his finite god is not Christian in any sense is a welcome breath of fresh air in an age when the same view of god is often called "Christian."

> The spirit of this book is like that of a missionary who would only too gladly overthrow and smash some Polynesian divinity of shark's teeth and painted wood and mother-of-pearl. To the writer such elaborations as "begotten of the Father before all worlds" are no better than intellectual shark's teeth and oyster shells. His purpose, like the purpose of that missionary, is not primarily to shock and insult; but he is

zealous to liberate, and he is impatient with a reverence that stands between man and God.[57]

The writer . . . declares as his own opinion, and as the opinion which seems most expressive of modern thought, that there is no reason to suppose the Veiled Being either benevolent or malignant towards man. . . . God presents himself as finite, as struggling and taking a part against evil . . . the reality of religion . . . is still our self-identification with God.[58]

Wells views the Christian God as an idol, which he is going to smash in order to liberate mankind. For himself, he believes in what he calls "The Veiled Being," which was one of the names used by the Greeks in speaking of the "unknown god." With missionary zeal, Wells seeks to destroy Christianity and its "tottering" idol of Jehovah.

In his first chapter, in a section entitled, "Modern Religion Has a Finite God," Wells argues:

Perhaps the most fundamental difference between this new faith and any recognised form of Christianity is that, knowingly or unknowingly, it worships *a finite God*. God is neither all-wise, nor all-powerful, nor omnipresent; that he is neither the maker of heaven nor earth, and that he has little to identify him with that hereditary God of the Jews who became the "Father" in the Christian system. On the other hand he will assert that his God is a god of salvation, that he is a spirit, a person, a strongly marked and knowable personality, loving, inspiring, and lovable, who exists or strives to exist in every human soul.[59]

The modern religious man will almost certainly profess a kind of universalism; he will assert that whensoever men have called upon any God and have found fellowship and comfort and courage and that sense of God within them, that inner light which is the quintessence of the religious experience, it was the True God that answered them. For the True God is a generous God, not a jealous God; the very antithesis of that bickering monopolist who "would have none other gods but me." . . . The True God has no scorn nor hate for those who have accepted the many-handed symbols of the Hindu or the lacquered idols of China. . . . The fact that God is *finite* is one upon which those who think clearly among the new believers are very insistent. He is, above everything else, a personality, and to be a personality is to have characteristics, to be limited by characteristics; he is a Being, not us but dealing with us and through us; he has an aim and that means he has a past and future; he is within time and not outside of it.[60]

What is amazing is that Wells did not realize that if god were as he claimed him to be and all religious symbols were good, then why did he scorn the Christian God as a "bickering monopolist"? Why did he mock this God as:

. . . a stuffed scarecrow of divinity, that incoherent accumulation of antique theological notions, the Nicene deity. This is certainly no God.[61]

Evidently Wells's universalism, which fawned on Eastern religions such as Hinduism or Buddhism, had no room for Christianity! Religious "universalism" has always been guilty of the most vicious forms of intolerance. Any religion and any god is "wonderful" *except* when it comes to Christianity and its God. He is reduced to a "stuffed scarecrow." Wells goes on to explain his new god.

The Infinite Being is not God. . . . The new religion does not . . . even assert that God knows all.[62]

God Is Within. God comes we know not whence, into the conflict of life. He works in men and through men. He is a spirit, a single spirit and a single person; he has begun and he will never end. He is the immortal part and leader of mankind. . . . He is by our poor scales of measurement boundless love, boundless courage, boundless generosity. He is thought and a steadfast will.[63]

The new religion has but disentangled the idea of him from the absolutes and infinities and mysteries of the Christian Theologians; from mythological virgin births and the cosmogonies and intellectual pretentiousness of a vanished age. Modern religion appeals to no revelation, no authoritative teaching, no mystery.[64]

He is a Being of the mind and in the minds of men . . . he exists in time just as a current of thought may do; that he changes and be-

comes more even as a man's purpose gathers itself together; that somewhere in the dawning of the mankind he had a beginning, an awakening, and that as mankind grows he grows. With our eyes he looks
out upon the universe he invades; with our hands, he lays his hands
upon it. All our truth, all our intentions and achievements, he gathers
to himself. He is the undying human memory, the increasing human
will.[65]

Wells's god does not know the future because he is only "undying
human memory." God has been reduced until he exists only in the will
and mind of man.

In Chapter 7, Wells proclaims that a "new religion" is coming in
which, like the Hindus, man will trust in no other god than the one
within himself. It will involve some form of pantheism in which man
participates in divinity. He sees a Western acceptance of Eastern religions resulting in a new world religion which will oppose the infinite
God of Christianity. He rejoices to see liberal clergymen already prepar-
ing the way for the new world religion by attacking all the "omni" attributes of God.[66]

Wells's prophecy has been fulfilled in our day with the rise of oc-
cultism, the New Age Movement, processianism, moral government,
and positive thinking. The day has finally arrived when so-called "evangelical" pastors and theologians are teaching the same finite god that
Wells imagined.

The "Trojan Horse" that has been used to penetrate evangelical
and charismatic theology is the process philosophy of Alfred North
Whitehead. Since it is often claimed that Whitehead was a "Christian"
theologian, we must take a close look at what he taught about Christianity.

Alfred North Whitehead (1861-1947) and God in Process

Although he was raised in a Christian home, Whitehead rebelled
against every aspect of Christian teaching. His influence was felt on
both sides of the Atlantic, as he taught at both Cambridge and Harvard.

Process philosophy or processianism has only recently been "discovered" by neo-evangelical theologians. As a general rule, liberal theological fads take at least ten years before they become evangelical theologi-

cal fads. Long after liberal theologians have abandoned the fad, some "evangelical" scholar will announce a "new" discovery. A flood of books will be written that explain the "new" insight. A fad will be launched and evangelical seminaries and colleges will jump on the bandwagon. Those who were "into" Barth a few years ago are now "into" processianism as the "latest thing."

Whitehead is increasingly viewed with awe by evangelicals. His writings are read in prominent seminaries and colleges, and his disciples, such as Pinnock and Rice, are spreading his ideas through evangelical publishers. It is thus important for us to examine what Whitehead taught.

In a book entitled *The Dialogues of Alfred North Whitehead*, Whitehead expresses his thoughts on God, the Bible, Jesus, Christianity, and other religious issues with remarkable clarity. The following readings are from these dialogues.

The Bible

Whitehead writes:

"How singularly humourless the Bible is," remarked the doctor.

"I wonder why?"

"You would be gloomy, too," said Whitehead gravely, "if you had Jehovah hanging over you."

"But what a contrast with the Greeks and their laughter," said Mr. Agassiz.

"Where does it come in?" asked Mrs. Nichols.

"Aristophanes."

"Yes," said Whitehead, "but I think humour is a bit later than the stage to which the prophets belong."

"Besides," said the doctor, "the Jewish scriptures were religious literature."

"Yes," said Whitehead, "and when writing is new, men don't set down what they regard as trivialities."[67]

As the evening went on we discussed whether there was much help in the Bible for people like us during the present world tumult. He (Whitehead) said there was no longer much of anything in it for him. I mentioned the Beatitudes, some of the sayings of Jesus, and the saga of Elijah on Mount Carmel.

"That is a great saga," said he, "but no more."

"The two who have never failed me," I said, "are Beethoven and Plato."

"Plato is the great one," he answered quietly.

He had given up the Bible.[68]

On Jesus

Whitehead continues,

Jesus would appear to have been one of those winning persons to whom good things get attributed, so that when those oppressed classes were making up a scheme of life whereby existence would be tolerable to them, it clustered around the figure of Jesus.[69]

We needn't go into the question of whether Christ was entirely an authentic historic personage, or one of those figures on whom are laid the needs and sayings and aspirations of a period.[70]

"The trouble," said he, "comes from intellectualizing upon a religion. Jesus was not very intellectual; what he had was a profound insight. . . . Paul comes as quite a drop from Jesus, and although his followers included many estimable persons, their idea of God, is, to my mind, the idea of the devil."[71]

On Christianity

According to Whitehead:

As for Christian theology, can you imagine anything more appallingly idiotic than the Christian idea of heaven? What kind of deity is it that would be capable of creating angels and men to sing his praises day and night to all eternity? It is, of course, the figure of an Oriental despot, with his inane and barbaric vanity. Such a conception is an insult to God. . . . I tell you, though, that on its emotional and aesthetic side, Christianity plays an enormous part in the lives of people who are not over-intellectualized; women especially.[72]

I consider Christian theology to be one of the great disasters of the human race.[73]

How is it that Hebraic thought gained over us Northern Europeans—for that is what we are?

It is peculiar. . . . I think that we must remember that it was a view of life that came in through the slave and proletarian populations. It was *their* view of how life may be well lived even though you are an underdog. And, of course, that view has coloured all subsequent European history. It is more Paul's than that of Jesus. There is no evidence that Paul ever saw Jesus, and he seems to have rather a patronizing view of his entourage. . . . Yes, one would have thought Paul would have gone to the apostles and said, "Come now, tell me all you can remember about him. Just how was it?"But no: instead, he says, "Now you sit there and I'll tell you what it all meant." . . . Christianity came into Europe through the lower classes."[74]

On the Christian God

Whitehead rejected the idea of "an omniscient, all-wise, all-powerful Being who has created this world."[75] He claimed that the Biblical God was his "idea of the devil."

Christianity is a fearful example. The Jews had originally a barbaric morality which was gradually undergoing humanization at the hands of their finer spirits, although it was from time to time rebarbarized by the coarser. I don't remember that the Buddhistic religion was ever guilty of such fearfully immoral ideas as the Hebrew theology in its earlier form or the Christian in its later: that mankind were to be saved or damned, and damned to eternal torment. Rather, the Buddhist held that we are, all of us, so imperfect that we must keep returning lifetime after lifetime for purification through experience until we are worthy to lose our identity in the all. But the Jews, looking over the world at large, thought there must be a despot over all, and the consequence was they conceived one of the most immoral Gods ever imagined.

"Fancy Jehovah telling Abraham to sacrifice his son!:" said Mrs. Whitehead.

"It is true," said Grace, "Jehovah did things which any one of us would have hesitated to do."

"Hesitated?" said Mrs. Whitehead, "You mean horrified. . . . How amiable the Grecian gods appear by comparison. They may have had their crimes and follies, and have been no better than they should have been, but their offenses were more urbane."

"Yes," I said, "even if they, too, went to the devil in the end, they had a good time going."[76]

"Where does this self-denigration come from?"

It is the 'sense of sin,' said Whitehead. 'The worst blight that ever fell on man."[77]

"It was a mistake," said Whitehead, "as the Hebrews tried to conceive of God as creating the world from the outside, at one go. An all-foreseeing Creator, who could have made the world as we find it now—what could we think of such a being? Foreseeing everything and yet putting in it all sorts of imperfections to redeem which it was necessary to send his only son into the world to suffer torture and hideous death; outrageous ideas. The Hellenic religion was a better approach; the Greeks conceived of creation as going on everywhere all the time *within* the universe; and I also think they were happier in their conception of supernatural beings impersonating those various forces, some good, others bad: for both sorts of forces *are* present, whether we assign personality to them or not. God is *in* the world, or nowhere, creating continually in us and around us. This creative principle is everywhere, in animate and so-called inanimate matter, in the ether, water, earth, human hearts. But this creation is a continuing process, and the process is itself the actuality, since no sooner do you arrive than you start on a fresh journey. Insofar as man partakes of this creative process does he partake of the divine, of God, and that participation is his immortality. . . . His true destiny as co-creator in the universe is his dignity and his grandeur."[78]

Christians can only feel the utmost pity and sorrow for such a pathetic figure as Whitehead. His hatred of God and the Bible led him to champion the pagan deities of Greece. He would rather have Zeus than Jesus.

Philosophical Works

The followings readings are from Whitehead's philosophical work, *Process and Reality*.

He begins by admitting that he is only reviving Greek philosophy. Thus his "organic philosophy only repeats Plato."[79]

He rejects the biblical account of Creation on the grounds that, "The book of Genesis is too primitive."[80] In terms of his god, Whitehead says,

> We must ascribe to him neither fulness of feeling, nor consciousness. He is the unconditioned actuality of conceptual feeling at the base of things. . . . He is the lure for feeling, the eternal urge of desire. . . . God, as well as being primordial, is also consequence. He is the beginning and the end. He is not the beginning in the sense of being in the past of all members. He is the presupposed actuality of conceptual operation, in unison of becoming with every other creative act. Thus by reason of the relativity of all things, there is a reaction of the world on God. The completion of God's nature into a fulness of physical feeling is derived from the objectification of the world in God. He shares with every new creation its actual world; and the concrescent creature is objectified in God as a novel element in God's objectification of that actual world. . . . Thus, analogously to all actual entities, the nature of God is dipolar.[81]

In his concept of a dipolar god, Whitehead is saying that god is the soul of the world just as the world is his body. The two are "One." Thus what can be said of one can be said of the other. They are merely two sides of the same coin or like the two poles on the same magnet. This is nothing more than the same pantheism that forms the basis if all pagan religion. He defines his dipolar god in the following way:

It is as true to say that God is permanent and the World fluent, as that the World is permanent and God fluent. It is as true to say that God is one and the World many, as that the World is one and God many. It is as true to say that, in comparison with the World, God is actual eminently, as that, in comparison with God, the World is actual eminently.

It is as true to say that the World is immanent in God, as the God is immanent in the World. It is as true to say that God transcends the World, as that the World transcends God. It is as true to say that God creates the World, as that the World creates God. God and the World stand over against each other, expressing the final metaphysical truth that appetitive vision and physical enjoyment have equal claim to priority in creation. But no two actualities can be torn apart: each is all in all.

Thus each temporal occasion embodies God, and is embodied in God. In God's nature, permanence is primordial and flux is derivative from the World: in the World's nature, flux is primordial and flux is derivative from God. . . . Neither God, nor the World, reaches static completion. Both are in the grip of the ultimate metaphysical ground, the creative advance into novelty. Either of them, God and the World, is the instrument of novelty for the other.[82] Whitehead's god is only as "divine" as the world is. Both the world and god are lesser beings who are being molded by the "ultimate ground," the impersonal force called "Creativity."

Utilizing the philosophies of both Plato and Aristotle, Whitehead sees "potentialities" becoming "actualities" in an eternal process. Everything including god is drawn toward the actual. Embracing Heraclitus' world of "flux," Whitehead sweeps away any permanence in god or the world.

Like Hegel, Whitehead's philosophy was self-refuting. If all things are in the grip of the flux of an eternally evolving "process" including truth, then his own philosophy was not "permanently" true. It would soon be swept aside with the march of time.

Conclusion

The Greek philosopher Cratylus took process philosophy to its logical conclusion. If all is flux (or process), then we must renounce all speech, for just as you never step into the same river twice, your words can never have the same meaning twice. Even as you speak, your words have gone through a dynamic change and no longer mean what you meant when you spoke them! Cratylus put his philosophy into practice and never spoke again. What a wonderful world it would be if the modern followers of Heraclitus would be as consistent!

No knowledge is possible in a world of constant change. There is no solid ground to stand on, no peg to place your hat, and no god to live or die for.

SEVEN

THE FINITE GOD OF EVANGELICAL PROCESSIANISM

W e must now deal with those theologians who have claimed to be "evangelical" and, at the same time, teach the doctrine of a finite god who cannot know or control the future. We realize that some of them will object to being called "Socinians" and "processians." But we have carefully traced the doctrine they teach throughout secular and church history and found that while it has a place in such heretical systems, it has *never* been a part of Christian theology. Anyone who limits the knowledge and power of God is doing something that the Christian Church has always considered heresy.

The Limited God of Anthony Kenny (1931-)

This Oxford scholar has spent most of his life in defense of man's "free will" as evidenced by the number of books and articles he has written on that subject. He places himself in the humanist tradition of such pagan thinkers as John Stuart Mill.[1] Thus "free will" for Kenny ultimately means pure chance or contingency. His goal is freedom *from* God.

It is interesting to note that with Kenny it is always *God* who is viewed as "the problem." It is God who stands in the way of man. It is God who is to blame if He dares to interfere with man and his plans.

When we look to see an in-depth discussion of the problem of man's sin and his desperate need for God to intervene in grace and mercy, we don't find anything. Evidently, the sinfulness of man, which gives a moral dimension to the question of "freedom" is never viewed as a problem.

For Kenny and those like him, there is nothing wrong with man. God is the problem. Also, when the choice comes down to either God's freedom to do as He pleases with what He made or man's freedom to do as he pleases free from any interference from God, why it is assumed that God must *always* give way to man? Why is the emphasis *always* on reducing God's power and knowledge? Why can't they consider that perhaps man should give way before his Maker? Why don't they reduce the knowledge and power of man and let God alone?

The Scriptures always defend God at all costs. Thus if all of mankind were to believe the opposite of what God has spoken in His Word, Paul declares, "Let God be true and every man a liar" (Romans 3:4). What adds considerable weight to this statement is that Paul is dealing with the objections of the humanists of his own day who argued that if God is glorified by all things, including evil, then we may do evil and God should not judge us because He derives a benefit from it.

> But if our unrighteousness demonstrates the righteousness of God, what shall we say? The God who inflicts wrath is not unrighteous, is He? (I am speaking in human terms.) May it never be! For otherwise how will He judge the world? But if through my lie the truth of God abounded to His glory, why am I also being judged as a sinner? And why not say (as we are slanderously reported and some affirm that we say), "Let us do evil that good may come." Their condemnation is just (Romans 3:5-8).

Notice that it is humanistic thinking (here called "human terms") that demands that God be limited. The point of the humanistic argument is to limit God from judging men for their sins.

On the contrary, Paul argues that all such attempts to limit God are really based on the immoral and depraved desire to exalt man, to absolve him from the guilt of his sin, and to escape the righteous judgment of God. With such evil motives behind their attempts to limit God, Paul pronounces that "their condemnation is just."

While Christian thinkers will always "let God be true and man the liar," humanistic thinkers will always "let man be true and God the liar." The battle will always boil down to Divine Revelation or autonomous human reason.

Kenny is bold to proclaim that "there is no such being as the God" of historic Christianity.[2] Why? "It . . . is an incoherent one."[3] That is, the Christian God is incomprehensible and cannot be reduced to his mind. Because God is "incoherent," he concludes:

> If God is to be omniscient . . . then he cannot be immutable. If God is to have infallible knowledge of future human actions, then determinism is true. If God is to escape responsibility for human wickedness, then determinism must be false. Hence in the notion of a God who foresees all sins but is the author of none, there lurks a contradiction. There cannot, if our argument has been sound, be a timeless, immutable, omniscient, omnipotent, all-good being . . . nothing can possess the totality of the divine attributes.[4]

Kenny is saying that the Christian God would be "responsible" for "man's wickedness" if He existed. This idea is based on the fallacious assumption that God is accountable to someone higher. But to whom, pray tell, is God responsible? To whom must the Creator answer? Who sits in judgment on the Holy One? Who will call the Almighty to judgment?

When humanists like Kenny discuss theodicy (the question of God's responsibility for evil), they begin with the false assumption that God is responsible to something or someone outside of His own nature. This is impossible because any discussion of "evil" assumes the existence of an infinitely good and righteous God. Otherwise the word *evil* has no meaning. Without the Christian God, the terms *evil* and *good* lose all meaning.[5]

Kenny is smart enough to know that once you take one infinite or "omni" attribute away from God, all such attributes must go. We can't just say, "God does not know the future," and then go merrily on our way with the rest of God still intact.

Just like unraveling a sweater by pulling only one thread, once God's omniscience or any other infinite attribute is "pulled," the entire biblical concept of God unravels. Once he rejects the omniscience and omnipotence of God Almighty, Kenny has to go with his reductionism until God is no longer GOD.

To Kenny the issue is simple. Either he knows *more* than God or God is *equal* to him in knowledge. In this way God is either "less" than he is or else his "equal." The Christian God is not acceptable to him because "an immutable being cannot know what we know."[6]

Kenny's solution is to limit God's knowledge to "all that we know."7 But this can be true only if god is limited in the exact ways that our knowledge is limited, that is, "he must be subject in some degree to change."8 This means that god is not infallible and immutable in his knowledge of the future. Thus, if god is limited by the knowledge of man, he cannot know the future.

What disturbs us with Kenny's line of reasoning is that he never considers the idea that God may know *more* than man in ways which far exceed man. A god who knows *less* than we do or is only *equal* to us is hardly worthy of the name "GOD." He who made man's mind is not ignorant of what goes on in that mind. God is not ignorant of the thoughts of man. He is not defiled because He *knows* all our evil and perverted thoughts. The Day of Judgment will reveal that His knowledge and power are not limited by man or by his idols.

Can a Finite God Really Be Called GOD?

If we answered the question on the basis of the conclusions reached by Steuer and McClenden, we would have to say no. The god of Steuer, McClenden, etc., is not the GOD of Scripture.

Steuer complains that in the Christian view, "God's being and God's properties are seen as different in kind, or qualitatively different, from those of his creatures."9 He goes on to claim that this is "Platonic metaphysics." Instead, we should see God and man as sharing the *same* being and properties or attributes. This is another way of saying God must be like us. He is not allowed to be "better" than we are, qualitatively speaking, or "greater" than we are, quantitatively speaking.

Up until this time, humanistic thinkers such as Mill, Wells, Brightman, and Whitehead did not hesitate to state that the concept of a finite god who cannot know or control the future came from Greek philosophy. Indeed, they actually boasted of this fact. But as the doctrine of the finite god comes closer to the evangelical Church, suddenly the approach flip-flops and the historic Christian concept of God is now rejected as "Greek philosophy"! This claim is so outlandish that anyone who makes it is either ignorant of the rudiments of philosophy or willfully deceptive. This ploy is used by Steuer, who dismisses the Christian God on the grounds that He is "a Platonic creation," when in reality it is Steuer who is trying to resurrect Plato's finite god.

Christians have always believed that God's being and properties are qualitatively different from man's. God's being is self-existent and independent while man's being is dependent on God for existence. God's being is eternal and man's being is temporal. The radical distinction between the Creator and the creature is the very essense of Biblical Christianity.

Steuer follows Greek philosophy in saying that God is *either* infinite *or* personal.[10] Since he assumes such Greek dichotomies as truisms, the God of the Bible, who is *both* infinite *and* personal, is "incoherent" to him.

This touches on the underlying issue of why the Christian God is always labeled as "incoherent." If one begins with pagan assumptions, then the Christian God will be "incoherent" in that He cannot be reconciled with those assumptions. The Christian God becomes a round peg that will not fit into the square hole of pagan thought. It is on this basis that God is declared "incoherent."

The trick played by the Socinians is now reproduced. God's knowledge is reduced to what is "knowable," because Steuer has decided that the future is "unknowable" because *man* cannot know it. God's knowledge is restricted to being "just like ours."[11] Thus God cannot know the future. "Man is the measure of all things," including God's knowledge!

But don't worry, God is still "omniscient," if we give this term a radical redefinition. God can see future possible "options" and "choices"; however, "he does not and cannot foreknow (infallibly foresee) the outcome of each individual free deliberation."[12]

Since God's knowledge of things that might happen in the future is finite and mutable, Steuer concludes that God's knowledge is neither infallible nor perfect.

> . . . the free actions of other agents cannot be predicted infallibly even by deity. . . . No one, even . . . God, can predict infallibly and therefore foreknow the outcome of a truly free choice of another agent.[13]

But what about all those prophecies found in the Bible? Aren't they infallible predictions of the future? Steuer states, "God's predictions . . . will not be infallible."[14]

This comment by Steuer reveals why "evangelical" processians usually deny the inerrancy of Scripture. If the Bible is not infallible in its knowledge of the future, how can it be infallible on anything else?

What is the bait that Steuer uses to lure Christians away from the God of their fathers? It is the same old idol of "free will" that pagans and heretics have always used. The "freedom" they desire is freedom *from* God. This "freedom" is nothing more than the old Greek gods "Chance" and "Lady Luck." Steuer argues that if man is "really" free, then the universe is closed to God.[15] Absolute freedom is possible only in a world "open" to chance and "closed" to God. Fallen man has always wanted a "closed" universe that God could not penetrate. Such a universe is "open" only to blind chance. The trick is to tell people that only a chance-based freedom can make the universe "open" to man without letting them know that such a universe is "closed" to God.

Utilizing once again the "either-or" dichotomies of Greek philosophy, he sets up the issue as:

> . . . either the denial of divine omnipotence or the denial of human freedom.[16]

> God's omniscience seems to make human freedom logically impossible.[17]

> . . . either . . . give up the claim that human beings possess the sort of freedom requisite . . . or . . . deny the traditional notion of God's omniscience.[18]

Steuer is always very careful to state that the only "sort of freedom" he will allow in the discussion is *his* personal idea of what "real" freedom is. The outcome of the discussion is already settled. The contest has been rigged from the beginning. If we begin by assuming a definition of freedom that arose out of a pagan worldview, of course it will be incompatible with the concept of God that arose out of the Judeo-Christian worldview as revealed in Scripture.

What is astounding about Steuer and others like him is that they can claim to be teaching "Christian" theology while never once going to the Bible to see what it has to say about God! The entire process of reducing God to a finite god is carried on in the name of "reason." Obviously, Steuer realizes only too well that if he gets too close to the Bible it will give the kiss of death to his god.

Richard Rice and the "Open" God

The finite god tradition has always been a part of the cults and the occult since the time of the Gnostics. It is a vital part of such groups as the Latter-Day Saints (Mormons), Jehovah's Witnesses, and the World-wide Church of God.

Rice is a Seventh-day Adventist and is an associate professor of theology at Loma Linda University, one of the top Adventist schools. Although the first edition of his book, *The Openness of God*, was published by Review and Herald, the S.D.A. publisher, his attempt to introduce process theology into Adventist circles met with stiff resistance from such "old-line" Adventist thinkers as Carsten Johnsen.[19]

Rice will have a difficult time convincing his fellow Adventists that God does not know the future. After all, the founder of his church, Ellen G. White, claimed to *know* the future so well that she even set a date for the Second Advent of Christ! How can God be ignorant of the future when Ellen White was able to predict it? It would seem that Rice's view destroys the very foundation of the Adventist Church.

In order to avoid Adventist criticism, Rice devoted the Appendix of his book to statements found in the "inspired" writings of White, which he claimed supported "the open view of God." But in the very passages he cites it is clear that she believed that the future was both knowable and predictable. Thus, Rice is not reflecting Adventist theology when he defines god as a finite being who is ignorant of the future and is himself caught up in the "process of becoming," not even knowing what he will be or do tomorrow.

Keeping in line with the finite god tradition, Rice is a rationalist. The Christian God is rejected not because the Bible tells him so but because Rice's "reason" and "intuitions" tell him so.[20] Rice claims that the orthodox concept of God is not "logically coherent" because it is "not faithful to human experience."[21] In other words, God must be a "coherent conception" or out he goes.[22] Rice's finite god "makes more sense on a rational basis" because it is "more internally consistent."[23]

Having stated that he is going to operate "on a rational basis," he charges those who would appeal to the orthodox doctrine of the incomprehensibility of God with using "piety as a cover for intellectual laziness."[24]

Rice's finite god is described as:

. . . an alternative to the traditional Christian understanding.[25]

God experiences the events of the world . . . as they happen, rather than all at once in some timeless, eternal perception.[26]

This all sounds just like Alfred North Whitehead. Rice admits this:

> Readers familiar with contemporary Christian theology will notice a resemblance between the view of God as presented here and the concept of God found in the writings of Alfred North Whitehead, Charles Hartshorne, and their followers.[27]

How Whitehead could be classified as a "Christian" theologian is beyond us. He was an "antichrist" in the full Biblical sense of the term (1 John 2:18-23). It would seem that Rice calls process philosophy "Christian" in order to palm it off in that guise to an unwary public.

> The concept of God proposed here shares the process view that God's relation to the temporal world consists in a succession of concrete experiences, rather than a single timeless perception. It too conceives God's experience of the world as ongoing, rather than a once-for-all affair.[28]

Rice's god, like Whitehead's deity, struggles from day to day never knowing what tomorrow may bring. At this point, Rice uses the Socinian trick of restricting God's knowledge to what is "knowable," having already decided that the future is "unknowable."[20]

But will Rice go so far as to adopt Whitehead's "dipolar" deity?

> It also shares with process theism the twofold analysis of God, or of dipolar theism.[30]

As we have seen, Whitehead's "dipolar view of god" is a form of pantheism called "panentheism" and is not to be confused with the theism of the Bible. Rice agrees with Whitehead's core idea that what god is to the world, the world is to god. Rice's god in this sense becomes:

- absolute and relative,
- necessary and contingent,
- eternal and temporal,
- changeless and changing.[31]

Rice has no problem with a god who is being "created" by the moment to moment turn of events. In this sense, god is always *changing* from moment to moment. What he is now is not what he will be two seconds from now, for he is changing all the time as he learns new things. What he thought he was going to do yesterday was based on the limited knowledge he had at that time. Now that he knows more today, his plans may change. Every "roll of the dice" makes god "new" and "different." This is why he rejects the historic Christian doctrine that God is infallible, changeless, immutable, and perfect.[32]

But Rice claims that, as of yet, he has not gone "all the way" with Whitehead. Even though he desperately wants people to accept Whitehead's god as "Christian," he knows that it is a panentheistic god. This would be hard for most Adventists to swallow. So, Rice meekly states that he still believes in a few aspects of Christian teaching such as "creation" and that his finite god has "ontological independence" of the world. What he means by these terms is not clear.

Rice then muddies the picture once again by saying that his god is the same as Paul Tillich's "ground of being."[33] Tillich was a pantheistic atheist! He hardly qualifies as a "Christian" by any stretch of the imagination. If this is what Rice believes, he is a pantheistic atheist as well.

The arguments Rice uses against the Christian God are the same ones used over and over again by the heretics throughout Church history. He repeats Whitehead, who admitted that he was only repeating Plato! Rice uses all the "either-or" dichotomies of Greek philosophy. Man is "free" only if he is free *from* God. We are told to choose between God and man. Either God is perfect, immutable, infallible, allwise, and all-knowing, or man is free in the sense of pure chance.

There are dire consequences of his view for the atoning work of Christ. If god does not know the future, then he did not know that Jesus was going to come to earth. As a matter of fact, Rice believes that not even Jesus knew the when, where, why, or what of his atonement! The events in the life of Jesus were not foreknown by god. That Jesus became incarnate and what happened to him afterward was left up to pure chance.

Rice argues that since the future is really "open," i.e., unknown, then god did not know if "his son would fail in his struggle with temptation."[34] That god did not know if Jesus would be deceived by the Devil will come as a shock to most Christians. But since Rice denies the immutability of God, he is forced to say that Jesus could have failed.

Rice's god did not even know that Jesus would die on the cross. His death was not predestined or known ahead of time. He believes that god did not have a clue as to what Judas, Pilate, Herod, or the Jews would do. The death of Christ must have been quite a shock to god!

According to Rice's "reason," the fact that the atonement was a chance happening that was unknown and unplanned by god is wonderful. It means that god took a "risk" in sending his son to do something, not knowing what it might be. Evidently, Jesus simply ran out of luck and got crucified.

But this means that the Trinity itself was at risk. God was:

> . . . running the risk of permanent disastrous consequences to the God-head itself.35

Rice is right when he places the Trinity in danger, because the historic doctrine of the Trinity cannot survive the assault of process theology. Even if god is *now* a Trinity, he *is* constantly changing into something else. What god will be in the future is left up to chance. Rice even states that the Trinity could self-destruct!

Some feminists claim that Mary has become a part of god and that god is now a Quaternity! This is an example of where Rice's "open god" can lead. Such a view of the Trinity is not the historic Christian concept of God.

The reason Rice can deceive the average Adventist and Christian is that he uses such orthodox words as "Trinity," "omniscient," "perfect," and "infallible" in reference to his god. But each of these terms have been radically *redefined* to mean the exact *opposite* of what they have always meant! Once again we are faced with the old Socinian trick of redefining orthodox terms to cover up a denial of orthodox doctrines.

Let the evangelical who is tempted by Rice's free-willism consider the fact that Rice does not believe in the Christian concept of the Trinity. This is no "tempest in a teapot." Rice has openly denied the historic and creedal concept of the Trinity. He must be judged as being as heretical as the Jehovah's Witnesses, who also deny that God knows all the details of the future.

A second edition of his book was published by an evangelical publisher under the title, *God's Foreknowledge and Man's Free Will*.36 This edition neglected to inform its readers that Rice is a Seventh-day Adventist. Whatever the reason for this, the Christian public should have been told who the author was, where he taught, and that he was a Seventh-day Adventist.

Evangelical publishers must understand that Christianity is a *historical* religion and that its concept of God, as found in all the great creeds of the Church, cannot be denied without causing great harm to the cause of God and truth. It is also important to remember that there is a history to ideas. If someone wants to believe in an idea that has historically never been a part of the Christian faith, then that idea has no right to bear the title "Christian." If an idea has historically been a part of pagan, cultic, occultic, and heretical traditions, then it is heretical.

The problem we face today is that people want to use the term "Christian" to cover ideas that have never historically been a part of Christian thinking. When we let a word mean anything and everything, then it means nothing. The word "Christian" loses all meaning if it is cut free from history.

Stephen T. Davis and the God Who Can Lie

Davis is another example of a nonevangelical whose book was published in its second edition by an evangelical publisher. As a result, Davis's book can be found in evangelical bookstores.

As a typical processian, Davis is a committed rationalist. His book is filled with appeals to "reason" as if human reason were the final authority in all things.[37] He is only interested in what his "intuition" tells him.[38] Whatever is "incoherent" to him, i.e., incomprehensible, is denied, "if we want to be rational."[39] Christians are told to "explain how" this or that aspect of God is rational.[40] When he lists his criteria for truth, he states,

> First, it must be coherent. Second, it must roughly agree with our intuition.[41]

But what about the Bible? Davis's rejection of Scripture is clear from his attack on the inerrancy of Scripture.[42] Thus he states in his introduction,

> I do not propose to do serious exegesis or biblical theology in this book.[43]

Davis's view of god is as follows.

> I abandon the notion of God's timelessness . . . and the notion of God's immutability.[44]

> . . . it is possible for God to do evil.[45]

... a temporal God who is "in" time just as we are[46] ... he cannot be immutable.[47]

My intuitions are such that God can, if he wishes, take away his own omnipotence.[48]

God is able to do evil.[49]

God is free to do evil ... it is logically possible and within God's power to do evil.[50]

God has the ability to tell a lie.[51]

God has the ability to break a promise.[52]

Now, lest Christians get upset over his idea that "god *can* sin,"[53] Davis assures us that while god can sin, he won't really do it. But when the basis of that hope is examined, it ends up being what Francis Schaeffer appropriately called an "upper-story leap of faith." God will not do evil because "he doesn't want to." But Davis never explains what happens if god's desires change. Such a god *could* decide to become the Devil tomorrow!

If God is not immutable, infallible, and perfect in His nature and attributes, then there is *no* guarantee that He will be good, loving, kind, or faithful one minute from now. It gives us no comfort whatsoever when Davis encourages us to take a blind leap of faith into the unknown future of god and hope for the best.

Clark Pinnock and the God Who Isn't There

At one time an evangelical and a strong defender of the inerrancy and authority of Scripture, according to Koivisto, Pinnock, "has changed his entire epistemological approach to the Bible."[54]

That Pinnock has rejected the orthodox view of the Bible is also documented by Holloman, who states that Pinnock,

... clearly departs from the traditional orthodox view of the Bible. [55]

Underlying Pinnock's thought is his conviction that "the New Testament does not teach a strict doctrine of inerrancy."[56]

Since Pinnock has rejected the inerrancy of Scripture, it is no surprise to find him now teaching that the Bible is flawed because of the human weakness of its authors; some of the miracles of the Bible are legendary; portions of Matthew's Gospel are fictional embellishments; some of Paul's teaching is not inspired; some of the early chapters of Genesis are sagas; Jonah is a "didactic fiction;" Daniel was written in the Maccabean period; and the Pauline authorship of Ephesians and the Pastoral Epistles is doubtful.[57]

In a recent book issued by an evangelical publisher, Pinnock argues against creationism and for evolution,[58] and that it is not necessary to believe in Jesus Christ or His Gospel to be saved![59] Evidently, if a pagan is sincere in his heathen religion, he can be "saved" without Jesus. What this does to missions is obvious.

Not only does Pinnock reject the Christian concept of the Bible, creation, and salvation, but now it seems that he denies the Christian concept of the afterlife. It looks as if he no longer believes that there is a hell to shun or a heaven to gain after death. The cultic doctrines of "soul sleep," conditionalism, and annihilationism are more to his liking.[60]

Like all the other defenders of the finite god tradition, Pinnock is a rationalist. This explains his "epistemological change." In a recent book published by another evangelical publisher, instead of appealing to Scripture, he constantly appeals to human "reason" as the final authority.[61]

He also appeals to such things as:

- our intuition[62]
- the demands of reason[63]
- the requirements of intelligence[64]
- rational hypothesis[65]

Pinnock starts out by using Steuer's trick of labeling the Christian view as "Platonic." His argument is either based on a sheer ignorance of Greek philosophy or willful deception. The irony is, of course, that it is actually Pinnock who is reviving Plato's finite god who does not know the future. At least Brightman and Whitehead were more honest!

But under this guise, Pinnock sneaks in all the old Greek dichotomies. His view of god is always presented in the "either-or" formula:

> If God is changeless in every aspect of his being and knows history, there cannot be genuine freedom.[66]

> Omniscience in the sense of a complete knowledge of all future contingents does not make sense.[67]

> God . . . interacts with his creatures in a changing situation. His experience of the world is open and not closed. He learns about our decisions as they happen, not before they happen . . . his experience of the world is open and he is involved in the ongoing course of events.[68]

> . . . philosophically . . . a future free action . . . cannot be known ahead of time by God or anyone else.[69]

> . . . history cannot be predicted even by God.[70]

With such beliefs, Pinnock could only conclude, "I stand against classical theism."[71]

Pinnock now uses the Socinian trick of limiting God's knowledge to what is "knowable," having already decided that the future is "unknowable" even to God.[72] Such circular arguments fail to impress us no matter how many times they are recycled. Pinnock arbitrarily decides what God can or cannot know.

Pinnock also rejects God's immutability, infallibility, and perfection. He admits that what he is saying is what Alfred North Whitehead taught. But using the exact same words as Rice, he tries "to ward off suspicion" by stating he still believes in a few things like "the ontological independence of God."[73]

This disclaimer is not worth much. Once you have torn the omni-attributes out of God and reduced him to a finite deity, to say that he is floating around somewhere in a universe that is out of control and headed toward possible oblivion, is not saying very much.

Once God is viewed as finite, fallible, imperfect, and mutable, how could such a god give us an infallible Bible which is perfect? Such a god would not and could not *control* the human authors of the Bible to *prevent* them from lying, embellishing, exaggerating, or giving fairy tales.

Given the kind of god that Pinnock now believes in, he is forced to abandon not only the Christian God but also the Christian Scriptures. Let Pinnock's apostasy serve as a warning to all those who in their zeal to exalt the Greek view of man's freedom are willing to reject the Christian God.

Pinnock has simply followed the same logical path that Marcion, Valentinus, Socinus, and almost every other heretic has followed. If man is "free" in the Greek sense of pure chance, then God is not sovereign. And, if God is not sovereign, then we must give up the inspiration and authority of the Bible. Man is thus left only with his "reason" as the origin and judge of truth.

Conclusion

We have surveyed the finite god tradition and have discovered that it is rooted in ancient pagan religions and has been held by almost all heretical groups down through the ages. The defenders of such a view are usually the most bitter enemies of Christ and His Church.

They are committed rationalists who begin with pagan assumptions that render the Biblical God "incoherent." They are reductionistic in their approach to God, shrinking Him until He "fits" into their preconceived mold of what God must be. They do not look to Scripture as the final authority but only to their own "reason" and "intuition."

As Gresham Machen pointed out the last time this controversy arose, liberalism is *not* "Christian." The term "Christian" has an historical meaning that cannot cover such pagan doctrines as a finite god.[74]

If someone finds the Greek gods more to his taste, fine. But let him not play the hypocrite and claim such gods to be "Christian" or "evangelical." Let him be honest and courageous enough to leave the Christian Church and join one of the cults that worship a finite god, and let God be GOD and the Church, the CHURCH.

PART THREE

THE GOD OF THE BIBLE

EIGHT

RELIGION, REASON, AND REVELATION

Having examined the finite god tradition throughout history, we now turn to the basis of the historic Christian conception of God. We must emphasize at this point that we are not defending *our* view of God as if *we* invented it yesterday. We have no desire to be novel or creative in our doctrine of God. The historic faith of the Christian Church as found in her greatest creeds, such as the Westminster Confession of Faith, is more than sufficient for us.

The main problem we face today when discussing the nature of God is that people are not willing to limit their beliefs to what the Bible clearly teaches. Throughout the present controversy over the omniscience of God one searches in vain to find a single finite god advocate who bothers to give any serious exegesis of Scripture. Why is this?

Instead of a careful exegesis of Scripture, "evangelical" processians and "moral government" teachers appeal to "reason," "intuition," and "experience" as all the proof they need. Thus they never bother to let the Bible decide such issues because their doctrines are chosen on the basis of what feels "comfortable" or sounds "reasonable" to them. Doctrinal truth is often decided on the basis of how it will supposedly affect prayer, evangelism, or missions.

Among liberals and neo-evangelicals, the Bible is ignored for the most part because it is assumed that the Scriptures do not contain any propositional revelation and hence cannot be used for theology. It is claimed that the Bible is not the Word of God but that it "becomes the Word of God" when it speaks to us, or that revelation is limited to a nonrational personal encounter with God who is identified as "unknown X."

The Christian Church has always taught that the God who created man in His image has no difficulty in communicating truth to man. God reveals in Scripture true propositions about Himself, and also personally confronts man in grace or judgment.

The liberal bias against the Bible is based on a humanistic either/or dichotomy. It is assumed that either God reveals only Himself or else He reveals only facts about Himself, but not both. Such men refuse to consider the rather obvious alternative that God's revelation is both personal and factual. Not only is the Bible a record of man's encounter with God, but it also contains God's revelation of truth to man. God acts in history and then gives us an infallible interpretation of those acts. For these theologians, however, regardless of what the hidden humanistic assumptions are, the end product is that the Bible is ignored or attacked.

In opposition to this, we state without hesitation that the Bible is the final authority in all matters of doctrine and morals. We are to speak where the Bible speaks and to be silent when the Bible is silent. Speculation is not the way to do theology. The historical and grammatical exegesis of relevant passages in Scripture is the only safe path for those who look to God as the Origin of truth.

Humanistic thinkers have a totally different approach to truth. They assume that:

1. Man is the origin of truth and morals, not God.
2. Man can be the final judge of truth and morals when some part of his being is absolutized, made into the origin of meaning, and everything else is reduced to it.
3. Man's reason, feelings, or experiences are absolutized and are made into rationalism, mysticism, and empiricism.
4. Our conception of God is accordingly to be derived from what man thinks, feels, or experiences.
5. The Bible is not the *final* authority. The Bible is to be accepted to the degree it agrees with our reason, feelings, or experiences.

This approach to truth and morals is particularly dangerous because it forms the basis of the truth claims of the New Age Movement. New Age leaders such as Shirley MacLaine do not hesitate to claim that their ideas about religion are true because they have *experienced* them. On this basis we are told that reincarnation is true, that man is a god, etc.

The Christian who bases his doctrines on his reason, feelings, or experience has no way to counter someone whose reason, feelings, or experience tells him that witchcraft is good. Once we assume that "man is the measure of all things," then all our beliefs become relative and subjective. Religion is reduced to "paying your nickel and taking your choice." Religious truth as *truth* becomes a farce.

In this light, it has become necessary to remind evangelicals that there is a distinctively Christian way of knowing truth that does not fall into rationalism, mysticism, or empiricism. It is historically known as Biblicism. It assumes that:

1. God is the Origin of truth and morals, not man.
2. God's revelation in Scripture is the final authority in all matters of doctrine and morals.
3. Man's reason, feelings, and experiences are not to be viewed as the origin or final judge of truth, justice, morals, or beauty.
4. The Bible contains propositional truths that give us facts about God, the world He made, man's origin, Fall, and need of salvation. Revelation contains inerrant information as well as providing a record of man's experience with God.
5. The only *valid* way to find out such things as whether God knows the future is to examine what the Scriptures have to say on the issue. What someone's reason, intuition, feelings, or experiences have to say on the subject has no ultimate bearing on the issue whatsoever.
6. It really does not matter to us if someone feels comfortable or uncomfortable with what the Bible teaches. The basis of historic Christianity, Reformation theology, and evangelical doctrine is the whole Bible and nothing but the Bible, so help us God.

With these few introductory words, let us examine the truth claims of rationalism, mysticism, and empiricism in the light of the infallible and inerrant Word of God.

Rationalism

One of the greatest challenges the Church faces today is the rationalism which grew out of the humanism of the Renaissance during the fifteenth and sixteenth centuries in Western Europe. The philosopher Descartes is usually designated as the "Father" of modern rationalism because he believed that while he could doubt the existence of God, the world, other people, and even his own body, there was one thing that he could not doubt: that *he* existed—because he was the one doubting!

Descartes thus began with *himself* and tried to work up to an explanation of the existence and form of the universe and the nature of God. He assumed that man could start from himself, by himself, without any outside revelation from God, and still come to a true understanding of the world around him. He began with man and not God because he assumed that "man is the measure of all things" including God, truth, and morals.

Descartes was following the same path that unbelief has always taken. Some aspect of man was abstracted from his being and made into the origin of truth. Man's feelings, experience, or reason took the place that God alone can occupy. In this case, the rationalists took human reason and turned it into an ideal, abstract, absolute, transcendent "Reason" which was the origin, basis, and judge of all truth.

To the rationalist, "reality" is limited to what *he* thinks it to be in *his* own mind. Whatever is "unthinkable" to *him* cannot be true or even exist. He assumes that he can simply sit down in a dark room and through "Reason" alone come to understand everything. Divine revelation is not needed.

The rationalists developed various phrases and slogans that expressed the supremacy of reason. All ideas must be "in accord with reason." They must be "tried before the bar of reason." Any idea that does not "satisfy the demands of reason" must be rejected. All ideas must "justify themselves before reason." Philosophy begins and ends with the "first principles of reason." They also appeal to such words as "intuition," "intelligent," "logical," and "educated," as if anyone who disagrees with them is obviously stupid.

Rationalists do not hesitate to demand that such things as the existence of God and the inspiration of the Bible must be "justified before the bar of reason." They will accept the Bible only insofar as it is "in agreement with reason."

The Mysteries of the Faith

Rationalists have always attacked certain Christian doctrines as being "irrational" and "incoherent" because they are "mysteries" of the faith. They gleefully denounce such doctrines as the Trinity, the foreknowledge of God, the sovereignty of God, the imputation of Adam's sin, election and predestination, creation, the inerrancy of Scripture, and Christ's substitutionary atonement as "not in accord with reason."

They demand to know "how" God can be one and three at the same time, foreknow the future, and be the sovereign Creator and Sustainer of all things? How can the imputation of Adam's sin to us, our sin to Christ on the cross, and His righteousness to us be "justified before reason." Since they don't see how God's sovereignty and human responsibility can both be true, they simply throw out God's sovereignty. Everything must be reduced to their idea of what is "reasonable."

If they can't understand something, it is rejected. If they must choose between the "free will" of man and the "free will" of God, they always exalt man and dethrone God. Man becomes the measure of all things, including religious ideas. This is the heart and soul of religious humanism.

Is Reason Really Sufficient?

The problem with appealing to "reason" as the sole basis of truth is that it is not infallible and hence it is not as trustworthy as rationalists assume. Also, each rationalist has his own personal tastes and prejudices in view when he speaks of "reason" with hushed tones. Rationalists have always disagreed among themselves as to whose "reason" is ultimate. Each one in turn tries to claim the honor for himself and to refute all the rationalists who went before him. No wonder rationalism fell into disgrace in secular philosophy!

We wish that we could say that rationalism perished from off the face of the earth many years ago. But, sad to say, we have encountered more committed rationalists in the Christian Church than we have found in the world. Religious rationalists are always difficult to nail down because no matter how many Biblical passages you show them in support of a doctrine, they can always wave them aside in the name of "reason." Because they don't see how this or that doctrine can be reconciled in their mind with another doctrine, they will pick one and reject the other. But in all their picking, *man* always comes out on top.

The Role of Human Reason in Scripture

The first thing that strikes the reader of the Bible is the conspicuous absence of any reference to any abstract concept of "Reason." The authors of Scripture never claimed that their doctrines were true because they were "reasonable." They never referred to or viewed human reason as "the ultimate court of appeal." They never demanded belief or obedience "in the name of reason." And, at no time did they ever justify their teachings "before the bar of reason."

The various Hebrew and Greek words that are translated as "reason" in our English versions always refer either to sanity or to common sense (Daniel 4:36; Acts 6:2 KJV). Since the abstract concept of "Reason" was not developed until the Renaissance, this is to be expected.

Instead of seeking to justify Divine revelation before human reason, the authors of Scripture always demanded that human reason justify itself before revelation! Human reason was correct to the degree it agreed with revelation and not the other way around.

Moses is a good example of the way Biblical writers viewed human reason. He began the Bible with the existence of God (Genesis 1:1). He did not begin with an attempt to justify the existence of God before man's reason. Moses did the exact opposite. He justified the existence of man on the basis of the existence of God! When Moses gave the Law to Israel he never said, "Do this because it is reasonable." He said, "Do this because God said so." The supremacy was always given to revealed truth.

That the authors of Scripture viewed Divine revelation as the ultimate court of appeal is clearly seen from the way they handled all conflicts between human reason and revelation. Whenever a conflict arose between human reason and revelation, human reason was rebuked as rebellious (see Romans 9:10-21).

Indeed, even if all of mankind were to rise up and call a certain revealed truth "irrational," "not in accord with reason," "unjust," or even "wicked," the Apostle Paul said, "Let God be true and every man a liar" (Romans 3:4). It is interesting to note in passing that when Paul in the book of Romans had to deal with the conflict between sinful human reason and revealed truth, the focus of controversy was usually the doctrine of God's sovereignty (see Romans 3:1-19; 9:1-33; 11:1-36). The rejection of this Biblical doctrine is viewed as rebellion against God.

Throughout Scripture, man is viewed as the *receiver* of truth and morals and not its creator. God is the Author of all truth and morals and the Source of all wisdom and knowledge (see 2 Chronicles 1:10-12; Proverbs 1:1-7; Daniel 1:17; 2:23; John 1:17; Romans 1:25; James 1:5).

The Limitations of Reason

"Reason" cannot be viewed as the origin or judge of truth because of inescapable Biblical realities. First, human reason is finite. Thus it is not an infinite reference point, which can give meaning to the particulars of life. Second, human reason is sinful. It cannot be trusted, according to the Bible. Third, man's mind is not capable of an exhaustive understanding of truth or morals. We can only go so far before our reason "runs out of steam."

The intrinsic limitations of human reason forever disqualify it as the origin or final judge of truth. It is thus not surprising in the least to find that revealed truth goes beyond the ability of the human mind to understand. Indeed, if the human mind could understand everything the Bible teaches, this would prove that the Scriptures were of human origin and not inspired by God!

The fact that the Bible goes *beyond* human reason does not mean that it goes *against* rationality or logic. The seeming contradictions and irreconcilable truths found in Scripture only point us to the Infinite Mind who gave it. Man's failure to understand completely the truths revealed in Scripture does not imply an inherent irrationality in God or His revelation. It simply shows the limitation of our minds.

In reality, there are no inherent contradictions in God or His Word. Some of the truths of the Bible are incapable of human reconciliation because we don't have all the facts before us and our minds are not capable of understanding anything in an exhaustive way. But faith can always swim when reason can no longer feel the bottom.

The person committed to the supremacy and sufficiency of Scripture is not bothered by the fact that he cannot completely understand or explain the doctrine of the Trinity, the decrees of God, creation, original sin, predestination, or the atonement. They are called "mysteries" in Scripture because they are truths that did not originate in the mind of man and that he cannot fully understand. In the Old Testament, the passage that fully sets out the finite nature of human reason is found in Job 38-40. (See also Job 5:9; 11:7-9). In the New Testament, the same doctrine is taught in Romans 11:33-36; Ephesians 3:8, 19 and Philippians 4:7.

Revelation Goes Beyond Reason

The Christian is not under any Biblical constraint whatsoever to justify revealed truth before the bar of a mythological "reason" created by rationalists. For example, the doctrine of the Trinity is *true* because it is a *revealed* truth. It is not true because it is "reasonable." It is reasonable because it is true!

As a revealed truth, the doctrine of the Trinity is not irrational, unreasonable, or antilogical. The failure of our reason and logic to explain everything about the Trinity reveals our finiteness. Being infinite, God does not have any such difficulties and He understands His Triune nature completely.

Human reason is not only finite but also corrupted and twisted by sin. Thus the human mind or heart is morally incapable of submitting to revealed truth. Christian theologians speak of the "noetic effects of the Fall," by which they mean the effects of sin on the human mind and thinking ability. The noetic effects of the Fall focus on a moral problem of man. To put it bluntly, by nature man is *biased* against God and His Law/Word (Romans 8:7). Man's depravity is moral and not physical or metaphysical.

As soon as Adam and Eve fell into sin, their reason became darkened and they thought and did the most wicked and stupid things (Genesis 3:8-12). How then can man be the final judge of truth when he is biased against God to begin with? By nature we are "children of wrath" who "hate the light and love darkness" (John 3:19-20, Ephesians 2:1-3).

All the same, the moral implications of the Fall should not be twisted to mean that man's ability to think logically or rationally was destroyed by Adam's Fall into sin. Man is still in the image of God (James 3:9) and can still know that $1 + 1 = 2$ or that the law of non-contradiction is true. Man's rationality, like fire, must be kept in its place. But when man's rationality is made the alpha and the omega of all knowledge, it becomes destructive. Thus we have no problems *per se* with human reason as a finite reflection of the rational mind of God. But when reason is exalted into "Reason," it becomes a false god and serves as an example of man's propensity to idolatry.

The Mind and Heart of Man

In Scripture, the mind, heart, and conscience of man is described in the following ways:

- evil (Genesis 6:5; 8:21)
- corrupt and vile (Psalm 14:1-3)
- futile (Psalm 94:11)

- senseless (Jeremiah 10:14)
- deceptive above all things (Jeremiah 17:9)
- beyond cure (Jeremiah 17:9)
- hostile to the Light (John 3:19-20)
- suppressing the truth (Romans 1:18)
- darkened (Romans 1:21)
- foolish (Romans 1:22)
- idolatrous (Romans 1:23-26)
- carnal (Romans 8:6)
- dead (Romans 8:6)
- rebellious and hostile to God and His Law (Romans 8:7)
- incapable of pleasing God (Romans 8:8)
- blinded by Satan (2 Corinthians 4:3-4)
- corrupted (2 Corinthians 11:3; 1 Timothy 6:5; 2 Timothy 3:8)
- futile and darkened (Ephesians 4:17-19)
- unspiritual (Colossians 2:18)
- defiled (Titus 1:15)

The New Testament describes the total depravity of human reason in Romans 1:18-32. In this passage, Paul says that the mind of man suppresses the truth revealed by God in both general and special revelation. He says that man's reason is without excuse, futile, foolish, darkened, idolatrous, sinful, immoral, depraved, and full of hate toward God. He describes what man is really like if God does not intervene by His sovereign grace.

Summary

Since human reason is finite and has been corrupted by sin, we must not "lean on our own understanding" or "be wise in our own eyes" (Proverbs 3:5-7). Human reason must bow before Scripture and admit that some things revealed in it "transcend all understanding" (see Philippians 4:7).

God's revelation is "unsearchable" and it "surpasses all understanding" (Ephesians 3:8, 19). We must confess with the Psalmist that such knowledge is "too wonderful" and "too lofty" and "cannot be fathomed" by the mind of man (Psalm 139:6; 145:3).

For who has understood the mind of the Lord, or instructed Him as His counselor (Isaiah 40:13; 1 Corinthians 2:16)?

The Role of Human Reason in Theology

Having seen that human reason is not the abstract and absolute "Reason" found in the myths of the rationalists, we must emphasize that one can be rational without being a rationalist. We can use reason without absolutizing it into the origin and judge of all truth. Human reason is to function as the *servant* of revelation and not its judge. Once man's reason bows to the supremacy of God's Reason, then it is set free to be what God intended it to be.

In God's wondrous work of salvation, He illuminates, regenerates, and renews the corrupt mind of man which has been darkened by sin and blinded by Satan (2 Corinthians 4:4-6; Matthew 16:17; Ephesians 1:18; John 3:3, 5; Romans 12:2). Once the mind is set free from its bondage to sin and guilt, it is then ready to fulfill its role by studying God's revelation in nature and in Scripture. We are to use our minds to plumb its depths and scale its heights; to clarify and refine its concepts; to discover its principles; to obey its commands; and to defend its truthfulness. This is God's plan for man's reason according to Genesis 2:19-20.

Logic and the Bible

We can use logic as a tool without being a rationalist because logic itself finds its ontological basis in the nature of the Creator of all things. In terms of its nature, a particular principle of human logic is valid if it reflects the Mind of God as revealed in Scripture. Logic thus has an ontological basis and is not to be reduced to a relative and cultural psychology.

Man was made in the image of God, and part of this image is his capacity for logical thought, which is simply thinking God's thoughts after Him. While man's understanding is finite, it is nevertheless *true* because it comes from the image of God within him. Thus $1 + 1 = 2$ is true for both God and man with the main difference being that God understands it infinitely and man finitely.

A close study of Scripture reveals that logic is used to convey, clarify, and defend revealed truth because it finds its own validity in God's nature. For example, the "law of non-contradiction" is rooted in the very Being of the God who cannot lie (Titus 1:2). When Paul said that God cannot both be God and a lying God at the same time, he was actually saying:

$$\sim [\, a \wedge \bar{a} \,]$$

The rule of logic which is called "the denial of the consequence" is used in such places as Galatians 5:18-21; 1 Corinthians 6:9-11; 2 Corinthians 5:17, etc. In such places, Paul did not hesitate to argue:

> If someone is in union with Christ, then he will be a new creature. *If someone is not a new creature*, then he is not in union with Christ.

The Apostle Paul had no problem whatsoever "reasoning" from the Scriptures (Acts 17:2; 18:4, 19, etc.). In all his writings, Paul constantly used logically valid forms of argumentation to demonstrate from the Old Testament that Jesus was the Messiah.

We must also remember that although human logic can tell us if the structure of an argument is *valid*, it cannot tell us if it is *true*. Indeed, an argument can be logically valid and materially false at the same time! Observe the following example.

- *Premise 1:* Something which is correct part of the time is better than something which is never correct.

- *Premise 2:* A stopped watch is correct twice a day while a fast or slow watch is *never correct*.

- *Conclusion:* It is better to wear a stopped watch than one that is fast or slow.

The above argument is logically valid but false! While something that is true will always be logically valid, the converse is not the case.

The logic or Logos of God is Jesus Christ, the Second Person of the Trinity. As the personification of divine logic, Jesus is the servant of the Lord and He does not sit in judgment on Divine Truth but seeks to serve it with reverence and humility. This is the true role of human reason.

Mysticism

One of the most perplexing problems we face today is the resurgence of mysticism in the Church of the twentieth century. We are encountering more people everyday who choose their views of God and His salvation solely on the basis of their "feelings." They do theology on the basis of, "If an idea *feels* good, we believe it."

The History of Mysticism

As a distinct philosophy, mysticism arose out of the humanism of the Renaissance. In mysticism, the emotions or the feelings of man are isolated from the rest of his being and then absolutized into the origin of all meaning and the basis and judge of all truth. Thus the "feelings" of man become the measure of all things, including truth, justice, morals, and beauty. Whatever feels "good" or "comfortable" is assumed to be true.

Most mystics have come to the depressing conclusion that a rational understanding of the universe is not really possible. Neither can the universe be understood by experimentation as the empiricists claim. There must be some other way of knowing the truth than by human reason or experience.

One would have hoped that having seen the futility of beginning with man's reason or experience as the measure of all things, they would have realized that the root problem was *beginning* with man in the first place. The book of Ecclesiastes teaches us that when we begin with finite man, we always end in skepticism (i.e., we cannot know truth from error) and relativism (i.e., we cannot know good from evil). Everything becomes vanity or emptiness.

The humanists have always begun with man as a self-sufficient being who does not need God's grace or revelation. Instead of looking away from themselves to the God who made them, they turned to what they thought was a "new way" of knowing. This new way was to look within themselves for the truth.

Although this notion had served as the basis of Eastern religions for thousands of years, the idea that truth could be found by simply "looking within" themselves to their emotions was quite new to the men of the Renaissance. This meant that they did not need a great intellect or vast scientific experience to understand the universe. Man's heart, i.e., his feelings, was the best guide to what was good, just, and true.

To the Christian, the idea that we should trust our heart to tell us the truth is foolish, for God has warned us, "the heart is deceitful above all things and desperately wicked" (Jeremiah 17:9).

The question as to how one went about "looking within" himself proved to be a tricky problem. Some said that truth could be found only after various ceremonies such as fasting or prayer. Others said that they instantly knew the truth when they heard it because their hearts felt a certain chill when the truth was being expressed. Still others required people to go into trances before the truth could be found.

The mystics could never agree as to how to "look within" yourself, and neither could they agree as to what is good, just, or true. These problems proved to be insurmountable. Mysticism fell into disrepute as the mystics fought among themselves over whose feelings were the ultimate judge of truth.

While mysticism is no longer a popular philosophy in the world, it is alive and well in the Christian Church. Indeed, it has become a dominant force in some Christian circles. Christian mystics identify themselves by their dependence on feelings for their doctrines and morals. And this is where the problem lies.

Mystics and the Bible

The Bible clearly teaches that our doctrines and morals should arise from a careful study of the Scriptures (2 Timothy 2:15; 3:16-17). But instead of studying the Bible to see what it says, the mystic will try to "feel" his way to the Truth. He is not interested in a careful study of the text of Scripture. He is only interested in how he "feels." He assumes that truth will conform itself to what his feelings tell him is true or false, right or wrong.

When confronted with a doctrine he does not like, such as original sin, a mystic will usually say something like:

> My feelings tell me that this doctrine is not true. I feel uncomfortable with the very idea. So, I must reject it.

The mystic is not saying that he will examine Scripture and let Scripture decide his doctrines. In reality, his doctrines come from his mysterious "feelings" which, supposedly tell him truth from error and right from wrong.

Whenever you hear someone saying that he will "pray about it" in order for him to "feel" what the Lord "says" to him "in his heart," you are dealing with a mystic. This person is assuming that truth is discovered by looking to his feelings instead of reading the Scriptures!

As a way of obtaining doctrine, morals, or guidance, mysticism has a poor track record. If the truth can be known through feelings, then all mystics should perceive the same truth. But there is nothing more fickle than human emotion. Thus the mystics always disagree among themselves, and the same mystic will change his mind as many times as his feelings change.

Human Emotion in Scripture and Theology

In Scripture, neither reason nor emotion is the determining factor in doctrine or morals. Not once did God ask people how they *felt* about His Laws. They were to obey regardless of their feelings. Revealed truth was never said to be true because someone felt good or comfortable about it. As a matter of fact, the history of the people of God as given in Scripture reveals that people did not generally *like* God's laws at all. And they certainly had some very bad feelings about the judgment of God on their sins.

Human emotion cannot be the measure of all things because it is finite. It is therefore insufficient as a basis for truth. It is not only finite but also sinful, according to Scripture (Genesis 6:5; Romans 3:10-18). Our emotions are hostile to God and our hearts actually hate God (Romans 1:30; 8:7). Our hearts are deceitful and cannot be trusted (Jeremiah 17:9). We do not want the light of truth but the darkness of error because our deeds are evil (John 3:19-21). No one seeks after or understands the true God (Romans 3:11).

Whenever a conflict arose between human emotion and revealed truth, the authors of Scripture rebuked that emotion as rebellion against God (Romans 9:14-23). It also comes as no surprise to find that it was over such humbling doctrines as God's sovereignty that sinful emotions rose up against God (Romans 4:4-8; 9:14-23; Psalm 2:1-12).

Just because we do not "like" a doctrine or we are not "comfortable" with it does not mean that it is not true. Most of the doctrines of Scripture are very hard on the emotions of man. We are told that we are wicked sinners on our way to an eternal hell which we justly deserve. Our pride is trampled to the dust and the Holy Spirit makes us feel guilty and afraid. Nevertheless, the doctrines of the sinfulness of man and the justice of hell are clearly taught in the Bible.

Does this mean that there is no place for human emotion in the Christian life? Of course not! We can state that human emotion has a role to play without becoming a mystic. It is the attempt to make emotions into an idol to which we object.

Human emotions such as guilt and fear are often the very means God uses to bring us to true repentance (2 Corinthians 7:10). The joy of His salvation comes to us at conversion (Psalm 51:12). Emotion has a very powerful role to play in the salvation of lost sinners. Until they feel as well as understand their need of salvation, they will not seek the Lord.

Emotion plays a powerful role in the Christian life. In the Psalms, we find human emotion in all its forms from the heights of joy to the depths of depression (Psalm 6; cf. Psalm 8). There are "songs in the night" as well as "joy in the morning." There is an appropriate Psalm for every occasion and condition of the human heart. This is why it is the favorite prayer book and hymn book of true Christians.

Throughout the Scriptures, "happiness depends on happenings," i.e., our emotional state usually depends on the circumstances around us. In some times and situations, we should sorrow and weep (Romans 12:15; 1 Corinthians 12:26; James 4:9-10). Even Jesus wept at the grave of Lazarus (John 11:35). The idea that Christians have to be happy all the time violates Scripture as well as sound human psychology. It burdens the people of God with an impossible task. It leads to a kind of hypocrisy that drives the unsaved away from the Gospel. We must not wear a mask of happiness when we are sick, sinful, or sorrowful.

While "happiness" comes and goes with the ebb and flow of daily events and can be affected by such things as the level of sugar, iron, or calcium in the blood, monthly cycles, personal tragedy, amount of sleep, etc., our ability to "thank God for everything" remains firm because giving thanks is an act of the will and not an emotion. Regardless of how we feel, we are to trust God and thank Him that He knows "why" things happen. We can commit our souls to our Maker and trust His sovereign will (1 Thessalonians 5:18).

Certain emotions such as joy, peace, patience, etc., should be cultivated in the Christian life (Galatians 5:22-23). Sinful emotions such as lust, anger, envy, hate, etc., should be "put to death" or "put off" (Romans 8:13; Colossians 3:8-9).

We should express our emotions in public and private worship (Psalm 150). The idea that "emotions" are intrinsically bad and should never be expressed in the worship of God flows out of the Greek deification of the mind and not from the Scriptures. Human emotions are never condemned in Scripture because they are *human* or because they are *emotions*. Only if an emotion was *sinful* (hate, lust, etc.) was it condemned.

The Lord Jesus expressed every valid emotion of the human heart without sin being involved at any point. We should never be ashamed of our tears or our laughter because the Lord Jesus Christ Himself wept and rejoiced openly.[1]

Summary

Human emotion must be made the servant of the Lord. As a humble servant, it will not try to judge truth or be the origin of morals. Instead of looking within ourselves, we need to look away from ourselves to God, His Word, and His grace. Instead of conforming Scripture to our feelings, we need to conform our feelings to Scripture. We need to trust in the Lord and His Word instead of trusting in our deceitful feelings.

Empiricism

Humanism has always taught that man is the measure of all things. Thus man's experience has been viewed by some as the origin of all truth. We can know what is true, just, and moral from human experience. Thus there is no need for Divine revelation. Man can discover the truth by himself.

This humanist view gave rise to such principles as:

- If it works, it's true.
- The end justifies the means.

That such principles should be utilized by unbelievers is not surprising. But when we find Christians using such principles as the basis of their doctrines and morals, it is scandalous.

Humanism has always rested on the doctrine of human autonomy, i.e., man has everything he needs within himself. He does not need God, or His Word, or His Grace. Man is self-sufficient. Man is his own god.

Humanism can express itself in religious terms as easily as in secular terminology. There are those within the Church of the twentieth century who boldly teach that man is his own "god." Man has all the power he needs within himself. The "free will" of man is absolute and thus he is not a helpless sinner in need of God's intervention by way of revelation or grace.

The only way that these Christian humanists can exalt man is by dethroning God. Instead of man's being dependent on God, God is said to be dependent on man! It is said that God is helpless and impotent.

He is not allowed to intervene or to interfere with the affairs of almighty man. This "God" is a poor, pathetic being who deserves our pity. Man is on the throne now and God waits to do his bidding. God has been reduced to being a mere puppet with man pulling the strings.

One of the clearest expressions of humanistic pragmatism is found in the idea that truth and morals depend on one's personal experiences. Instead of studying Scripture to see what God has revealed, the Christian humanist will base his beliefs on human experience.

An Example of Religious Empiricism

One example comes to mind which clearly illustrates this problem. The following is a dialogue between Sam and Bob over the issue of being "slain in the Spirit."

Sam: Oh, what a wonderful time I had last night in church! I was "slain in the Spirit" and I must have lain there at least an hour. When Kathryn touched me, I felt the electricity of the Spirit and it knocked me down flat. Isn't that wonderful?

Bob: I'm glad that you had a wonderful time in church but I'm not altogether sure that this "slain in the Spirit" stuff is Scriptural.

Sam: Don't be silly! Of course it is true, because I *experienced* it and a lot of other people have experienced it too. And, it felt so good to be slain. Kathryn came by me and I reached out and touched the hem of her garment and down I went. What could possibly be wrong with that?

Bob: But where in the Bible or church history do you find this stuff? Aren't you concerned in the least if "being slain" is true according to God's Word? We must not interpret the Bible according to our experience. Instead, we must interpret our experience according to the Bible. Wouldn't you agree?

Sam: I don't see what you are getting all hyper about. I know it is true because I experienced it. I don't have to run around and prove it by the Bible or church history. But I'll ask my pastor for the proof tonight and I'll tell you tomorrow.

The next day . . .

Bob: Well, what did your pastor say?

Sam: He told me that I should not talk to you anymore. He said that you are guilty of something called "bibliolatry" because you think that the Bible is God.

Bob: But I don't think that the Bible is God and neither do I worship it as God. But the Bible does tell us that what we believe and how we live are to come from it and not from human experience. I guess that he could not come up with any proof and just told you to avoid me.

Sam: No, he gave me all the proof I needed. Being "slain in the Spirit" is clearly taught in John 18:6 and Revelation 1:17. There! Does that satisfy you?

Bob: I don't really think that you can legitimately use those passages. First, let me ask you something. Was being "slain in the Spirit" a blessing or a judgment of God?

Sam: It's a wonderful blessing! I know because I experienced it.

Bob: But if this is so, how can you use John 18:6, when in that passage Jesus judged his enemies who were coming to kill him by knocking them down? Furthermore, they did not become unconscious. It was also a very unpleasant experience for them. Remember, this was not a worship service! Jesus did not touch them. As a matter of fact, in the Gospels whenever Jesus touched people, or they touched him, no one ever got knocked down.

Sam: Well, I must admit that John 18 doesn't exactly prove my case but Revelation 1:17 does.

Bob: Sam, did you bother to look at the text at all? It isn't enough to cite a verse. You have to examine it. Was there a worship service going on? Did an evangelist touch him? If you read the text you will find that John actually fainted in fright. He was so frightened by the appearance of Jesus that he fainted. Are you going to say that whenever someone faints in fright that this is what "slain in the Spirit" is all about? I thought you told me it was a pleasant experience. Did you faint in fright the other night?

Sam: You are doing exactly what my pastor said you would do. He warned me that you would try to rob me of my experience.

Bob: But Sam, all I did was to look at the context and the wording of those passages. Isn't this what we are supposed to do as Christians?

Sam: I'm not going to talk about it anymore with you. I know I am right because I experienced it and you could show me all the verses in the Bible until you are blue in the face and I still will not believe you.

This illustration is based upon an actual conversation. Although we do not deny that Sam was "saved," in his thinking he was still a humanist because he assumed that his experience was the measure of truth. He did not need the Bible to tell him right from wrong, or truth from error. It did not matter what the issue was. It could be tongues, worship, healing, salvation, or God's foreknowledge. In all these issues his experience was ultimate.

Human Experience in Scripture and Theology

Human experience is never appealed to in Scripture as the basis or judge of truth or morals. Since our experiences need to be interpreted and understood, how can they serve as the basis for anything? The real issue is, "How do we interpret our experiences?"

The humanist will interpret his experiences according to what he thinks or feels that they mean to him. He does not go outside of himself for an interpretation. For example, Saul went to the Witch of Endor because others had gone there and experienced what they claimed was communication with the dead (1 Samuel 28). So, he went and asked her to call up Samuel. After the seance, Saul thought that he had talked with Samuel.

Now, the theist will not trust his reason or emotions to interpret his experiences (Proverbs 3:5-7). Instead, he goes outside of himself to God's Word to seek an explanation. In the case of Saul, we would interpret Saul's experience at Endor differently from the way he did. On the basis of other texts of Scripture, such as Deuteronomy 18:9-14, we would say that Saul was actually talking to a demon who pretended to be Samuel. Saul was deceived and tricked by the old witch.

Now, no one denies that Saul had an experience. The issue comes down to how we interpret it. The humanist will look to himself for the interpretation, while the theist will look to Scripture (2 Timothy 3:16-17).

Truth and morals cannot be decided by our experience, because each experience itself must be judged as to whether it is true, just, or moral according to Scripture. Just because something works, gets the job done, or feels good, does not mean that it is true, just, or moral (Deuteronomy 13:1-5). The ends do not justify the means (Romans 6:1-2). We must interpret our experiences according to the Word of God.

> To the Law and to the Testimony! If they do not speak according to this Word, they have no light (Isaiah 8:20).

Divine Revelation

God has chosen in His sovereign mercy to reveal Himself to a fallen humanity. He was under no obligation to do so, because we all have sinned against His grace and provoked Him to His face (Romans 3:23). We have trampled His Law under our feet. The only thing God owes us is eternal punishment!

How did God reveal Himself? In Paul's Epistle to the Romans, he points out that all men are without excuse and are under the wrath of Almighty God because they have rejected God's revelation. This revelation is twofold: general and special.

General Revelation

There is, first of all, the general revelation of God as found in the creation around us and our conscience within us. The existence and form of the universe are such that, what

> is known about God is evident within them; for God made it evident to them. For since the creation of the world His invisible attributes, His eternal power and divine nature, have been clearly seen, being understood through what has been made, so that they are without excuse (Romans 1:19-20).

Again,

The heavens are telling of the glory of God; and the firmament is declaring the work of His hands (Psalm 19:1).

General revelation from the creation around us is going on twenty-four hours a day, seven days a week, in every part of creation; to every human being. It does not matter if man through his own wickedness has blinded himself to the light of creation, the light is still shining.

Day to day pours forth speech; and night to night reveals knowledge (Psalm 19:2).

Not only does the existence and form of the universe reveal the hand of the Creator, but the uniqueness of man as particularly displayed in his conscience reveals that the Creator is also the Law-Giver and Judge.

For when Gentiles who do not have the Law do instinctively the things of the Law, these, not having the Law, are a law to themselves, in that they show the work of the Law written in their hearts, their conscience bearing witness, and their thoughts alternately accusing or else defending themselves (Romans 2:14-15).

The conscience of man, although defiled and scarred by sin, reveals that man is not a brute beast kicked up by some unlucky fluke of a meaningless and purposeless evolutionary process. He is the image-bearer of God.

Special Revelation

Psalm 19 moves from general revelation (vv. 1-6) to special revelation (vv. 7-11) as David considers the revelatory nature of the Holy Scriptures. In the same way, having spoken of creation in Romans 1 and conscience in Romans 2, the Apostle Paul in Romans 3 speaks of the "oracles of God" as given in Scripture.

General revelation cannot save anyone, for it does not reveal salvation or the Savior. Paul argues that creation and conscience can only bring us into further condemnation. By these things we know that we are creatures of God who are in rebellion against Him and under His wrath. That is all.

It is only in special revelation that we are told of a way to escape the just judgment of the Creator on rebel sinners. The Scriptures reveal the truth about God, man, and salvation. They tell us in language that cannot be misunderstood that we are in need of salvation and a Savior. Man cannot "go it alone."

The Bible is God's infallible and inerrant written Word just as much as Jesus was the infallible and inerrant Living Word. The two Words are one in that Jesus is the Speaker and His words, the Scriptures. As the divine Logos (John 1:1), Jesus is the basis of all revelation, particularly propositional revelation. He forms the point of contact or bridge between the infinite mind of God and the finite mind of man. Jesus can do this because He is *both* God and man.

The full authority of Scripture rests on the fact that it is "God breathed" (2 Timothy 3:16). Because it comes from an infallible and inerrant God, it is,

> profitable for teaching, for reproof, for correction, for training in righteousness; that the man of God may be adequate, equipped for every good work (2 Timothy 3:16-17).

Conclusion

Why depend on the quagmire of "reason" when we have a sure foundation in Scripture? Why follow the fantasies of "feelings" when we have the facts of Scripture? And why be deceived by "experience" when the truth has been revealed in Scripture?

The Bible never changes. It is not caught up in any "process." Its truths are immutable and infallible. Its words are "perfect" (Psalm 19:7) and come from the Holy Spirit as He moved the prophets of old (1 Corinthians 2:13; 2 Peter 1:21).

What is God like? Is He infinite in His nature and attributes? Has God revealed Himself or are we left to the conceit of our own vain speculations? Does God know the future? Is He the Creator of space and time or do they create Him?

Thanks be unto God for He has made Himself known in Scripture! His Word is the final judge of truth, justice, morals, and beauty. Its doctrines shall stand long after the cavillings of rationalists, mystics, and empiricists, secular or religious, have long been forgotten.

To God be all the glory!

NINE

THE DANGER
OF IDOLATRY

I n Christian theology, God is a theological "Given" who has revealed Himself in Scripture. Thus we are *not* free to "pick and choose" among the attributes of God as if we were in an ice cream parlor. What God is like in His nature and attributes is *not* left to our personal tastes.

Humanistic thinkers assume that they are "free" to reject any attribute of God that they cannot fully understand, completely explain, rationally reconcile, and feel happy about. If they don't *like* a certain attribute of God, they have no qualms about throwing it out. But God demands that we accept Him as He has revealed Himself in Scripture. Anything less than this is a rejection of God.

The God who has chosen to reveal Himself in Scripture is a very jealous God. He condemns as idolatry any attempt to add to or subtract from His revealed nature. This is so important that God devoted the first two Commandments of the Decalogue to a condemnation of all attempts to mold God into a manmade image. It does not matter if the image is mental or metal, wooden or woolly, all manmade ideas of God are idolatry.

The First Commandment

In the First Commandment God tells us, "You shall have no other gods before Me" (Exodus 20:3).

In this commandment we find that:

1. There is only one God.
2. The God who has revealed Himself in Scripture is this God.

3. He alone is to be worshiped, feared, loved, and obeyed.
4. We are not free to make up any ideas on our own of what God is like. It does not matter if our ideas seem "reasonable" or "practical" to us. We cannot have any ideas of God except those revealed in Scripture.
5. Man is not a god-maker or a god-in-the-making. Any concept of the "divinity of man" is idolatrous.
6. God is His own interpreter. He has revealed Himself and interpreted this self-revelation in Scripture.
7. Rationalism, empiricism, mysticism, and all other forms of humanism are hereby condemned as idolatry for they would exalt man's opinion over God's self-revelation as given in Scripture.

The Second Commandment

In the Second Commandment God warns us:

You shall not make for yourself an idol, or any likeness of what is in heaven above or on the earth beneath or in the water under the earth. You shall not worship them or serve them; for I, the Lord your God, am a jealous God, visiting the iniquity of the fathers on the children, on the third and fourth generations of those who hate Me, but showing lovingkindness to thousands, to those who love Me, and keep My commandments (Exodus 20:4-6).

The text clearly teaches that the greatest evidence of *hatred* toward God is the refusal to accept Him as He has revealed Himself in Scripture. The converse is also true. The greatest evidence of *love* toward God is the acceptance of God as He has revealed Himself in Scripture.

Just as the degree to which we accept revelation is the measure of our love of God, even so the degree to which we follow "reason," "intuition," or "feelings" instead of revelation is the measure of our hatred of God.

Any attempt to construct a deity on the basis of what is palatable to our rational or aesthetic tastes is sheer unmitigated idolatry. Here is no middle ground, no two ways about it, no compromise on this point. Either we accept God as He has revealed Himself in Scripture or we are idolaters.

This position is quite humbling to fallen man. We don't like the idea of God's *telling* us what He is like. We would much rather make up our own ideas of what God is. Neither do we like the idea of God's *commanding* us to obey Him according to what He says is right or wrong. We would much rather make up our own ideas of what is right and what is wrong.

Haters of God

Our natural hatred of God comes out in our rebellion against His Word and Law. It is no wonder that we find the Apostle Paul describing fallen men as "haters of God" (Romans 1:30). This hatred of God focuses on a rejection of God's revelation in Scripture (Romans 8:7).

The desire to be "free" from God's revelation and God's Law is the very soul and substance of *all* forms of humanism, religious or secular. To a heart filled with hatred toward God, man is not "really" or "genuinely" free unless he can think and do as he pleases as if there were no God or because there is no God. All the humanistic talk about "free will" is nothing more or less than a cheap trick used to deceive Christians.

The Scriptures declare that when man tries to "go it alone" in truth, justice, morals, and beauty, he turns freedom into slavery, liberty into license, good into evil, justice into injustice, truth into error, and beauty into ugliness. All these things can be clearly seen in modern philosophy, theology, and the arts.

But the Christian takes a path to the knowledge of God that is different and more challenging because it takes courage to venture out *beyond* reason and experience into the truths of revelation. Only a bold and daring spirit will be able to cast itself wholly upon God. Only a mighty faith can launch out and swim in unfathomable depths, while those who trust in their reason can only wade in the shallows.

The Loss of Mystery

One of the greatest problems we face in theology today is the lack of any sense of mystery. No one wants to believe in anything that goes beyond the capacity of man to comprehend. Thus the awe and the wonder of the mysteries of God are entirely absent in modern theology. Everything must be explained, sewn up, tied up, and put away in neat little packages.

With the demise of the awe and wonder of mystery in modern theology, faith is not desirable. Humanistic philosophers such as the processians demand "comprehension," not mystery; "coherence," not faith; "reason," not revelation. The absence of true mystery has always been the breeding ground of heresy.

No wonder modern theology is quite arid and sterile. It is insufferably boring. Its world is drab and gray. It is totally bereft of the bright colors of wonder, awe, and mystery. It merely apes the fads of secular philosophy. Thus it is one vast wasteland littered with the bones of those foolish enough to enter it.

But the Bible begins and ends with mystery. Thus the Biblically informed Christian can rejoice in his God. He is not depressed because he can't explain everything and answer every question. He frankly admits that he does not have everything tied up in neat little packages. By faith he can venture out *beyond* the shallows of reason into the uncharted and unfathomable depths of God's mysteries. He is not afraid of accepting by faith alone those mysteries revealed in Scripture.

The word *mystery* is found twenty-seven times in the New Testament. In the Gospels, Jesus often spoke of the "mysteries of the Kingdom" (Matthew 13:11). In the Epistles, Paul uses the word no fewer than twenty times. He spoke of God, His Word, His Will, the Gospel, the Faith, and the Church as "mysteries" (1 Corinthians 4:1; Ephesians 1:9; Colossians 1:26; 1 Timothy 3:9; Ephesians 5:32).

The Biblical concept of "mystery" had no relationship to the Gnostic idea of an esoteric secret told only to an initiated few, as in the ancient mystery religions and modern-day cults and lodges that have secret words, symbols, and rites. The Biblical concept simply meant that God had revealed an idea no human mind ever conceived.

For example, in 1 Corinthians 2:7, Paul speaks of the "mystery" of God's wisdom as displayed in the Gospel. In this passage Paul tells us that this wisdom was a "mystery" because:

1. It was "hidden" from man's sight and perception (v. 7).

2. It was "predestined before the ages to our glory," i.e., it was an idea conceived in the mind of God in eternity before time began (v. 7).

3. It was something "none of the rulers of this age has understood; for if they had understood it, they would not have crucified the Lord of Glory" (v. 8). If they understood that Christ had come to die according to an eternal predetermined plan, they would have rebelled and refused to murder the Son of God.

4. This mystery was something "which eye has not seen and ear has not heard," i.e., something *beyond* human experience.

5. It contained ideas that "have not entered the heart of man," i.e., things *beyond* human reason and comprehension. This "mystery" was something man could never discover on the basis of his own experience or reason. The only way for man to know of it was through Divine revelation. Thus Paul goes on to say that this was a mystery that "God revealed through the Spirit, not in words taught by human wisdom, but in those taught by the Spirit, combining spiritual thoughts with spiritual words" (vv. 10-13).

Not only is a mystery something man would have never conceived on his own, it is also something that goes beyond his capacity to comprehend. For example, in Ephesians 1:4-11, when Paul touches on God's sovereign will and His decrees of election and predestination, which took place "before the foundation of the world," he speaks of all these things in terms of "the mystery of His will" (v. 9).

Paul speaks of God's electing will as a "mystery." Who can explain how "He is working all things together according to the counsel of His will" and, at the same time, is not the Author of evil?

How is it that we are told in James 1:13-14:

Let no one say when he is tempted, "I am being tempted by God"; for God cannot be tempted by evil, and He Himself does not tempt anyone. But each one is tempted when he is carried away and enticed by his own lust.

Yet, at the same time, we are told to ask God *not* to lead us into temptation (Matthew 6:13)? Or, that God provides us with an escape from the temptation which He also provided (1 Corinthians 10:13)?

Who can fully explain how "God is working *all* things together for our good" (Romans 8:28)? Or how was Judas to blame for betraying the Lord when Jesus said that it "had been determined" by God for him to do it (Luke 22:22)?

What is important for us to understand is that questions relating to God's will and human destiny are placed in the category of "mystery" by the authors of Scripture. Just as the doctrine of the Trinity is a "mystery" and no one will *ever* explain how God can be Three but One and One but Three, neither will anyone cut the "Gordian knot" of Divine sovereignty and man's accountability. Our responsibility is not to pass judgment on revealed truth but to submit to it in awe.

But what if we decide that we will accept only those doctrines of the Bible that "agree with reason"? Those who have an evangelical background will usually reject God's sovereignty, divine election, God's foreknowledge, original sin, and the vicarious nature of the atonement.

But once the principle is laid down that only what is "reasonable" can be accepted, such doctrines as the deity of Christ will have to be rejected, for who can fully explain how Jesus can be *both* God and man? How can one person have *two* natures? Who can make the incarnation "coherent"?

We freely admit that it is a complete mystery to us how Jesus was both God and man. But it is a *revealed* mystery we gladly accept by faith on the authority of Scripture. Why should we abandon the authority of God's Word for the authority of the word of His enemies? But rationalists cannot live in the same universe with mystery.

Conclusion

Over the years we have observed a process of apostasy that begins with the rejection of the mystery of God's sovereignty and then proceeds to the rejecting of the mystery of the inerrancy of Scripture, the authority of Scripture, the incomprehensibility of God, the infinite nature of God, the Trinity, the deity of Christ, the personality and deity of the Holy Spirit, the sinful nature of man, the historicity of Biblical miracles, the accuracy of the Gospel narratives, and the eternal punishment of the wicked.

The driving force that pushes people down this path of apostasy is their refusal to bow in humility before the Word of God. They will not accept the many seemingly conflicting statements of Scripture. They cannot abide mystery in any form. Whatever cannot be rationally explained, they will eventually throw out. They always assume the Greek "either-or" dichotomy in every issue and refuse to acknowledge the "both-and" solution of Scripture because it would throw the issue back into mystery.

We grow weary of hearing that we must choose *either* God's sovereignty *or* man's responsibility. Why is it always assumed that we can't accept *both*? Why do processians assume that if man is free, God must be bound? Why is it assumed that divine election and evangelism cannot both be true? So what if we can't resolve all the questions that humanistic philosophers raise? Ought we not to please God rather than man?

We desire not to judge God's Word but to be judged by it. We strive not to conform the Word to our opinions but our opinions to the Word. We demand not that revelation be in accord with reason but that reason be in accord with revelation. We seek not to master the Bible but to be mastered by it.

TEN

THE ATTRIBUTES OF GOD

The first thing that must be established is that God has attributes and we can discuss them. This position is clearly based on such Scriptures as Romans 1:20, where the Apostle Paul speaks of God's "attributes."

Secondly, these attributes are not something that man makes up and then projects to God. God has revealed His own attributes in Scripture. Thus we have no choice in the matter whatsoever. We have no freedom to add or subtract to the revealed nature of God. We either accept Him "as is" or reject Him out of hand.

Since God has chosen to reveal Himself in Scripture, the attributes of God found in the Bible are to be accepted by faith and not debated by unbelief. Figure 10.1 on the next page illustrates the nature of the revealed attributes of God.

Humanistic theologies such as processianism assume that God is really unknowable. Since God is unknowable in nature, all His "attributes" are reduced to *man's* subjective and relative descriptions of what he "thinks" or "feels" this god is like. The attributes of God in this sense are things man attributes to God. They do not really say anything about God *per se*. They only point to man's ideas about God. Thus modern theology either denies outright that God has any attributes or reduces them to some aspect of human psychology.

With its assumption that no objective revelation of the attributes of God exist, modern theologians are particularly hostile to the idea of God's having any "essential" attributes. If He did have "essential" attributes, this would limit man's freedom to mold God into whatever he pleased. This would also make it impossible to view God as only a part of this world. Thus the idea of "essential" attributes is rejected.

Figure 10.1: Biblical Theology Verses Manmade Religion	
Biblical Theology	**Manmade Religion**
God → man	Man → god
revealed by God	created by man
objective	subjective
immutable	mutable
transcendent	cultural
absolute	relative
universal	contextual
knowledge	speculation
truth	myth

God's Essential Attributes

Why has historic Christian theology always believed that God has "essential" attributes? The only way we can distinguish one object from another is to identify those "attributes" or qualities that belong exclusively to one of the objects and without which the object cannot exist or be distinguished from anything else.

For example, how do we distinguish between a circle and a square? Can we draw a square circle or a circular square? No. The very attempt is absurd. It is obvious that a circle is not a square and a square is not a circle. But how do we *know* this? The essential "attribute" of a circle that makes a circle a "circle," and that no circle can exist without, in distinction from a square, is that the distance from the center of a circle to any point along its circumference will always be the same.

In the same way, God has "attributes" or qualities that make God GOD and without which He could not exist and could not be distinguished from anything else. These attributes cannot be applied to any other being. They belong only to God. Thus it is only by virtue of God's essential attributes that we can distinguish Him from the world and from the false gods of the heathen.

How do we identify the essential attributes of God? Christian theology has always taken the position that those attributes that are necessary for the existence of God and that describe His intrinsic nature or being are essential. Those attributes which refer to the works of God are not necessarily "essential."

For example, while the love of God is an essential attribute that makes God GOD, the act of sending His Son into the world was not "essential" or "necessary" for the existence or nature of God. He did not have to save anyone. He would still be GOD regardless if He threw everyone into the hell they so richly deserve.

It is in this sense that Christian theology has always viewed God's attributes of timelessness, omnipotence, omniscience, omnipresence, immutability, perfection, and sovereignty as "essential" attributes. To deny that God knows the future is to deny one of the essential attributes of God. To deny that God is timeless, immutable, or perfect is to deny that God is GOD.

The essential attributes of God are nonnegotiable. They all rise or fall together. In principle, if just one attribute is rejected, they must all be rejected. You can't have one without the others.

ELEVEN

MAKER OF HEAVEN AND EARTH

W hat is truly wonderful is that Scripture not only teaches us that God has attributes, but it also tells us where to begin. The very first thing that God wants us to understand about Himself is that He is the Creator of heaven and earth. Thus the very first attribute is that God is the Creator.

> In the beginning, God created the heavens and the earth (Genesis 1:1).

The early Church understood this in a deeply profound way. They faced a pagan world that believed the universe was eternal and whatever gods existed were only finite parts of this world. Thus, according to the early Church, the first essential difference between the Christian God and the gods of the pagans was that He was the "Maker of Heaven and Earth."

In the theology, hymns, and creeds of the early Church, the doctrine of creation was viewed as the beginning point of all theology. All of the other attributes of God made sense only in the context of a God who existed prior to, independent of, and apart from the space-time universe that He created out of nothing for His own glory. If God is not the Creator, then He is not GOD. If someone accepts this fact, he will not have any problem with accepting anything else in Scripture.

The early Church was right in starting with the doctrine of creation, for it is the most mysterious and incomprehensible doctrine contained in the Bible. After all, what human mind can possibly fathom the act of Creation? Who can fully understand how God "spoke" the worlds into being? How did He bring everything out of nothing? How did He make life from nonlife? Why did He create angels and men, knowing that they would sin? Who can give a "coherent" explanation of Creation? Who can know the mind of the Creator and tell us the hows, whys, and wherefores of Creation?

We must bow in humility and awe before the God who is there in the very first sentence of His revelation. We must confess that creation out of nothing is beyond human reason and experience. This is why the author of Hebrews stated, "Faith is the conviction of things not seen" (Hebrews 11:1).

This is why the world focuses its main attack on the Biblical doctrine of creation. They revived the old Greek idea of evolution in order to cut the main taproot of Christianity. Once God is no longer viewed as the Creator of heaven and earth, then He is no longer the God who gives the world its existence. He becomes just one of many gods, all of whom derive their existence from the world!

The doctrine of creation is always the starting point throughout Scripture in any discussion of the "Gordian knots" of theology. Thus when Paul dealt with the issue of Divine sovereignty and man's moral accountability in Romans 9, he immediately turned the discussion to the doctrine of creation (vv. 20-21). When dealing with why wives are to submit to their husbands, he appealed to creation (1 Corinthians 11:7-9; 1 Timothy 2:12-13).

Is God the Author of Evil?

When dealing with the "problem of evil," the first step taken by Scripture is to affirm that "evil" is not eternal and thus it did not coexist with God as a rival god. The Zoroastrian idea of an eternal conflict between good and evil is refuted by the doctrine of creation. Evil is a finite part of the world God made.

But does this mean that God is the "author" of evil? If by "author" one asks if God is the "agent" of evil, the Biblical answer is no. When we sin, *we* do the sinning, not God. He does not *force* or *tempt* anyone into evil according to James 1:13-17. We sin because *we* choose to do so.

If by "author" one asks if God is "responsible" for evil, the answer is still no. The word *responsible* means accountability to a higher power to whom something is owed and who can demand payment of it. But there is no "higher power" to whom God is accountable. God is not accountable to anyone or anything outside Himself. God has no "Day of Judgment." Whatever God does or says is always consistent with His own immutable nature.

If by the word *evil*, one means "an accident of chance or luck," the answer is no. There is no such thing as "luck" or "chance." Sin is not an "accident" that we can blame on God, the stars, the cards, or on Lady Luck. The concept of chance totally removes any human responsibility.

But while the Bible clearly teaches that God is not the "author of evil," at the same time, dozens of passages speak of God creating, sending, planning, and foreordaining evil! These passages are enough to show that while God is not the "author of evil" in the sense of being the agent of it, or of being accountable for it, yet, in some sense God "creates evil," "sends evil," "means it for good," etc. Surely these passages mean *something* and not nothing! (See: Isaiah 45:7; Amos 3:6; Job 2:10; Genesis 50:20; Deuteronomy 29:21; Joshua 23:15; Judges 2:15; Judges 9:23-24; 1 Samuel 18:10, 11; 1 Kings 9:9; 1 Kings 21:21, 29; 2 Kings 6:33; Exodus 4:11; 1 Samuel 2:6-7; Proverbs 16:4; Romans 11:36.)

Some theologians have tried to avoid the force of these and many other like passages by arguing that the "evil" spoken of is only "nonmoral evil." It is assumed that nonmoral evil is not *real* evil and hence not part of the issue of the problem of evil *per se*.

Several serious problems are found with this approach. First of all, the concept of nonmoral evil cannot be found anywhere in the text of Scripture. The Bible uses the same Hebrew and Greek words for "evil" whether speaking of sin or sickness. No exegetical basis for the distinction between moral and non-moral evil exists. The distinction between moral and nonmoral evil was a refinement of medieval theology and should not be arbitrarily read back into the text of Scripture.

The second problem with the idea of nonmoral evil is that this does not lessen the reality or gravity of the evils in view. Since the Bible calls all these things "evil," how these things are not *really* evil has yet to be explained.

We cannot imagine trying to comfort someone whose child was born blind by claiming that this was not a *real* evil, or, that the pain and suffering caused by a hurricane or an earthquake are not *really* evil.

While all evil is not sin *per se*, all evil comes from sin. For example, while sickness and death are not sins, they are "evils" that come from the Fall of man into sin (Romans 5:12).

Third, when the problem of evil is discussed, the kinds of evils that are raised as objections to God's foreknowledge, power, goodness, and existence are the *exact* evils mentioned in the texts. Anything that causes *pain* and *suffering* is assumed to be an "evil." Such things as disease, birth defects, blindness, lameness, ignorance, poverty, deception, war, and death are all considered as "evils."

The obvious solution is that what the Bible means by the word "evil" is not what pagan philosophers such as Epicurus meant. This never seems to occur to modern theologians. They assume the humanistic definitions of all the key terms used in the "problem of evil." Like Pavlov's dogs, whenever they see the word "evil" in the Bible, they yelp that it means "chance-produced evil." They never bother to exegete the text to see what the Bible means by such words.

Thus when they see the word *evil* in the above texts, this throws them into a state of confusion because God is pictured as *sending* evil upon people. In fact the Bible states many times that God *predestines* and *predetermines* evil. Evil is a part of His plan, called "His-story." Thus evil is not "chance-produced." It is *planned* by God Almighty!

Biblical Meaning of Evil

In the Bible, the different words for evil (Hebrew *ra*; Greek *kakos*, *poneros*) are used in the following ways:

1. The word *evil* is used as a description of the nature of man after the Adam's Fall. In Luke 11:13, Jesus describes man as "being evil." The present participle of the verb can be translated, "being and remaining evil."

2. Because man by nature is evil, all his thoughts, words, and deeds are called "evil" (Genesis 6:5; Mark 7:21-22; Romans 3:10-18).

3. The act of sin is "evil" (1 Kings 11:6).

4. Evil is not only the act of sin but also its resulting pain, suffering, or death. Thus evil can be the result of sin on one's self or the harm that one can do to others (2 Kings 22:16-17; Jonah 1:7).

5. God uses evil for His own purposes. (Genesis 50:20; Psalm 119:67, 71).

The fourth problem with the idea of nonmoral evil is the fact that such a concept does not solve the problem of evil. It is assumed that it is all right to say that God "creates," "plans," or "sends" *nonmoral* evil. Otherwise how can we explain the judgment of God on sinners? The plagues of Egypt are a good example of God's causing pain, suffering, and death. Hell, of course, is the greatest *evil* God ever created.

But when it comes to *moral* evil, it is claimed that we must never say that God "creates," "plans," or "sends" moral evil, for this would make God the "author" of evil.

The problem with this line of reasoning is that the Bible clearly speaks of evils that cannot be viewed as anything other than *moral* evils, and that God not only *foresaw* but also *planned* from all eternity! The greatest evil ever perpetrated in human history was the murder of the Son of God. Here we have a real moral evil. Does the Bible tell us that this evil was foreknown and foreordained by God, or does does it say that God did not know that Christ would die on the cross for our sins?

In terms of man's responsibility in the whole affair, Peter laid the entire evil on the shoulders of those who did it.

> You have taken and by *wicked* hands have crucified and slain (Acts 2:23).

The early Church agreed with this and saw Herod, Pontius Pilate, the Gentiles, and the Jews as the "author" of this, the greatest of all evils (Acts 4:27).

Yet, while man was "accountable" for this evil because he was the "agent" who did it freely and not under any external constraints, Peter and the early Church believed that this evil was foreknown, predestined, preordained, decreed, predetermined, and planned by God. Thus Peter said that Christ was:

> . . . delivered up *by the predetermined plan and foreknowledge of God* (Acts 2:23).

To this the Church agreed saying,

> For truly in this city there were gathered together against Thy holy Servant Jesus . . . both Herod and Pontius Pilate, along with the Gentiles and the peoples of Israel, *to do whatever Thy hand and Thy purpose predestined to occur* (Acts 4:27-28).

How can we explain this seeming contradiction? Herod was responsible for doing something not only foreknown but also predetermined by Almighty God! The text cannot be any clearer.

There are only two possible ways of handling this. One way is to pretend that these passages do not exist. The tension is "solved" but at the expense of God's Word. This is what processian and moral government teachers do.

The second way is the historic Christian response, which is to bow before the mysteries of Revelation. When humanistic thinkers demand, "But *how* does God do this?" we respond that we don't know. All we know is what we have been told in Scripture. And Scripture tells us that God is "working all things together for our good" (Romans 8:28). This we believe although we cannot explain it.

Conclusion

Biblical Christians believe in God the Father Almighty, Maker of heaven and earth, and that everything that exists is part of the Creator's plan that will bring Him glory and honor both in this world and in the next.

TWELVE

THE INCOMPREHEN- SIBILITY OF GOD

The God who has revealed Himself in Scripture tells us that He is going to be "incomprehensible" to us. But does this mean that God is going to be irrational or illogical? No. It means that God is *beyond* man's capacity to understand or explain exhaustively. In this sense, God is *beyond* human reason and logic because He is infinite and we are finite.

The doctrine of incomprehensibility is the opposite of rationalistic "reductionism," which reduces God to human categories in order to make Him "manageable," "coherent," and "explainable." Incomprehensibility allows God to be GOD. It reveals that God is infinitely better and greater than man. Thus we can build all the little theoretical molds we want, and we can try to force God into these molds, but in the end God will not "fit." He will always be *beyond* our grasp. He is too high for us to scale and too deep for us to fathom. We cannot get God in a box. The finite span of the human mind will never encompass the infinite God of Scripture.

But does this mean that God is "unknowable"? If by "unknowable" we mean the Greek philosophic dichotomy that "man must know either all or nothing," this is not what Christian theology means by its doctrine of incomprehensibility. We can have a true but finite knowledge of God on a personal and intellectual level because God has revealed Himself. Thus while we cannot fully understand the God who has revealed Himself, yet we can and do know Him. (See Jeremiah 9:23, 24; Daniel 11:32; John 17:3; Galatians 4:8-9; 1 John 4:4-8; 5:18-21.)

The doctrine of incomprehensibility means that we can only go so far and no further in our understanding of God because we are *limited* in three ways.

First, we are limited by the *finite capacity* of our minds. This is a "problem" that cannot be avoided any more than it can be overcome. So, we might as well as admit that we are not gods. Since we are finite creations of an infinite God, we will *never* understand it all.

Second, we are also limited by the *sinfulness* of our minds. Thus we have a *moral* problem as well as a capacity problem. By nature, we do not want the light of Truth. We prefer the darkness of error (Genesis 6:5; John 3:19-21). Sin and Satan have darkened and blinded our minds lest we see the Truth (Romans 1:28; 2 Corinthians 4:4). Only God's wondrous grace can overcome our moral aversion to truth and righteousness.

Third, we are limited by revelation. Paul warned the Corinthians "not to go beyond what is written" because it would lead to arrogance (1 Corinthians 4:6). The constraints of revelation are given in order to restrain man's depraved lust to make gods for himself. We are not free to speculate and come up with our own ideas of God. We are to study the Bible in order to learn *God's* ideas about Himself, to think God's thoughts after Him.

What are the consequences if we reject the doctrine of the incomprehensibility of God? While we might "cheer" at first because this gives a cheap and easy way to resolve the antinomies and paradoxes of Scriptures, it ultimately leads to a rationalistic denial of all Christian doctrine.

Stephen Davis is a good example of this process. He demands a "precise explanation" that is "coherent" to him, or he will not believe. In other words, if he cannot fully understand some aspect of the Christian God, he will throw it out because "man (in this case Davis) is the measure of all things." This is the basic assumption of secular and religious humanism.

Davis first applies his humanistic assumption to the issues of divine sovereignty and human accountability. He understands that the historic Christian solution beginning from the Apostolic Fathers is that *both* divine sovereignty and human accountability are true. Christians for two thousand years have also believed that no one is able to reconcile these two ideas. It is a Biblical mystery that demands faith, not explanation. Since those who hold to both doctrines at the same time openly admit that they cannot give a "precise explanation" of *how* divine sovereignty and human accountability are *both* true, Davis has no choice but to reject the Christian position that both are true. He must now choose one and reject the other.

But does he now choose God and exalt His glory? No, as a humanist, Davis will always exalt *man* at the expense of God. When the choice comes down to either God's being "free" to do as He pleases with what He made, or man's being "free" to do as he pleases, a humanist will always make man "free" and God "bound." Thus Davis argues;

> Take the person who tries to reconcile divine predestination of all events with human freedom by saying, "Well, I'm talking about a kind of predestination which allows for human freedom." Until it is explained precisely what this species of predestination is, we will be suspicious that the proposed reconciliation is spurious.[1]

While this is a quick and easy way of philosophically dismissing the position of the early Church and the Reformation, we should warn the reader that having established the *precedent* that "whatever cannot be precisely explained is spurious," Davis goes on to apply it to such doctrines as the indwelling of the Holy Spirit.

> Similarly, we would be suspicious of a person who tries to explain how an incorporate being can be spatially located somewhere by the use of what this person calls "an aspatial concept of inside of." Again, until it is explained precisely what this species of "inside of" is, we will reject the proposed reconciliation.[2]

Since no one can "precisely explain" *how* an "incorporate being," either the Holy Spirit or a demonic spirit, can exist "inside of" someone, Davis rejects the idea. He also calls into question the *omnipresence* of God, for who can "precisely explain" *how* God is everywhere present?[3] Davis concludes,

> If we want to be rational we have no choice but to reject what we judge to be incoherent.[4]

We had better consider the *way* that someone does theology because it sets a *precedent* that will be relentlessly applied to more and more Christian teaching until nothing is left. While a denial of predestination is exegetically foolhardy, it is not damnable. But it *is* damnable to deny the essential attributes of God, such as His omnipresence, or the doctrine of the indwelling of the Holy Spirit. Christians need to understand that they must first look at where a line of reasoning will take them before they unknowingly start down the "primrose path" to apostasy.

Let us now examine some of the Scriptures which clearly teach the doctrine of the incomprehensibility of God. We will begin with the book of Job as it contains the fullest treatment of the doctrine in the Bible.

The Book of Job

This book is the passage of full mention in the Bible concerning the problem of evil. And it is *also* the passage of full mention on the subject of the incomprehensibility of God. Thus any discussion of the problem of evil must involve an affirmation of the incomprehensibility of God.

In Job the problem of evil is "solved" by the doctrine of the incomprehensibility of God. In other words, Job's solution was to accept *both* that God is sovereign and that man is responsible. He did not try to explain this. He simply left such mysteries in the hands of God.

It is interesting to note that when we examined the books that claim to "solve" the problem of evil by reducing the power and knowledge of God, not one of them even mentioned the book of Job. Why is Job ignored? Perhaps they don't *like* the answer God gave Job out of the whirlwind, because this answer is the incomprehensibility of God.

Now, we must point out that the problem of evil was not an academic issue for Job. The pain and suffering caused by the death of his children, the theft of his goods, the loss of his health, the ruination of his marriage, and the criticism of his friends, were all real evils to him.

But when Job said that he was willing to receive "evil as well as good from God," he meant what he said (Job 2:10). He was even willing to worship the God who "took" away his children, wealth, and health, saying:

> The Lord gave and the Lord has taken away.
> Blessed be the name of the Lord (Job 1:21).

When his wife told him to curse God for all the evils He had sent their way, Job refused (Job 2:9). In the face of unbelievable pain and suffering, Job exclaimed,

Though He slay me,
I will hope in Him (Job 13:15).

This passage is very important, for in his mind, Job viewed God as his "Slayer." He did not say that "chance" or "bad luck" or even "the Devil" was the cause of all the evils which came upon him. He always assumed that God was in control of this world. Although the *agent* who *caused* the evil may have been the Devil, the Chaldeans, etc., Job bowed before God as the One who sent the evils his way. Yet, he did not "blame" or "curse" God as if He were the agent or cause of these evils.

Job held to two seemingly contradictory doctrines. On the one hand, God was not the author of evil in the sense of being its agent, and He was thus not accountable for it. Therefore God should not be cursed. On the other hand, God is sovereign and He sent all these evils on Job. Thus he states over and over again that it is God who "took" away his children, wealth, health, and happiness (Job 12:9). No other exegetical conclusion is possible. As we shall see, Job could live with two seemingly contradictory doctrines because he had a very deep belief in the incomprehensibility of God.

But *how* could he endure all these things and believe in God's sovereignty and not curse God? Why didn't he give up his belief in God and become an atheist? Why didn't he trade in his infinite God for a finite god like the gods of the heathen? They were "guilty but forgiven" because they were limited in power and could not know the future. Did Job ever limit his God in these ways? How did he handle it?

Job handled all the evils in life the same way true believers have always handled them. Faith! Mighty faith! Faith that looked to God alone! This was his secret.

Job ultimately accepted the fact that his "reason" was incapable of comprehending the Being and works of God. So, he simply trusted in God that He knew what He was doing. Job did not presume to instruct the Almighty or to be His counselor.

But Job and his friends had to learn the hard way to trust in God and not to lean on their own understanding. At the beginning they still tried to reason it out all by themselves. But after all their discussions, they never solved anything. The book of Job concludes with the solution that Divine revelation is the only way for man to find an answer. This is the enduring message of the Book of Job and God's eternal answer to the problem of evil.

Several passages in Job deserve close study.

> But as for me, I would seek God;
> And I would place my cause before God;
> Who does great and unsearchable things,
> Wonders without number (Job 5:9).

How does Job resolve the fact that God is good and, at the same time, that "He inflicts pain" (Job 5:18)? The answer given in Job 5:9 is that when we try to search out the whys and wherefores of God's actions, we will always find that His ways are "unsearchable," i.e., incomprehensible. His "wonders are without number" and cannot be counted and measured by man.

> Who does great things, unfathomable,
> And wondrous works without number.
> Were He to pass by me, I would not see Him;
> Were He to move past me, I would not perceive Him.
> Were He to snatch away, who could restrain Him?
> Who could say to Him, "What art Thou doing?" (Job 9:10-12)

Starting with the doctrine of Creation (v. 8), Job proceeds to the incomprehensible nature of God and His works. What God does is so "great" that no one can "fathom" its depths. This makes His works "wondrous" or "awe-inspiring."

Job now proceeds to the fact that we cannot "see" God. Thus we cannot "perceive" His motives or goals. Neither can we "restrain" Him from doing whatever He wants. Thus we have no right to challenge God by demanding, "What art Thou doing?"

> Can you discover the depths of God?
> Can you discover the limits of the Almighty?
> It is high as the heavens, what can you do?
> Its measure is longer than the earth,
> And broader than the sea.
> If He passes by or shuts up,
> Or calls an assembly, who can restrain Him?
> For He knows false men,
> And He sees iniquity without investigating (Job 11:7-11).

The impact of these rhetorical questions cannot be avoided. No one can "discover the depths of God" for the depths are bottomless. No one can "discover the limits of the Almighty" for He is limitless. The text states that even if we could search out all of creation in terms of its height, depth, length, and breadth, we still could not "discover," i.e., comprehend, the *infinite* nature of the Almighty.

This is also applied to the sovereign will of the Almighty. If He wants to "pass by or shut up" something (v. 10), no one can restrain Him. He will do as *He* pleases.

God's omniscience is then defined in terms of an *immediate* and *perfect* knowledge of all things including the sins of man (v. 11). God's knowledge does not "grow" because He does not have to investigate a matter to learn about it. No, God knows all things "without investigation," i.e., without waiting until the event and its investigation occurs. The incomprehensibility of God is the context for both God's sovereignty and God's omniscience.

> Then the Lord answered Job out of
>   the whirlwind and said,
> "Who is this that darkens counsel
> By words without knowledge?
> Now gird up your loins like a man,
> And I will ask you, and you instruct Me!
> Where were you when I laid the foundation of the earth!
> Tell Me, if you have understanding,
> Who set its measurements, since you know?" (Job 38:1-5)

Job and his friends had sat around discussing the problem of evil in terms of what had come upon Job. On the basis of human reason, they engaged in endless philosophical speculation and, in the end, failed to resolve anything. Although a great deal of heat was generated during their discussions, little light came of it.

At last, God gives a revelation to the problem of evil. The first thing that He does is to dismiss all the conclusions of human "reason" as "words without knowledge" that only "darken counsel." Paul echoes this thought when he states that the world with all its philosophical wisdom is sheer "foolishness" (1 Corinthians 1:18-21).

Then God challenges their ability and capacity to understand the questions and the answers to those questions. In fact, they had asked questions that were "too deep" for them. Not only did they not understand their questions, but even the answers were also beyond their capacity to understand. They were "in over their heads" and did not know it! This is why so many people drown in unbelief. And even when we toss out to them the lifeline of Scripture, they would rather drown in unbelief than accept God's revelation by faith.

For four chapters, God challenges them,

> So, you think that you are so smart that nothing is "beyond" you? You don't even hesitate to tell Me how to run the universe I made! Well, I have a few questions for you. We'll see if you are as smart as you claim. Since you think that you can comprehend Me, let's see how well you comprehend the world around you. After all, this should be easy for you since you claim to understand Me!

God then proceeds to put Job and his friends in the "hot seat" and give them "the third degree." Under divine interrogation, they soon realized that their "reason" and "intuition" were not sufficient. The sovereignty of God was the solution to the problem of evil.

> Then Job answered the Lord, and said,
> "I know that Thou canst do all things,
> And that no purpose of Thine can be thwarted.
> Therefore I have declared that which
> I did not understand.
> Things too wonderful for me,
>   which I did not know.
> Hear, now, and I will speak;
> I will ask You, and You instruct me.
> Therefore I retract,
> And I repent in dust and ashes" (Job 42:1-4, 6).

Under the rebuke of God for trying by "reason" to solve the problem of evil, Job "repents" and "retracts" all the things he and his friends had said. He now bows before revelation and submits to the Divine glory. He admits that God can do whatever He wants and no one can frustrate or condemn His sovereign will. He admits that such questions are "too wonderful," i.e., mysterious, for him. He will leave such things to God.

Other Passages

The rest of Scripture follows Job in resolving the problem of evil by submitting to the incomprehensibility of God. Let us examine a few of these passages.

Such knowledge is too wonderful for me;
It is too high, I cannot attain to it (Psalm 139:6).

In this Psalm, David first introduces the subject of God's omniscience in verses 1-5, which leads him to the incomprehensibility of God in verse 6. Then he goes on to describe the omnipresence of God in verses 7-12. David did not become depressed over the fact that God's omniscience and omnipresence are concepts that were "too high" for him to comprehend. The opposite was true. The incomprehensibility of God enhanced his worship. He could worship such a God because He is so *wonderful.*

Great is the Lord, and highly to be praised;
And His greatness is unsearchable (Psalm 145:3).

In the context, David has in mind not only the "greatness" of God's being, but also of His works. The word "unsearchable" is often translated "unfathomable." A nautical term, it meant that the plumb line of human reason will never discover a bottom to God in His nature or deeds. The true God has no "bottom" or limit for man to discover. Such a God is alone worthy of our worship.

Why do you say, O Jacob, and assert, O Israel,
"My way is hidden from the Lord
And the justice due me escapes the notice of my God"?
Do you not know? Have You not heard?
The everlasting God, the Lord, the Creator of the
 ends of the earth,
Does not become weary or tired.
His understanding is inscrutable (Isaiah 40:27-28).

The apostate among Israel cherished two vain hopes. First, they hoped that God was limited in His knowledge and thus did not know about their sin. If He did not know about it, they would not get punished for it.

Second, they hoped that if God were not ignorant, at least He would be distracted by far more important things than meting out the justice due to them. If He were going to punish anyone, He would have to begin with people who are really wicked, not them. Or, perhaps, He was just uninterested in them and wouldn't care.

The prophet Isaiah dashes to the ground all such finite views of God that would see Him as "growing" or "learning." God is not ignorant, distracted, or uninterested, because the eternal God is the Creator of all things including man. His "understanding" or "knowledge" is not limited in any way by what He has made. It is thus "inscrutable," i.e., unlimited.

> Oh the depths of the riches both of the wisdom
>   and knowledge of God!
> How unsearchable are His judgments
>   and unfathomable His ways!
> For who has known the mind of the Lord,
> Or who became His counselor?
> Or who has first given to Him
>   that it might be paid back to him again?
> For from Him and through Him and to Him
>   are all things.
> To Him be the glory forever. Amen (Romans 11:33-36).

This is one of the most beautiful statements on the incomprehensibility of God in the New Testament. It is brought in by the Apostle Paul as the doxological climax to his discussion of election, predestination, God's sovereignty, and human responsibility in Romans 8-11. The Apostle Paul calls us to worship a God who is *beyond* our capacity to comprehend in either His being or works. This God is "unsearchable" and "unfathomable." No one will ever "know" all the "ins and outs" of the mind of the Lord. If someone could, he would "become His counselor," for he who can understand God would be greater than God.

The immediate occasion of this doxology to the incomprehensible God is his discussion of the inclusion of the Gentiles into the covenant of grace and the exclusion of Israel. Paul states that God's election is based on His grace and not on some condition of man such as race or parentage (Romans 11:.6-7).

But what about all the "whys," "hows," and "wherefores" that naturally arise? Paul does not claim to know all the answers. He knows only what has been revealed. Thus he can now freely worship God because he leaves such mysteries in the hands of his Creator:

The love of Christ which surpasses knowledge (Ephesians 3:19).

Paul prays that the saints might "comprehend" and "know" the love of Christ (vv. 18-19). But while they can have a finite but true knowledge of such things, they cannot exhaustively comprehend the Lord Jesus Christ or His love. Christ is God as well as man. He is infinite in His being and love. We will never be able to understand the "whys," "hows," and "wherefores" of His love for sinners.

Let us point out that if we begin with the rationalistic assumption that everything must either be "precisely explained" or we must reject it, then we must reject the love of Christ because it "surpasses comprehension." God's election and love are so joined in Scripture that they either stand or fall together.

The peace of God which surpasses all comprehension (Philippians 4:7).

Who can "precisely explain" *how* the peace of God can "indwell" us and gives us comfort? Who can make "coherent" the ways of the Spirit of God? Is not the work of God in the soul like the wind which comes and goes without our permission or knowledge (John 3:8)?

If we are limited to what can be "precisely explained" and "made coherent," then we will have to reject the peace of God as well as the love of Christ! But if we accept the incomprehensibility of God, we can have both His peace and His love. By this faith we can live without fear, being confident in His sovereign love and power.

Conclusion

From just these few passages of Scripture it is abundantly clear that the Christian doctrine of the incomprehensibility of God is a revealed truth. It follows naturally after the doctrine of creation and forms the context of all the other attributes of God.

It is also clear that the authors of Scripture were not embarrassed by the incomprehensibility of God but proud of it. They did not apologize for it but boasted of it. They did not agonize over it but rejoiced in it. They were not driven away from God by it but were drawn nigh unto God because of it. They did not curse God but fell at His feet in wonder, awe, and praise.

THIRTEEN

THE INCOMPARA-
BILITY OF GOD

The God of the prophets and apostles is so wonderful in all His being and attributes that He cannot be reduced to the level of the pagan gods or man. God simply cannot be "compared" to the gods or man as if they were His equals. What the gods are like has *no* bearing whatsoever on the God who is there and who has revealed Himself in Scripture.

The incomparability of God has always been denied by humanistic thinkers because they think God is no "better" or "greater" than themselves. They assume God must be "like" the other gods and "like" man himself. This leads to a theology in which the nature of God is determined by looking at the gods of the heathen and at man himself. Whatever limitations man has, God is said to have, because He is "just like us."

As we saw in the Chapters 5 and 6, pagan thinkers always argue from what *they* can or cannot do to what God can or cannot do. Since *they* cannot know the future, then God cannot know it either. Since *they* cannot rule the world, then neither can God. Since *they* have to learn things by trial and error, then God must do likewise. Since *they* have to wait around until things happen before they can know them, then so must God. Since *their* understanding is finite and *their* power is limited, then so is God's. Since *they* are neither perfect nor immutable, then God is neither perfect nor immutable. In short, *they* create God in *their* own image and likeness!

But God has revealed that He is *not* like man or his false gods. Thus God cannot be compared to them, for He is "better" in quality by being

Divine and "greater" in quantity by being Infinite. This is one of the *major* Biblical themes of God's glory.

The following texts will demonstrate two things. First, the very "God-hood" of God is involved in His incomparability. God is GOD because He is *not* like man or his gods. Second, God is not like man or his gods because of those very attributes of God which pagan thought has always rejected. God is the incomparable GOD because He is the Creator, the sovereign Lord of all things, and the omniscient One who foreknows the future!

> Who is like Thee among the gods, O Lord?
> Who is like Thee, majestic in holiness,
> Awesome in praises, working wonders (Exodus 15:11)?

Miriam's song of triumph after Pharaoh's army perished in the Sea magnifies the sovereign power of God. Which of the finite pagan gods can do what Yahweh has done? He is incomparable in His character and power.

> There is none like the God of Jeshurun. . . .
> The eternal God is a dwelling place,
> And underneath are the everlasting arms. . . .
> So Israel dwells in security (Deuteronomy 33:26-28).

In Moses' farewell blessing, he blesses Asher by teaching him the incomparability of Yahweh. He alone is the "eternal God" who transcends space and time. His sovereign power, or "everlasting arms," is the only basis of security for God's people.

> My soul shall rejoice in the Lord;
> It shall exalt in His salvation.
> All my bones will say, "Lord, who is like Thee,
> Who delivers the afflicted
>   from him who is too strong for him" (Psalm 35:9-10).

As David sees his enemies approaching with a force too great for him to overcome, he cries out to God for deliverance. In his prayer he reminds the Lord that He is incomparable in His mercy as well as in His judgment.

> But to the wicked God says,
> You thought that I was just like you;
> I will reprove you (Psalm 50:16, 21).

God begins His address to the wicked in verse 16. They are condemned because they hypocritically speak of God's statutes and covenant while rejecting God's revelation! But their greatest crime is their wicked assumption that God is limited just like them. They are able to abandon themselves to sin because they think that God is limited in knowledge and does not know what they are doing, and that God is limited in power and cannot do anything about it anyway. God is going to "tear them into pieces" because they have "forgotten" what God is really like (v. 22). Humanists always assume God is "just like man."

> For Thy righteousness, O God,
>   reaches to the heavens;
> Thou who hast done great things;
> O God, who is like Thee? (Psalm 71:19)

In the context, the Psalmist focuses on the "righteousness," i.e. justice, of God because it "reaches to the heavens," i.e., is infinite. This infinite justice of God is declared to be incomparable and becomes the basis of his hope that God will deliver him from his enemies.

> There is no one like Thee among the gods, O Lord;
> Nor are there any works like Thine.
> For Thou art great and doest wondrous deeds;
> Thou alone art God (Psalm 86:8, 10).

David cries out for deliverance to a sovereign God who is "great" in His being and works. God's sovereignty is so complete and universal that even David's enemies are under the control of God! David's enemies can "choose" to do him harm, but God is in control and will deliver His people.

> The Lord is high above all nations;
> His glory is above the heavens.
> Who is like the Lord our God,
> Who is enthroned on High,

> Who humbles Himself to behold
> The things that are in heaven and in the earth (Psalm 113:4-6)?

The Psalmist begins in awe with a vision of the transcendence of God over man ("the nations") and nature ("heavens and earth"). This transcendent God is sovereign over all things for He is "enthroned on high." He is called "the Most High God" no fewer than forty-six times in Scripture.

But does this mean that He is not immanent "in" the world because He is transcendent "above" it? No, the Psalmist believes that God is *both* transcendent and immanent. The Lord "humbles Himself to behold" all that takes place in heaven and in the earth.

The Psalmist thus concludes that God is incomparable because He is transcendent, sovereign, and omniscient. The gods of the heathen are *not* transcendent, sovereign, or omniscient. They are "of" the world as well as "in" the world. But the True God is "above" the world (transcendent), "over" the world (sovereign), "in" the world (immanent), and knows all "about" the world (omniscient). God is GOD because of these things.

> To whom then will you liken God?
> Or what likeness will you compare with Him (Isaiah 40:18)?

Isaiah 40 is the passage of full mention on subject of the transcendence of God. He is depicted as the sovereign Creator and Ruler of the universe, who sits enthroned far above all earthly powers. The nations are only "a drop in a bucket" or "a speck of dust on the scales" (v. 15). All the inhabitants of the earth are "like grasshoppers" (v. 22).

Thus it is absurd to make an idol and compare it to God (v.18). What is an idol but a manmade god (vv. 19f.). How can such ignorant gods compare to the True God, who is omniscient (vv.13-14)?

> "To whom then will you liken Me?
> That I should be his equal?" says the Holy One.
> Lift up your eyes on high
> And see who has created these stars,
> The One who leads forth their hosts by number
> He calls them all by name;
> Because of the greatness of His might and the
>   strength of His power
> Not one of them is missing (Isaiah 40:25-26).

God is not only incomparable because He is transcendent and omniscient, but also because He is omnipotent. His omnipotence is revealed in creation and providence. He created the stars. This shows His omnipotence. He knows them all by name which reveals His omniscience. And His power sustains them in their orbits, which reveals His Providence. The gods of the heathen are limited in power and knowledge. The God of Israel should not be compared to these idols.

> I am the first and I am the last,
> And there is no God besides Me.
> And who is like Me? Let him proclaim and declare it;
> Yes, let him recount it to Me in order,
> From the time that I established the ancient nation.
> And let them declare to them
>   the things that are coming
> And the events that are going
>   to take place (Isaiah 44:6-7).

Isaiah now bases the incomparability of God on His eternity. As "the First and the Last," God is transcendent over time itself. Thus he appeals to God's absolute and infallible foreknowledge of the future as proof of His uniqueness. Which of the gods of the heathen can "recount" history from "the beginning to the end"? Which of them can tell us future events? Only the true God can do this.

> I am God, and there is no one like Me,
> Declaring the end from the beginning
> And from ancient times
>   things which have not been done,
> Saying, "My purpose will be established,
> And I will accomplish
>   all My good pleasure" (Isaiah 46:9-10).

No wonder pagan philosophers have always attacked God's foreknowledge and foreordination of the future! Since Isaiah records God's claim that He is GOD because He foreknows and ordains the future, the heathen have always made their chief attack on those very attributes. Once God is denied knowledge and control of the future, then He is "just like" their gods.

"For my thoughts are not your thoughts,
Neither are your ways My ways," declares the Lord.
"For as the heavens are higher than the earth,
So are My ways higher than your ways,
And My thoughts than your thoughts" (Isaiah 55:8-9).

Isaiah now tells us that God's thoughts and ways cannot be compared to man's thoughts and ways. The limitations of man's thoughts and ways should not be placed on God. Man is *not* the measure of all things. God is His own interpreter and He has made it plain that He is *not* a man and should not be limited in power and knowledge as if He were a man (Numbers 23:19; Hosea 11:9).

Humanistic theologians are forever trying to instruct God as to what He may and may not do. They try to inform the Holy One about what is just and unjust. They are cosmic "back-seat drivers" who gripe and complain about the direction in which history is going, and who then take it upon themselves to tell the Almighty how to run the world He made for His own glory! Their conceit and imprudence know no bounds!

There is none like Thee, O Lord;
Thou art great, and great is Thy name in might.
Who would not fear Thee, O King of the nations?
Indeed it is thy due!
For among all the wise men of the nations,
And in all their kingdoms,
There is none like Thee. . . .
But the Lord is the true God;
He is the living God and the everlasting King. . . .
Thus you shall say to them,
"The gods that did not make the heavens
    and the earth shall perish
    from the earth and from under the heavens."
It is He who made the earth by His power,
Who established the world by His wisdom;
And by His understanding
    He has stretched out the heavens. . . .
Every man is stupid, devoid of knowledge;
Every goldsmith is put to shame by his idols;
For his molten images are deceitful,

And there is no breath in them. . . .
The Portion of Jacob is not like these;
For the Maker of all is He,
And Israel is the tribe of His inheritance,
The Lord of hosts is His name (Jeremiah 10:6-16).

The true God cannot be compared to such absurdities. He is the omnipotent Maker and Sustainer of all things. All attempts to lower God down to the level of the finite gods of the heathen are sheer "stupidity," says Isaiah.

Conclusion

These Biblical passages are clear enough to establish the doctrine of the incomparability of God. Why then should we follow the processians in rejecting those very attributes of God which make Him different from and superior to the gods of the heathen? Why reduce God to the level of pagan deities by claiming that He cannot know or control the future? If God is no better or greater than man or his manmade gods, why believe or worship Him? Are we really any better off if God is no longer GOD?

Such searching questions as these can be ignored only at the peril of one's immortal soul. Theology is not a game but a matter of eternal life or death. If you want a finite god, then you must choose Baal and serve him. But if you want to serve Jehovah, then you must accept Him as He has revealed Himself in the Bible: the omnipotent, omniscient, sovereign Creator and Sustainer of heaven and earth.

FOURTEEN

THE UNITY OF GOD

The pagan doctrine of polytheism can be successfully refuted by the Christian doctrine of the unity of God. The "unity" or "oneness" of God teaches us several different things about God.

First, the True God is ONE in *number*. There never were, are not now, and never shall be any other true gods. That this is the clear teaching of Scripture cannot be denied. (See 1 Kings 8:60; Isaiah 43:10; 44:6,8; 45:5, 18, 21, 22; 46:9; Jeremiah 10:10; John 17:3; 1 Corinthians 8:4, 6; 1 Thessalonians 1:9; 1 Timothy 2:5.)

Second, God is ONE in *nature*. He is a divine Person and not just a random collection of independent attributes. This means that we cannot simply "pay our nickel and take our choice" when it comes to the attributes of God. The attributes of God are so interrelated that one cannot be rejected without rejecting all of them. The attributes are defined in terms of each other. They modify one another and form the context of their mutual understanding. They stand or fall together. Thus the unity of God means that we must accept *all* of God as He has revealed Himself in Scripture. We cannot "cut" God into pieces.

Processians are in the nasty habit of thinking that they can pick and choose among the attributes and still end up with the Christian God. They assume that they can reject some attributes of God and this will not affect the remaining attributes. But when anyone tries surgically to remove any of the essential attributes of God, the patient dies just as surely as when someones has his heart, lungs, and brain removed!

When a moral government teacher denies the sovereignty, foreknowledge, perfection, immutability, and omnipotence of God, the remaining product is only a god and not God at all because all the attributes have been radically altered.

For example, processians "like" the attribute of the love of God. We are not aware of any of them that throw it out, even though Scripture describes it as "beyond understanding." But they "dislike" the sovereignty of God as much as they like His love. So, while they gladly accept the love of God, they throw out His sovereignty.

The only "fly in the ointment" is the exegetical fact that the only "love" of God spoken of in Scripture is a *sovereign* love. God's love is never described in the Bible as a weak pathetic sentimentalism. God is not wringing his hands and whining that he "loves" man but can't "interfere" because of man's "free will."

If we take the Bible seriously, the love of God for His people is sovereign and it led Him to predestine them to adoption as sons before the world was created (Romans 8:28-30; Ephesians 1:4, 5, 11). He sovereignly "draws them" to Himself (Jeremiah 31:3; Psalm 65:4; John 6:44), sovereignly "opens" their hearts (Acts 16:14), and sovereignly gives them the gifts of repentance and faith (Acts 11:18; Philippians 1:29).

But we cannot stop here. The processians also deny the immutability and perfection of God. This means that God's love can no longer be understood as changeless or perfect. God's love becomes fickle, defective and hence unreliable. This stands in dark contrast to the love of God spoken of in Scripture, which is both immutable and perfect!

The Bible and the Gods

Third, the Bible uses the word "Elohim" (gods) in a figurative and symbolic way to refer to men and angels when they carry out a God-like function. Moses (Exodus 4:16) and the judges of Israel (Exodus 21:6; 22:8, 9; Psalm 82:6) are called "gods" because, like God, they held the power of life and death over men.

While the idols of the heathen are also called "gods" (1 Corinthians 8:5), the authors of Scripture are careful to state that they were "false gods" and that there is actually only one God "by nature" (1 Corinthians 8:6; Galatians 4:8).

The figurative use of the word "gods" in the Bible should not be confused with polytheism, which is the belief in many gods. In John 10:30-36, when Jesus quoted Psalm 82:6 to the Jews who were about to stone Him, He was not saying that his enemeies were "gods" in the sense of real deity. He was not saying that we should pray to or worship them. What He was doing was answering their objection to His claim of deity in verse 30. How could they get so mad at Him for claiming to be "God" when the word *Elohim* was at times even used of mere men such as the judges of Israel? He was greater than they because He was one in nature with the Father. The Jews got the point and picked up stones, saying, "You being a man, make yourself out to be God" (John 10:33). They knew He was not just claiming to be "a god" in a figurative sense like the judges of Israel. He was claiming to be the one true GOD! This is why they screamed, "Blasphemy!"

The Bible has some very harsh things to say about the gods of the heathen. Their "gods" are not "true" or "real" but only "nonexistent" fictions. The idols that represent them are only wood, stone, or metal. They are "nothing" because they are "lifeless." They are thus "profit-less," "speechless," and "powerless." They are "dumb idols" which only "stupid" people worship. When an idol is worshiped, this worship goes to demons, not God. (See 1 Chronicles 16:26, cf. Psalm 96:5; 2 Kings 19:18, cf. Isaiah 37:19; 2 Chronicles 13:9; Jeremiah 2:11; 5:7; 10:8-10; 16:20; Habakkuk 2:18-20; Acts 19:26; 1 Corinthians 8:4-5; 10:20; Galatians 4:8.)

It is interesting to note that in the passages above, the gods were not true deity because they could not know or foretell the future.

Conclusion

There is but one true eternal Triune God of Father, Son, and Holy Spirit. He alone is worthy of our worship and praise.

FIFTEEN

THE SELF-EXISTENCE
OF GOD

The Scriptures reveal an eternal, transcendent God who existed prior to, independent of, and apart from the universe He created out of nothing for His own glory. This is in direct conflict with the processian heresy of a "dipolar deity" in which God is as dependent on the world for His existence as the world is dependent upon God.

The historic Christian position is that God's existence is:

- real and not mythological
- eternal and not temporal
- independent and not dependent
- infinite and not finite
- perfect and not imperfect
- absolute and not relative
- immutable and not mutable

God is the "self-existent" One because God "has life in Himself" and not in some "ground of being" outside of Himself (John 5:26). He is not dependent on space or time for His existence because He pre-existed them and they were created out of nothing.

The attribute of self-existence is directly involved with the issue of whether God is "timeless." Is God "in" time and, therefore, dependent on TIME for His own existence? Or is time "in" God and dependent on GOD for its existence? Who is the ultimate "ground of being"? Is Time the GOD of God?

It is claimed by processians that God is as dependent on time as man is because time is as eternal as God. Thus God exists "in" time like man. Time is the ultimate "ground of being," not God. God is thus a dependent being like man and the gods of the heathen.

The Christian Church has always taught that God is timeless for two reasons. First, God is the only *eternal* Being and nothing is eternal along side of, beneath, or over God. If time were eternal, then it would be a rival god or a higher god upon whom God depended for His existence. Second, God created the space-time universe out of nothing. God is not dependent on the space-time world for His existence, for He existed prior to it. He does not depend on time or space for He is GOD.

As we have already seen, the attributes of God stand or fall together. If we deny that God knows or controls the future, we have to tamper with all of the other attributes until nothing of GOD is left. If God's timelessness is denied, He is no longer the living God of Scripture.

That this is the clear teaching of Scripture can be seen from the following passages.

The Living God

God is described as the "living God" thirty times in Scripture, with the New Testament using the phrase at least fifteen times. The "living God" is often contrasted to the "lifeless" gods of the heathen who were dependent upon time and space for their existence. (See Deuteronomy 5:26; Joshua 3:10; 1 Samuel 17:26; Psalm 42:2; Isaiah 37:4; Jeremiah 10:10; Matthew 16:16; Acts 14:15; 1 Thessalonians 1:9.)

In Exodus 3:14, we are told that God's name is "I AM." This word in the original means that He is the eternally existent One who always was, is, and shall be the same throughout all eternity. He is the Eternal I AM.

It is thought by many that the book of Job was the first book of the Bible ever written. Thus it is the earliest record of God's self-revelation in Scripture. In Job, God is described as the One:

In whose hand is the life of every living thing, and the breath of all mankind (Job 12:10).

In Job 33:4, Job tells us that:

The Spirit of God has made me, and the breath of the Almighty gives me life.

Job did not think that God was receiving His life, i.e., His existence, from time or anything else. God was the GIVER and not the receiver of life.

When Daniel rebuked Belshazzar and foretold his doom and the destruction of his kingdom, he not only revealed that God knows all about the future, but he also instructed him concerning the true nature of God.

> You have praised the gods of silver and gold, of bronze, iron, wood, and stone, which do not see, hear, or understand. But the God in whose hand are your life-breath and your ways, you have not glorified (Daniel 5:23).

Belshazzar made a big mistake when he assumed that he was "free" from God. His life's breath was in the hands of the Almighty who was the Creator and Sustainer of all things.

The Apostle Paul in his address to the Greeks on Mars Hill was careful to point out that the God whom he represented was self-existent. He was not dependent like their gods. He was the One upon whom all things depended for their existence.

> The God who made the world and all things in it, since He is Lord of heaven and earth, does not dwell in temples made with hands; neither is He served by human hands, as though He needed anything, since He Himself gives to all life and breath and all things; . . . for in Him we live and move and exist (Acts 17:24, 25, 28).

Here Paul teaches that God's existence is *independent* and does not rely on anything outside Himself. It is *perfect* and is not lacking in anything. And it is *immutable* and *absolute*, for all things including time and space depend upon Him. God does not "need" time or anything else for His existence.

Conclusion

But how is God's "self-existence" possible? Can we give a "precise" and "coherent" explanation of God's self-existence? Can anyone fully understand how He has "life in Himself?" No! Does this bother us? No! Why?

Without faith it is impossible to please Him, for he who comes to God must *believe that He is,* and that He is a rewarder of those who seek Him (Hebrews 11:6, italics mine).

SIXTEEN

INVISIBLE AND INCORPOREAL

According to Jesus, God is *spirit* in His essence or nature (John 4:24) and a "spirit" by definition does not have a physical body (Luke 24:39). Thus we should not think of God as the "Man Upstairs," because He does not have a male human body. "God is not a man" (Numbers 23:19).

Since God is spirit, He is invisible (Colossians 1:15; 1 Timothy 1:17; Hebrews 11:27). Thus, no one has seen God the Father, for there is nothing physical to see (John 1:18). The only way to see God is to see Him in His Son, who became a real man of flesh and blood (John 1:14-18; 14:9).

In John 4:24, Jesus did not say that "God is *a* spirit" but "God is spirit." The distinction is crucial. If God were "a spirit" this would imply that He is only one *finite* spirit among many others. He would be in essence no different from the Devil and his demons. But when Jesus said that God was "spirit," this implied that He is spirit in an *infinite* sense. God cannot have a body because He is infinite spirit. Those who deny God's infinite nature are actually robbing God of His spirituality.

This also applies directly to the issue of whether God is "timeless." If God is not timeless and spaceless but "in" time and space like man, then God's being is reduced to some kind of "matter" or "form" and must "struggle to overcome" such problems as gravity, the speed of light, entropy, and inertia. This was clearly believed by Whitehead and most processians.

Christians have always believed that time and space are attributes of created things, not of the Creator. Thus God is described as the "eternal Spirit" in Hebrews 9:14. God is not only spaceless but also timeless.

One error is consistently made by processians at this point. When the creeds of the early Church stated that God did not have a body and thus He did not have "parts or passions," some processians have twisted this to mean that the God of historic Christian theism is devoid of any "emotions." This is labeled as a "Platonic" element in Christian theology. Such a God does not "love" or "hate" because He has no "passions." Thus the historic Christian concept of God is defective. Clark Pinnock, for instance, gives this kind of argument.[1]

In reality, when the early Fathers and such creeds as the Westminster Confession of Faith state that God does not have any "passions," this has reference to God's not having any *bodily* passions. For example, since God does not have a stomach, He has no "passion" for food. Since God has no reproductive organs, He has no sexual "passions." This was said to distinguish God from the gods of the heathen who ate, drank, raped, and plundered. The charge that the creeds of the Church deny that God has emotions is absurd.

Conclusion

In His nature, God is both eternal and infinite in spirit and cannot be reduced to a finite time-bound being who struggles with a chance-directed universe. God is not a man.

SEVENTEEN

PERSONAL AND INFINITE

Christian theology has very carefully stated that while God is infinite and spiritual in His essence, this does not mean that He is an impersonal "it." The Greeks had fallen into the trap of assuming that God must be either finite and personal or infinite and nonpersonal. But this dichotomy is never found in the Bible.

God is "personal" in that He is a self-conscious ego who can say, "I AM" (Exodus 3:14). He has intellect (Romans 11:34), thoughts (Isaiah 58:8-9), will (Romans 12:2), emotion (John 3:16), and action (Ephesians 1:11). He cannot be reduced to a nonpersonal "ground," "force," or "energy." An "I AM" is far superior to an "it."

Some processians have argued that God "needs" the world to fulfill Himself. Since this "need" of God would be eternal, the world must be eternal. The doctrine of creation is thus rejected because God needs the world for His own growth and knowledge. It is by this assumption that they made time eternal, holding that God "needs" time to exist.

The historic Christian response to such pagan ideas is to point out that God is a Trinity: God the Father, God the Son, and God the Holy Spirit. Because the fellowship and communication within the Three Persons of the Trinity is both eternal and self-sufficient, God is not "lonely." He does not "need" man or the space/time world. The Father, the Son, and the Holy Spirit have gotten along just fine for all eternity without man or the world.

Only the infinite God of the Bible can give man a sufficient basis for universal truths and moral absolutes. Being infinite in nature, God, not man, is the "measure of all things." God, not man, is the Origin and Judge of truth and morals. God, not man, is the infinite reference point by which all the particulars of life can find their meaning.

Infinitude and Ignorance Do Not Mix

Now you would think that "evangelicals" would be the last ones to deny the infinitude of God. But this is what "evangelical" processians and "Arminian" moral government people do when they deny God's omnipotence, omniscience, immutability, sovereignty, and perfection. Why? The word "infinite" means *unlimited.* Thus when God's knowledge and power are *limited* by claiming that He cannot know or control the future, then God is no longer unlimited, i.e., *infinite.*

While the philosophically astute "evangelical" processians understand this, some of the moral government people, having no background in philosophy or logic, have naively assumed that God is still infinite, i.e. "unlimited," even though they have limited most of His attributes! This is totally irrational. To say that God is limited and unlimited at the same time is like trying to draw a square circle!

Once we deny any of the infinite attributes of God, He becomes a *finite* being. Once this happens, God can no longer be the Origin of universal truths and moral absolutes. Why? A finite god needs an infinite reference point to explain him! God becomes just one more particular in search of a universal! Everything becomes "relative," including God.

For example, if god does not know the future, then his present knowledge is *limited.* Since his present knowledge is limited, it becomes mutable, imperfect, and relative. What he knows *today* is incomplete and may need readjustment *tomorrow.* It may even be wrong because he did not have at that time all the information he needed. Thus whatever a finite god says today must be taken with a grain of salt because his understanding of the situation is as limited as man's understanding. Since a finite god cannot see the future, he cannot see the "big picture."

The modern attack on God's infinite nature is a master stroke of Satan. If he can get people to deny just *one* attribute of God, he has destroyed *all* the infinite attributes of God in one swoop.

The word "infinite" as used in Christian theology is not an independent attribute. It is actually an adjective, that when applied to all the other attributes, makes God GOD. In other words, it is the addition of the concept of "infinity" that makes God the Creator instead of a creature.

For example, what is the *difference* between the person and presence of angels and men as opposed to the person and presence of God?

While the person and presence of angels and men are both *finite* in that they are *limited* to being only in one place at one time, God's person and presence are both *infinite* in that He is *unlimited* and thus everywhere present in the totality of His person. God is omnipresent only by virtue of the fact that He is infinite!

God's knowledge is *different* from the knowledge of angels and men because it is infinite, i.e., omniscient. His power is *different* because it is infinite, i.e., omnipotent. And even His moral attributes of love, mercy, grace, goodness, and holiness are *different* from angels and men because they are infinite, i.e., without end or limitation.

This leads us to ask what it would mean if we deny that God's attributes are infinite, i.e., unending and inexhaustible? This would mean that the love and mercy of God are limited! The day may come when we ask forgiveness from God and He must say, "Sorry, I can't help you. I don't have any left. I'm only finite, you know."

Not only is the concept of "infinite" the only way we have to show how God is *different* from His creation, but it also reveals how God is *superior*. God's "infinity" should not be reduced to the mathematical idea of a "boundless quantity." While God is *quantitatively* distinct from His creation by being "infinite," i.e., not limited like the things He made, infinitude also means a *perfection* of God whereby He is *superior* to what He has made in a *qualitative* sense. Thus God's infinite presence or omnipresence is *superior* to the finite presence of men and angels. God's infinitude is a quality of perfection that makes all His attributes superior as well as different to those of angels and men.

God is GOD because He is different in a superior way to the world both quantitatively and qualitatively. God cannot be limited, exhausted, or quantified. His person, presence, power, prescience, knowledge, moral qualities, or glory have no end, boundary, or limitation. No one will ever find a "cut-off point" for God. We can never draw a line and then tell God that He can only go so far and no further. This is what Christians mean when they say that God is "infinite."

The Evidence for God's Infinitude

The evidence for the infinite nature of God rests on the clear Biblical teaching that He is the Creator of all things. When God created the world, His power was not exhausted or depleted by the act of creation because His power is infinite. But the limited power of a finite god would have been exhausted. The idea of a "tired" god who is too worn out and weak to do anything sounds more like Zeus than Jehovah! We shudder to think of the implications for prayer of such an idea.

Evidence can also be drawn from the fact that the Bible describes God as the self-existent One, the eternal "I AM," and the "living God" who has "life in Himself." To be self-existent, God must be infinite in being and power or He would "run down" and "perish." God's existence must be infinite in order to be eternal, immutable, and perfect. Otherwise, we are left with a finite god no different from pagan deities who grow old and die.

> Great is our Lord, and abundant in strength,
> His understanding is infinite (Psalm 147:5).

In the context, God's glory is revealed by His omniscience because He can "count the number of the stars" and "give names to all of them" (v. 4). The universe may be vast and immeasurable to man but it is only a finite speck of dust to the Almighty. He knows its measurements because He made it.

In v. 5, the Psalmist gives a poetic contrast between the finite nature of the universe and the infinite nature of its Creator. He first says, "Great is our Lord." Leupold translates it as, "Great is our sovereign Lord," to catch the force of the Hebrew plural, a sort of plural of majesty.[1]

The Creator is the sovereign Lord of the universe. As such He is "abundant in strength," i.e., omnipotent. Since God is infinite in power, the creation of the world did not "drain" God. He was not "exhausted," "worn out," or "nearly out of gas" after speaking the worlds into being. But He is more than "abundant in power." But if we say that His power is finite, then there is a point at which it can be depleted or used up.

Now the Psalmist turns once again to the omniscience of God. He states that God's "understanding" or "knowledge" is "infinite." The Hebrew word translated "infinite" is a word that means without number, limitation, boundary, or end, i.e., infinite.

The Psalmist is using a poetic play on words by using the same word translated as "number" in verse 4, where God is said to be able "to count the number of the stars." He is able to do this because the stars are "limited," i.e., finite. They can be "numbered" because there is an "end" to them. There is a boundary to their number. We can draw a line and say that there are no more stars after this line.

But in contrast to the finite nature of the stars, it is impossible to "number" God's knowledge or understanding. It has no end, no boundaries, and no limitations. We cannot draw a line and say that God's knowledge ends with this line. The Hebrew word is emphatic, says Delitzsch:

> To His understanding there is no number, i.e. in its depth and fulness it cannot be defined by any number. What a comfort for the church as it traverses its ways, that are often so labyrinthine and entangled! Its Lord is the Omniscient as well as the Almighty One. Its history, like the universe, is a work of God's infinitely profound and rich understanding. It is a mirror of gracious love and righteous anger.[2]

The vision of God in Psalm 147 is an exalted one. The Lord is "great" because, as Moll points out:

> He has assigned a number to the stars which men cannot count (Gen. XV.5). This means that, in creating them, He called forth a number determined by Himself. It is also said that He calls all by name, i.e., that He knows and names them according to their special features, and employs them in His service according to His will, in conformity with the names which correspond to such a knowledge.

> The Omniscience and Omnipresence of God are thus presented at once to the soul. The greatness of God (v. 5) with respect to might (Job XXXVII.23) corresponds to the fullness of His understanding (Psa. CXLV.3), which no number can express. The same Lord who, with infinite power and unsearchable wisdom, rules the stars in their courses, rules also the world of man.[3]

The same vision of the infinite nature of God is found in Isaiah 40:12-17 where the entire universe is a like a "speck of dust" to the Almighty. The contrast between the finite nature of creation and the infinite nature of God is obvious.

Also, while the pagan gods were finite and could be "housed" in a temple because they were "contained" in the world, the Biblical God cannot not be "housed" or "contained" because He is infinite. If the earth is no more to Him than a "footstool," how can the world "contain" God? If the world cannot contain God, how much less could a temple "house" Him! (Isaiah 66:1-2; Matthew 5:35; Acts 7:49; 17:24-29).

Conclusion

Why do pagan philosophers such as Whitehead hate the infinite nature of God so much? God can be "infinite" only as long as He exists prior to, independent of, and apart from the world He made out of nothing. Thus the infinitude of God rests on the self-existence of God, the doctrine of Creation, and the timelessness of God.

But once God is *merged* into the world, or becomes identified as being the whole of it, or a part of it, He can no longer be infinite because He is no longer self-existent, the Creator, or timeless. Thus Whitehead's dipolar deity, finite gods such as Isis, or even a pantheistic god who is identified with the world, *cannot* be "infinite" by definition.

Neither can such a god create the world out of nothing. And, since the world "contains" god, then the world must be as "eternal" as he is. Since the world is eternal, and the world is "in" time, then time is eternal. Then nothing, not even god, is "timeless," for time is the ultimate and eternal "ground of being" for everything. Thus the hidden assumption of monism always lies behind every rejection of the timeless nature of the infinite/personal God of the Bible.

EIGHTEEN

THE PERFECTION
OF GOD

The early Christians faced a world that was hostile to their idea that God is totally and absolutely "perfect." This was in conflict with the gods of the heathen who were *imperfect* because they were in the *process* of "growing" and "learning."

These gods were in the "process of becoming" because they were born, grew into maturity, and then eventually passed away into obscurity. They could "increase" and "decrease" in being, power, and knowledge. A god could go from strength to weakness just as easily as he could from weakness to strength.

Thus the gods of the pagans were not "perfect" because they were not "finished" or "complete." What they were today was not what they would be tomorrow. Their future was "open" because they could become good or evil, smaller or bigger, greater or lesser, ignorant or knowledgeable.

This "open" view of God tried to invade the early Church but it was condemned by the Church as a damnable heresy incompatible with Biblical Christianity. The idea that God was imperfect and still in the process of becoming something no one knew, not even God, was taught by Gnosticism, Valentinianism, Marcionism, and, later, by Socinianism. Today the same heresy is taught by processianism and moral government which have their roots in Whitehead's Platonic philosophy.

One of the chief reasons why the pagans gave up their gods and accepted the Christian God was that He was perfect while their gods were imperfect. God's perfection is part of the essence of His Godhood. This made Him not only *different* from the gods of the heathen but also *superior* to them.

When Christian theology states that God is "perfect" it means that God is complete; finished; whole; lacking in nothing; not defective; has no blemishes or imperfections; does not increase or decrease; does not get smaller or bigger; does not grow older or younger; is not evolving; is not in the "process of becoming;" is not dependent but independent; and is the same eternal I AM who was, is, and forever shall be perfect in His existence, being, attributes, and works.

God's perfection is not an independent attribute. Perfection is a word that is essential to the definition of all the other attributes of God and raises them to divinity.

First, God is perfect in His existence in that He is the eternal self-existent One. His existence is "perfect" because it is complete, finished, whole, independent, not lacking in anything, needing nothing, does not increase or decrease, does not get older or younger, bigger or smaller, and is not evolving or "becoming." God's existence is thus not "open" but closed. It is not insecure but eternally secure.

Second, in the same exact way, God is perfect in His Being because He is complete, lacking nothing, and has no imperfections or blemishes that need correcting, does not need growth or development, will not get bigger or smaller, older or younger, and is not in need of any more "being" or "becoming."

Third, all of God's attributes are "perfect" and could not be divine attributes if they were not so. God is not partial but whole, not incomplete but finished, not defective but perfect.

Fourth, all of God's works are perfect because He is perfect. When He made the world, it could not have been anything but perfect and good. To deny that God is perfect means that we do not even have a perfect Bible, for an imperfect God can only give an imperfect revelation.

This is the root reason why the inerrancy of Scripture is denied by so many "evangelical" processians like Clark Pinnock. Once god is no longer viewed as perfect, how can he give a perfect revelation? Once you deny the Christian view of God, it will not be long before you deny the Christian view of the Bible, salvation, and eternal punishment.

God's Perfection and the Gospel

But does this issue mean anything to the average Christian? Yes, for the issue of the perfection of God either makes or breaks the Gospel itself. For example, is God's grace perfect or is there something wrong with it? Is it defective in some sense? Does it have blemishes? Is it in need of growth? If so, then it cannot serve as the basis of our salvation.

Likewise, is God's knowledge perfect? Or, is it imperfect, blemished, and lacking something? Does His knowledge get bigger or smaller, older or younger? Can it increase or decrease? Is God dependent on something or someone else to inform Him? Is His knowledge finite and incomplete, lacking many things? If so, then we cannot trust Him for He is as ignorant as we are.

Again, is God's power perfect or defective? Is it lacking in something? Does the Almighty need help? Is He in danger of running out of power? Does His power increase or decrease? If God's power is not perfect, then we cannot trust His power to keep us safe until He brings us to heaven. He may be too weak one day to defeat Satan.

Is God's goodness perfect? Is it complete, with no possibility of change? Or, is His goodness "open" to becoming evil? Must we wait every day for the "roll of the dice" to see if God is good? Or, is His goodness perfect?

When someone denies the perfection of God, he must be prepared to accept the consequences. The consistent processians are willing to do this. This is why they state that God can sin. They argue that God can lie and do evil and tempt others to do evil. This is what is meant by the "open view" of God! God is "open" to do evil but "closed" to sovereign acts of mercy and grace!

Some people have foolishly thought that they could deny the perfection of God's knowledge in order to get rid of the Biblical antinomy of divine sovereignty and human accountability without having to deny the perfection of all of God's attributes. What they fail to understand is that once imperfection, which is no more than the Greek philosophic concept of relativity, is injected into God, be it His knowledge or power, it destroys all of God.

For example, if God is not perfect in His knowledge, then He does not even have a perfect knowledge of Himself! He is unknown to Himself. He must wait until tomorrow for "the roll of the dice" to see what He will be. He doesn't even know if He will be a devil or an angel tomorrow!

It also means that He does not have a perfect knowledge of what man needs for salvation. He does not have a perfect knowledge of the present anymore than He has of the future. If God is not *perfect* in His goodness and in all His attributes, He is not a GOD worthy of our trust,

love, or obedience. He is no different and in no way superior to the
pagan gods.

No wonder the Scriptures and the Christian Church have always
confessed that God is perfect in all His attributes and works. This is
what made the Biblical God worthy to be GOD.

Biblical Passages

The word *perfect*, according to James means, "complete, lacking in
nothing" (James 1:4). This word is directly applied to God in both the
Old and the New Testaments.

> Ascribe greatness to our God!
> The Rock! His work is perfect (Deuteronomy 32:3-4).

Our God is "great," says Moses, because He is "perfect" in all His
works. The Hebrew word *tamim* means that which is complete, lacking
nothing, whole, pure, with no defects or imperfections whatsoever. The
word was used in its physical sense to describe the lamb used for Passover. This lamb had to be "perfect," i.e., without any defects, imperfections, or blemishes. The lamb could be lacking in nothing. It had to be
complete (Exodus 12:5). In the same way, whatever God does is "perfect."

> As for God, His way is blameless; . . .
> For who is God, besides the Lord?
> And who is a rock, besides our God (2 Samuel 22:31-32)?

The marginal notes of the NASV correctly point out that the word
translated "blameless" literally means "complete." It is once again the
word *tamim* and is translated as "perfect" in the KJV.

The word *blameless* opens up another aspect of the doctrine of the
perfection of God. If God is not perfect in His attributes, then we must
conclude that He is not *morally* perfect! This at once "opens" God to
moral guilt or blame. The Bible views "perfection" in the moral sense as
"blamelessness." The "open" view of God leaves Him "open" to make
mistakes caused by His ignorance and weakness! But if God is perfect in
all He does, then He is blameless in all He does.

> Stand and consider the wonders of God. . . .
> The wonders of One perfect in knowledge (Job 37:14, 16).

Delitzsch translates verse 16 as,

> The wondrous things of Him
> who is perfect in knowledge.

He comments that,

> God is called . . . the Omniscient One, whose knowledge is absolute
> as to its depths as well as its circumference.[1]

God is not lacking in knowledge in any sense. He is not defective or imperfect in His knowledge of the past, present, or future of the world He made. "The Law of the Lord is perfect" (Psalm 19:7).

The Bible is the inerrant Word of God because it is as perfect as the God who inspired it. Only a perfect God can give a perfect revelation.

> Neither is He served by human hands, as though He needed anything, since He Himself gives to all life and breath and all things (Acts 17:25).

In order to show the difference between his God and the gods of the Greek philosophers, the Apostle Paul declares that his God is "not in need of anything," i.e., perfect. He is the self-existent One who lacks in nothing. "The will of God is . . . perfect" (Romans 12:2).

Not only are God's ways, words, works, wisdom, and knowledge perfect but also His will. In that it is "perfect," it is also "good," "acceptable," and "blameless."

Conclusion

The fact that God's Word plainly states that God's knowledge is perfect is enough to prove that the Almighty is cognizant of all things including the future. But rationalists will not believe it unless they know "how," "in what way," and "why" God is perfect when man is not. They reject the plain teaching of Scripture and follow their own conceited ideas of what God is like.

While we may not be able to answer all the riddles that the pagans compose, we do know that we cannot run through the attributes of God selecting what we like and throwing out the rest. The attributes of God are not independent of each other but are so interrelated that if one is removed, they all fall. Either we accept all of God as He has revealed Himself, or we are left with nothing at all.

NINETEEN

THE ETERNITY OF GOD

C hristian theology has always begun its discussion of the relationship of God to time and eternity with the doctrine of Creation because this is where the Bible begins (Genesis 1:1). In the first verse of the Bible we are told that God *alone* is eternal. Everything else, be it invisible or visible, spiritual or material, is *not* eternal because God created *all* things. Thus God alone existed *before* all things and all things depend on His power for their existence.

This is also clearly taught in the New Testament.

> For by Him all things were created, both in the heavens and on earth, visible and invisible, whether thrones or dominions or rulers or authorities—all things have been created through Him and for Him. And He is before all things, and in Him all things hold together (Colossians 1:16-17).

In this passage, the Apostle Paul was emphatic that *nothing* existed alongside of God for all eternity. All things are created and hence not eternal. In order to make this clear he encompasses everything in heaven and in earth regardless of its spiritual or material nature. Whatever we may ask about has been created by God.

It is for this reason that Christians have always taught that space and time were both created and hence are not eternal. While the Greeks believed that space and time were eternal, and even deified time and made it into the god Kronos, the Christians rejected such an idea because space and time are attributes of *created* things.

Created things, by definition, occupy space and time. They are limited because they can only be in *one* place at any *one* time. Space and time are inseparable, like the two sides of a coin.

But is this true of the God of the Bible? Can He be in *more* places at one time or is He limited like Zeus and Baal? Are space and time eternal? Is God limited by them? Does He exist in them? Or, do they exist in Him?

The Vocabulary of Eternity

Every Hebrew and Greek word that could possibly signify "eternity" was applied to God in the Bible. Since He alone is the "eternal" God, the word *eternal* became one of the names of God, signifying one of the essential attributes that makes Him GOD as opposed to the pagan gods (Genesis 21:33; Romans 16:26).

The eternity of God is the basis of our confidence in His ability to care for us. Thus Moses could speak of "the everlasting arms of God" as carrying and protecting us because He is "the eternal God" (Deuteronomy 33:27).

The Hebrews used the word *olam* (forever, everlasting, eternal) in creative constructs in order to emphasize that God *alone* was the "Eternal I AM." God is viewed as being from "eternity" to "eternity" in such places as Psalm 41:13; 90:2; 106:48. If God were "in" time like the pagan deities, then He would have a "beginning" and an "end." But God has no beginning or end because He is from "eternity" to "eternity."

Even as Isaiah said,

> . . . thus saith the high and lofty One that *inhabiteth eternity*, whose name is Holy; I dwell in the high and lofty place (Isaiah 57:15 KJV, emphasis added).

While the NASV's text says, "lives forever," its margin records the literal Hebrew as "dwell in eternity." Other modern versions emphasize that God here claims that He alone has existed or lived from all eternity.

> Even from eternity I am He; and there is none who can deliver out of my hand; I act and who can reverse? (Isaiah 43:13)

The Hebrew simply says that God was the I AM "before the day." This is interpreted in the Greek Septuagint and the Latin Vulgate in the sense of "before the first day," i.e., before time itself began." The ancient and classical commentators all see God as claiming that He pre-existed time itself and is "eternal" in this sense.

Eternity and the Other Attributes

We have discussed the issue of the timelessness of God in connection with the other attributes of God to emphasize that timelessness cannot be separated from the Christian view of God. Everything that the Bible tells us about God is said in the context of His timelessness. All His attributes are *timeless* attributes.

God's existence is described as "eternal" because it is self-existent and independent. As such, it is perfect and does not increase or decrease. He always was, is, and shall be the same eternal I AM. He alone is eternal because He alone is GOD.

God's being and attributes are also described as "eternal" because they are likewise independent and self-existent. Thus Paul could speak of "His eternal power and divine nature" (Romans 1:20).

Since God's knowledge is part of the "divine nature," it too is eternal, independent, self-existent, and perfect. Therefore, any attempt to say that God's knowledge "grows" is a denial that it is eternal. The only way it can "grow" is for it to be dependent on time and space. Thus it is not self-existent. If it is not eternal, self-existent, independent, or perfect, wherein is it "divine"? It is more *human* than divine!

Is Time God?

The only way to deny that God is eternal in the sense of "timeless" is to hold that time is *not* created but is itself eternal. But for time to be eternal means that it must be self-existent and not dependent on anything, not even God. Like Zoroastrian dualism, in which two gods struggle to overcome each other, time becomes a rival "god" to Jehovah.

One of the more consistent modern pagan thinkers has been forced to the same conclusions. Stephen Davis argues that God is not timeless because such an idea is not "coherent" to him.

> . . . a timeless being cannot be the Christian God . . . [because] the notion of a timeless being is probably incoherent.[1]

As a rationalist, Davis demands complete coherence.

If we want to be rational we have no choice but to reject what we judge to be incoherent.[2]

In the place of the historic Christian doctrine that God is timeless, Davis proposes to "argue for the assumption that God is temporally eternal."[3] But if God is only "temporally eternal" and not timeless, this means that time is itself eternal and not created. And if it is eternal, then it does not depend on God for its existence.

Time is not a contingent, created thing like the universe.[4]

Since time was not created, then it must eternally exist alongside of God. Davis states that, "time has always existed alongside God."[5] But for time to exist alongside of God means that it too must be "divine" in that it is self-existent and not dependent on anything outside of itself including God. Time is not created.

. . . time was not created; it necessarily exists . . . it depends for its existence on nothing else.[6]

But which is "higher," God or time? Which is the "ground of existence" for the other? Is time "in" God or is God "in" time? Which of these two eternal gods is the "greater"? Davis decides that time is. Davis ends up believing in, "a temporal God who is 'in' time."[7]

The process is finally complete. Instead of being the creature, Time is now the "Creator" of everything including God! Jehovah has been kicked off His throne and Kronos put in His place! We have returned full circle back to the Greek view that TIME is GOD!

The Christian view has always taught that time was created by and dependent on the one true God who alone is self-existent and eternal. Thus time is "in" God as He is its Creator and Lord. But with Davis and other processians, time is not created but eternal, self-existent, and independent of God. Time not only eternally existed outside of and alongside of God, but time is a higher god "in" whom God must find the ground of His own existence!

When we look to Davis, Pinnock, or Olson to give just one Biblical text saying that time is not created; that it is eternal; that it has always existed outside of and alongside of God; that it is self-existent and independent of God; that God is dependent upon it; that God is "in" time; we look in vain. No one has ever come forth with such a text.

The entire argument against the timeless nature of God is merely *philosophical* and devoid of any Biblical support. After all, Genesis 1:1 does *not* say, "In the beginning Time." But it *does* say, "In the beginning God." The world was not created by Time *and* God. God alone is the Creator of *all* things including time.

When we took a close look at the philosophical arguments against the timelessness of God, we came to the conclusion that they were highly overrated and patently absurd. If the same line of reasoning is applied to space as well as time, the absurdity of the argument is obvious. If the arguments that are used to deny the omniscience of God are valid, then they would also refute His omnipresence. While the Socinians and Jehovah's Witnesses have already taken this next logical step, most "evangelical" processians are either not intellectually honest enough to admit it or emotionally ready for it.

- To say that God cannot act in time without being limited by time is the same as saying that He cannot act in space without being limited by it.

- To say that if God is timeless then time is an illusion is the same as saying that if God is spaceless then space is an illusion.

- To say that if God is timeless He cannot know the categories of time is the same as saying that if God is spaceless, He cannot know the categories of space.

- To say that since the Bible uses metaphors of time such as "past," "present," and "future" and such words as "foreknowledge," that God is limited by time is the same as saying that because the Bible uses metaphors of space such as "up," "down," "here," and "there" as in "God came down," that He is limited by space.

- To say that God cannot hear our prayers unless He is limited by time is to say that He cannot hear our prayers unless He is limited by space.

- To say that unless God is "in" time like man, man has a greater knowledge than God, is to say that unless He is "in" space like man, man has a greater knowledge than God.

The philosophical arguments against the doctrine of the timelessness of God are stupid as well as blasphemous. This is how the Fathers and the Reformers viewed such heretical attacks on the Divine Glory of God.

Conclusion

God is the Maker of all things including time. Nothing is "above" or "beneath" God as if He needed something to support Him. No eternal rivals are alongside God because He alone is the eternal infinite/personal God who is the sovereign Creator and Sustainer of all things. To Him be all the glory!

TWENTY

THE IMMUTABILITY
OF GOD

The historic Christian doctrine of the immutability of God is under special attack these days. The processians are particularly vicious in vilifying this doctrine by misrepresenting it.

Clark Pinnock is a good example of this procedure. He begins by calling God's immutability "Platonic" thinking based on a "Greek model."1 He then argues that if God is immutable, "there cannot be genuine freedom."2 He even claims that it came from "Aristotle's God."3

According to Pinnock, the orthodox view teaches that that God is "static" and "immovable." Then, having defined the doctrine by using Greek concepts, he turns around and condemns it as Greek philosophy! This is the logical fallacy known as "stacking the deck" or "building a straw man."

The early Church did not accept "thought thinking itself," the god of Aristotle. They condemned Aristotle as an atheist because he did not believe in a God who existed prior to, independent of, and apart from the world which He made out of nothing. Also, Aristotle believed in many finite gods. Thus he was an idolater as well as an atheist.

Christian theology derived its doctrine of the immutability of God from the Holy Scriptures and not from the atheistic philosophers of the ancient world. The God who has revealed Himself in Scripture is "faithful," "dependable," and "unchanging." This is what historic Christianity has confessed for two thousand years.

The processians consistently misrepresent the Christian doctrine of the immutability of God because, as humanists, they begin with false assumptions.

First, they assume the Greek dichotomy that God must be either Parmenides' static "being" or Heraclitus' dynamic "becoming." Humanistic theology will only recognize two gods. This is why they constantly harp on the "static versus dynamic" theme.

The history of philosophy demonstrates that humanistic views of God swing back and forth between a static god and a dynamic god. In one century they will champion a "static" god, and then in the next century they will champion a "dynamic" god. They simply "rebel" against the previous generation's god.

The contrast between the "static" god found in eighteenth-century Rationalism with the "dynamic" liberal god of the nineteenth century is a perfect example of how humanistic thought swings back and forth between Parmenides' god and Heraclitus' god.

It is also interesting to point out that when Parmenides's static god was in vogue among rationalists, the Christian God was rejected because He was too "dynamic." Today, now that Heraclitus' dynamic god is in vogue, the rationalists reject the Christian God because He is too "static"! Either way the God of the Bible loses out.

Second, the processians assume that when Christians speak of the "immutability" of God, they mean an "immobility" of God in which He does nothing and knows nothing. Why is this?

Some of the philosophic gods of the heathen are said to be "immutable" in the sense of "immobile," "unmoving," "unacting," "uncaring," and "unknowing," because they are nonpersonal gods that are defined as "ground of being," "power," or "energy."

We agree that a nonpersonal "it" cannot hear our prayers or interact with us. But we emphatically disagree with the attempt to impute such pagan concepts to the Christian doctrine of the immutability of God. It would help their case if the processians could produce just one orthodox theologian who denies the personhood of God. But they have never submitted such evidence.

The Christian View of God's Immutability

The Christian doctrine of God does not operate on the assumption that either Parmenides or Heraclitus had the "true" view of God. Such atheistical philosophers are best ignored as just another example of the "foolishness of the world." Our view of God must come from revelation alone.

The Christian God is in stark contrast to the gods of the heathen, who were *mutable* and hence always changing. The gods were born, grew old, and could even die. They could change morally and become good or evil. They could even change sexes, with male gods becoming female deities and vice versa. The Marcionite heretics even claimed that the god of the Old Testament was different from the god of the New Testament!

In the Christian view, God is immutable, changeless, consistent, faithful, dependable, the same yesterday, today, and forever in His existence, being, and attributes.

What does all this mean? It means that when we pray, we pray to the *same* God twice. The God who created the world is the *same* God who later spoke to Abraham, Isaac, and Jacob, who gave His law to Moses, sent His Son to be our Savior, inspired Paul, and in whom we believe today. He is the *exact* same God and not something *different*. The God of the New Testament is not *different* from the God of the Old Testament. He is not older, wiser, more knowledgeable, bigger or smaller, greater or lesser, stronger or weaker. Only ONE God, as the eternal I AM, is the same yesterday, today, and forever.

Notice that we did not say in our definition that God was immutable in His "works." The Scriptures do not teach that God is immutable in terms of His *relationship* to His creation. He is not "sitting on His hands doing nothing." He is the sovereign Creator and Sustainer of all things.

The Lord Jehovah invades and pervades both space and time and does His mighty deeds. His glory is revealed in every flash of lightning and peal of thunder. The roar of the sea is a testimony of His power. His providential care can be seen in His concern for the smallest sparrow. He makes the grass to grow and sends the rain. The mighty lions look to God for their food. The Lord God Omnipotent reigns over His creation (see Psalm 22; 104; 148).

By His omnipotent power, God intervenes in the affairs of men, raising up and putting down, killing and bringing to life. He interacts with men and changes His revelation, laws, and deeds from covenant to covenant. He is so involved by His providence in the affairs of the sons of men that His hand lies behind all things. Nations even rise and fall at His command (see 1 Samuel 2:6-10).

Those who are the "sons of Satan" are under Divine wrath. But God can change His attitude toward us, and we can become the "sons of God" under His blessing. Salvation is a transition from wrath to grace in which God's attitude toward us changes (Ephesians 2:1-4).

How different is this doctrine from the gods of the heathen who, if personal, are *subject* to change all the time or, if nonpersonal, know no change at all!

Both Static and Dynamic

God is thus not trapped into being either static or dynamic. He is both and neither. While in His relationship to the world He is the dynamic sovereign Lord of history, in His existence, being, and attributes, He is changeless.

First, God is not capable of change in terms of His existence. He cannot go out of existence like a flickering candle. He will not grow old or die. The eternal I AM will always be the same.

Second, God is immutable in His being and nature. He cannot become "non-God." He cannot become less or more than what He has always been. There are no "degrees" of God, as if He were sliding up and down some pagan scale of being. God is GOD and always was GOD and always shall be GOD. We do not have to wait for God to become GOD, contrary to what processians like Whitehead, Davis, Rice, and Pinnock claim.

This is why Christian theology has always been careful to say that Christ is *both* GOD and man. But if God is not perfect or immutable and is still awaiting the time when He shall become GOD, then Christ could not be GOD!

The divine nature of Christ as well as the divine inspiration of Scripture become absolutely impossible once the perfection and immutability of God are rejected. This is the conclusion that most modern processians have now accepted.

As a matter of historical record, we must add that *all* essential Christian doctrines from the Trinity to the atonement were conceived and confessed with the assumption that God is the infinite/personal, eternal, perfect, immutable, omniscient, omnipotent, omnipresent, transcendent, sovereign, immutable Creator of Heaven and earth.

This was the theology behind *all* the ancient creeds of the Church from the Apostles' Creed and the Nicene Creed to the Athanasian Creed, and *all* the creeds of the Reformation from the Augsburg Confession and the Thirty-nine Articles to the Westminster Confession of Faith. Thus it does not surprise us in the least that modern theology is slowly but surely rejecting *everything* these creeds confess. Once the Christian God is rejected, it is only a matter of time before all Christian doctrine is rejected.

Can God Become Evil?

The Bible clearly describes the Creator as "changeless." Immutability in this sense is applied to all the attributes of God and this makes God different from and superior to the gods of the heathen. For example, when Christians say that God is good, they mean He always was, is, always shall be, and cannot be anything other than good. In other words, He is *immutably* good. Thus He *cannot* do evil because He cannot *become* evil. We can trust Him for His goodness is "unalterable," "eternally consistent," and "ever the same." The problem of evil is solved by the Biblical teaching that God *cannot* do evil.

In contrast, processians such as Stephen Davis argue that God *can* become evil because He *can* sin. But this "open view" of God is possible only if God is imperfect or immutable. If God is neither perfect nor immutable, then He can sin. Thus the historic Christian doctrine of the impeccability of God and Christ is also rejected by such thinkers.

But in trying to absolve God from the problem of evil by reducing Him down to the level of Zeus or Baal, modern rationalists have actually accomplished what they set out to avoid. The moment they denied the perfection and immutability of God, they unwittingly established that God *can* become the author of evil *tomorrow!*

The more daring and bold among the processians state God *can* become the Devil! This is what they *must* say if they are consistent. After all, if the universe is *really* based on pure chance or contingency, and God does not know or ordain the future, then *anything* is possible— including God's becoming Satan!

How different is the attitude of Christian theology, which has always taught that God is *immutably* good, i.e., He *cannot* be the author of evil because He cannot become evil, do evil, or tempt anyone to do evil.

Biblical Passages

"Shall not the Judge of all the earth deal justly" (Genesis 18:25)? To Abraham, God was *immutably* just. It was inconceivable to him that God could do anything that was unjust because God is a righteous God and all His acts must be consistent with His nature. Thus God would do the right thing when it came time to deal with Sodom and Gomorrah.

We must also point out that such passages as this reveal that God does not have the absolute "freedom" found in Greek philosophy. The Greeks assumed that the gods were "free" to become demons if they so chose. Nothing was impossible to them.

But the Biblical God is "free" to act only in conformity to His nature. Thus God *"cannot* lie" because "it is *impossible"* (Titus 1:2; Hebrews 6:18, emphasis added). God is not free to become non-God or to do non-Godlike things. While He is free to do righteousness and to speak the truth, He is not "free" to do evil or speak lies, because He is not capable of doing so.

In the same way, man can act only in conformity to his nature. He cannot do that which is inconsistent with his nature. Thus the humanistic vision of a truly autonomous man who can do anything and everything in a world of chance is a delusion because the Greek ideal of absolute freedom is an illusion.

> And God said to Moses, "I AM WHO I AM"; and He said, "Thus you shall say to the sons of Israel, I AM has sent me to you (Exodus 3:14).

Even such names of God as "I AM" bear witness to the immutability of God. God is ever the same God. He is the eternal *I* AM because His nature is complete. He did not say, "I BECOME," but "I AM."

> God is not a man, that He should lie, nor a son of man, that He should repent. Has He said, and will He not do it? Or has He spoken, and will He not make it good (Numbers 23:19)?

> And also the Glory of Israel will not lie or change His mind; for He is not a man that He should change His mind (1 Samuel 15:29).

These texts clearly state that those who say that God can lie, that God can do evil, that God can repent, that God can promise to do something and then fail to do it, have made a god in the image of man. But God is *not* like mutable man, who is capable of lying because of his sinful and mutable nature. Neither is God like man, who needs to repent for doing evil.

According to Scripture, God is immutably faithful and true. Thus He is not "open" to lying or to failing to make good on His promises. Indeed, without the basis of the immutability of God, all the promises of God are rendered null and void. After all, a mutable God who is "open" to failure and sin cannot give man immutable promises to live and die by!

If we live in a universe where all things including God are "open," i.e., governed by chance, then we must wait for the "roll of the dice" to see if God's promises come true. God's promises are thus reduced to mere wishes and guesses which may or may not be fulfilled because not even God knows the future.

But if God is *immutably* and *perfectly* faithful and true, then we *know* that He will do all He has promised. His promises are not made in ignorance as some kind of "shot in the dark." He promises what He *knows* will happen because He guarantees it to come to pass by His almighty power.

> The Rock! His work is perfect,
> For all His ways are just;
> A God of faithfulness and without injustice,
> Righteous and upright is He (Deuteronomy 32:3-4).

One of the metaphors used in Scripture to illustrate the immutability of God is "The Rock." (See Genesis 49:24; Deuteronoy 32:15, 18, 30, 31; 1 Samuel 2:2; 2 Samuel 22:2, 3, 32, 47; 3:3; Psalm 18:2, 31, 46; 28:1; 31:2, 3; 42:9; 61:2; 62:2, 6, 7; 71:3; 78:35; 89:26; 92:15; 94:22; 1 Corinthians 10:4.) In the passage quoted, Keil and Delitzsch point out that the word *Rock*

> . . . is placed first absolutely, to give it the greater prominence. God is called "the Rock," as the unchangeable refuge, who grants a firm defense and secure resort to His people, by virtue of His unchangeableness or impregnable firmness . . . David, who had so often experienced the rock-like protection of his God, adopted it in his Psalms.[4]

Notice also that God's greatness, perfection, justice, faithfulness, purity, righteousness, and uprightness all flow out of and thus are intrinsically bound together with His immutable rocklike nature. God is called the "Rock" in Scripture in order to distinguish Him from mutable man. This is in stark contrast to the god of the processians, which can only be described as some kind of divine "Putty" that time and space mold.

The fact that God's perfection and immutability are joined together in this text from the Mosaic period also supplies us with an iron-clad refutation of the claim that the idea that God is perfect and immutable comes from Greek philosophy. Modern processians such as Pinnock dismiss the historic Christian doctrine of God by the cheap rebuff that it "is simply the Greek ideal of perfection."[5]

Of course, processians like Pinnock nowhere *document* the Greek origins of the Christian God. And, indeed, it will take a great deal of imagination to picture Moses and the prophets learning about God from Greek philosophers who were not even born until hundreds of years later!

The fact that the Bible, beginning in Genesis, speaks of the infinite/personal God who is the Creator and Ruler of all things forever reveals the Greek-origin charge as just another cheap Socinian trick.

> Thy years are throughout all generations.
> Of old Thou didst found the earth;
> And the heavens are the work of Thy hands.
> Even they will perish, but Thou dost endure;
> And all of them will wear out like a garment;
> Like clothing Thou wilt change them,
>   and they will be changed.
> But Thou are the same,
> And Thy years will not come to an end (Psalm 102:24-27).

The eternity and immutability of God are revealed and celebrated in this Psalm. That it is also applied to Jesus in Hebrews 1:1-12 makes it even more glorious.

The Psalmist begins by contrasting the shortness of human life with the eternity of God in verses 23-24. He then turns to consider the world around him. Instead of ascribing eternity to it as do the pagans, the Psalmist proclaims that it was created by the true God who existed prior to it, independent of it, and apart from it.

The world is dependent on its Creator for its very existence. It cannot exist autonomously apart from God. Indeed, He made the world with a mutable or changeable nature in that it decays and perishes. Just as a piece of cloth gets thinner and thinner until it must be thrown away, the world will one day perish. Then God will create a new heavens and a new earth.

While the world is mutable, decaying, and will perish one day, Jehovah is not like this at all. He is the eternal I AM, the Unchanging One. He is not "changing," "decaying," or "perishing." He is ever the same. But He could not be the *same* from eternity to eternity if He were changing into something new and different all the time. He can only be "the same" if He is what He has always been and what He will always be.

Down through the centuries, this passage has always been central in the Christian concept of God. The world may change but God does not change. Thus He is our refuge and our strength. Notice the profound comments of the great expositors of these verses.

Charles Spurgeon

When heaven and earth shall flee away from the dread presence of the great Judge, he will be unaltered by the terrible confusion, and the world in conflagration will effect no change in him; even so, the Psalmist remembered that when Israel was vanquished, her capital destroyed, and her temple levelled with the ground, her God remained the same self-existent, all-sufficient being, and would restore his people, even as he will restore the heavens and the earth, bestowing at the same time a new glory never known before. The doctrine of the immutability of God should be more considered than it is, for the neglect of it tinges the theology of many religious teachers, and makes them utter many things of which they would have seen the absurdity long ago if they had remembered the divine declaration, "I am God, I change not, therefore ye sons of Jacob are not consumed."[6]

Stephen Charnock

The text doth not only assert the eternal duration of God, but his immutability in that duration; his eternity is signified in that expression, "thou shalt endure;" his immutability in this, "thou are the same.". . . He could not be the same if he could be changed into any other thing than what he is. The psalmist therefore puts, not thou *hast been* or *shall be*, but *thou art* the same, without any alteration. . . . The psalmist here alludes to the name *Jehovah, I am*, and doth ascribe immutability to God, but exclude everything else from partaking in that perfection.[7]

Lange's Commentary

> Although the heavens and the mountains are termed everlasting with reference to the lasting duration of the order of things, . . . yet, when contrasted with God, they are not merely transitory and mutable, but will undergo a change by the power of God. In view of the contrast to this change to which the world will be subjected, [verse 28] is not to be understood as referring . . . to the fact that God is the only Being who can lay claim to the Divine name, but, as in Job iii.19; Isa. xli.4; xlvi.4, to the immutability in which God ever manifests himself as the *same*.[8]

J. A. Alexander

> The meaning then is, Thou art the Unchangeable One just described.[9]

Franz Delitzsch

> The expressive [Hebrew phrase], Thou art He, *i.e.*, unalterably the same One, is also taken from the mouth of the prophet, Isa. xli.4, xliii.10, xlvi.4, xlviii.12; [the word "same"] is a predicate, and denotes the identity (sameness) of Jahve.[10]

Matthew Henry

> It is likewise comfortable in reference to the decay and death of our own bodies, and the removal of our friends from us, that God is an everlasting God, and that therefore, if he be ours, in him we may have everlasting consolation. In this plea observe how, to illustrate the eternity of the Creator, he compares it with the mutability of the creature; for it is God's sole prerogative to be unchangeable. . . . God is perpetual and everlasting: Thou art the same, subject to no change.[11]

Jehovah is the one true God, for He is eternal and immutable. In Him we can trust, for He is ever the same and changeth not.

> For I, the LORD, do not change (Malachi 3:6).

For the Christian, this passage alone is sufficient to confirm that the historic faith of the Christian Church in the immutability of God arises out of Scripture. In the context, God claims that because He is unchanging, unalterable, and immutable, He does not destroy His people

Israel. He will keep His covenant with Abraham and thus "the sons of Jacob are not consumed" (Malachi 3:6). Let us again glance at some classic comments on this passage.

Matthew Henry

Here we have God's immutability asserted by himself, and gloried in. . . . We may all apply this very sensibly to ourselves; because we have to do with a God that *changes not*, therefore it is that *we are not consumed*. . . .[12]

E. B. Pusey

The proper name of God, He Who Is, involves His Unchangeableness. For change implies imperfection; it changes to that which is either more perfect or less perfect: to somewhat which that being, who changes, is not or has not. But God has everything in Himself perfectly.[13]

C. F. Keil

The unchangeableness of God is implied in the name *Jehovah*, "who is that He is," the absolutely independent and absolutely existing One.[14]

Thomas V. Moore

Let not the Christian heart grow timid in a time of prevalent wickedness and unbelief, in the fear that the ark of God may perish. The sons of Jacob shall not be consumed—the seed of Christ shall not perish. The unchangeableness of God is the sheet-anchor of the Church. He will be faithful to his Son, and to his word, however disheartening external circumstances may appear to our wavering faith.

The perseverance of the saints is guaranteed, not by their unchangeable love to God, but by his unchangeable love to them, and his eternal purpose and promise in Christ Jesus.[15]

These commentators point out that our reliance on God to do as He has promised is based on the immutability of His nature. But if God as well as all things are being tossed to and fro in some kind of Heraclitian flux, as the processians claim, then the god who promises something today will not be the same god tomorrow. He may have learned some new things and thus decided not to keep his word. Such a god is not trustworthy.

> Jesus Christ is the same yesterday and today, yes and forever (Hebrews 13:8).

Having already ascribed Psalm 102:25-27 to Christ in Hebrews 1:10-12, the author of Hebrews concludes with a ringing affirmation of the immutability of Christ in 13:8. But can the second Person of the Trinity be the "same yesterday, today, and forever" if God is mutable? If Jesus is "open" in the sense of the processian's chance-based world, then we cannot pray to the same Jesus twice! As a matter of fact, the processian Jesus is *never* the same. He is always changing. But is this the Jesus of the Christian Gospel? We think not.

> Him who is and who was and who is to come (Revelation 1:4).

The syntax of the Greek text of Revelation 1:4 is absolutely clear that Christ is immutable for what He *is* right now, is what He always *was* and what He shall always *be*. It is the Greek equivalent of the Hebrew, "I Am that I Am."

This is also why God is called "the First and the Last" and "The Beginning and the End." He is the *same* from the beginning to the end of the world (Isaiah 41:4; 44:6; 48:12; Revelation 1:17; 2:8; 22:13).

> The Father of lights, with whom there is no variation, or shifting shadow (James 1:17).

In this passage, James speaks of God as the unchanging and unchangeable One, He who is ever the same from age to age.

The context of James's statement on the immutability of God is also important. In the context James is discussing the origin of sin. The fact that God cannot be blamed for evil is based on the immutably good nature of God. In verse 16, he warns Christians, "do not be deceived, my beloved brethren." The expression, "Do not be deceived" is always associated with subjects which heretics try to use to deceive the elect (see 1 Corinthians 15:33; Galatians 6:7). As we have already seen, heretics usually use "the problem of evil" in order to undermine the faith of

Christians. Christians must be on their guard, says James, not to be misled by heretics on this subject.

James is quite aware that the pagan religions in his own day taught that god was the author of sin. It is this blasphemous idea that he attacks in this opening chapter of his book. He first states that God cannot be the author of sin because He is *incapable* of doing evil by nature. Thus He *cannot* be tempted by sin. Neither is He capable of tempting anyone into sin.

> Let no one say when he is tempted, "I am being tempted by God"; for God cannot be tempted by evil, and He Himself does not tempt anyone (James 1:13).

Notice that James proceeds from God's nature to His actions. God "cannot" by nature be tempted by evil. He is not "open" to sin. Therefore He "does not" in His actions tempt anyone to do evil. Notice also that James does not say that God could do evil if He "wanted," but that God "cannot" even be tempted by it, much less do it. In other words, God is not "free" to do anything that is inconsistent with His nature.

But if God *cannot* be the "author" of evil, who is? James points his finger at *man*.

> But each one is tempted when he is carried away and enticed by his own lust. Then when lust has conceived, it gives birth to sin; and when sin is accomplished, it brings forth death (James 1:14-15).

But what about God? Does James go on to say that God was not the author of evil because He did not foresee it? If the processians are right in limiting the power and knowledge of God, isn't this an ideal place for such an idea to be given? It is nowhere to be found! James does not limit the knowledge and power of God, but rather exalts them as immutable.

James goes on to guarantee that God will never become the author of evil by contrasting God to the "lights" He has placed in the heavens. While the sun, moon, and stars wax and wane, i.e., change because they are mutable, there is "no variation" with God or a "shifting shadow."

After meticulously tracing the two Greek words translated as "no variation" and "shifting shadow" throughout ancient sacred and secular literature, Joseph Mayor concludes,

The meaning of the passage will then be "God is alike incapable of change in his nature (*parallage*) and incapable of being changed by the action of others (*aposkiasma*).[16]

Notice that by using these two different words, James tells us that the immutability of God includes the idea that people, places, and events *cannot change God*. The idea that God is changing as events happen would be deemed blasphemous by James.

The Latin Vulgate renders the words as, *apud quem non est transmutatio nec, vicissitudinis obumbratio*. God is *not* "transmuting" into GOD. God *is* GOD and has always been so and will always be so throughout eternity.

The Repentance of God

But what about the few passages in Scripture that speak of God's "repenting?" (See Genesis 6:6; Exodus 32:14; 1 Samuel 15:11, 35.) Do these pose any problem to the doctrine of the immutability of God?

First, we have already stated that the immutability of God concerns the *being* of God. None of the passages in question speak of a change in God's *nature*, but rather describe some *act* of God. Second, all of these passages describe a change in God's works in terms of His revelation, relationship, or attitude toward man.

In Genesis 6:6, because of man's sin, God changed His attitude toward mankind from acceptance to rejection, from joy to grief, from tolerance to judgment.

In Ephesians 2:1-4, God's attitude changes toward us from wrath to grace when we come to accept His Son.

In Exodus 32:14, God changed the revelation of His will. He first told Moses that He was going to destroy Israel (v. 10). Then He revealed that He was not going to destroy Israel due to the intercession of Moses (v. 14).

The same thing can be said of the sacrifice of Isaac. God's revealed will first commanded Abraham to sacrifice his son (Genesis 22:2). Then as he lifted the knife, God revealed that he was not to kill his son (Genesis 22:12).

First Samuel 15 is a perfect example of the difference between God's being unchanging in His nature while being capable of change in His relationship to men. In verses 11 and 35, the Lord "repented," i.e., changed His revealed mind or will concerning Saul. Since Saul had rejected God's Word, God now rejected Saul's kingship, and David has to be anointed king in his place (v. 26).

But lest we assume that God can change in His nature, Samuel adds in verse 29 that God,

> . . . will not lie nor repent: for he is not a man that he should repent (KJV).

Thus in the same chapter where we are told twice that God "repented," we are also told that God never repents! The liberal theologian will jump at this and cry "contradiction." But we doubt that the author of 1 Samuel 15 was really so stupid as to compose so blatant a contradiction. Instead, Samuel is reassuring us that the Lord is unchanging in His being and nature even when He changes the revelation of His will or His attitude toward man. The NASV and other modern versions simply translate that God "regretted" or "grieved" instead of "repented." In this way, it can be clearly seen that it is God's attitude which is spoken of and not His essence or nature.

God's revelation of laws, institutions, and ceremonies change from covenant to covenant. Thus we can go from circumcision to baptism, Passover to the Lord's Supper, from the ceremonial law to freedom in Christ. But none of this requires a change in the being or nature of God. Only His administration changes.

Conclusion

As one of the perfections of God, the immutability of God is found throughout the Scriptures. It is viewed as an essential aspect of the greatness and glory of God. It is the foundation of the believer's hope and trust. And it enables us to live with confidence knowing that the Triune God is "the same yesterday, today, and forever."

TWENTY-ONE

THE OMNIPRESENCE
OF GOD

I t may come as a surprise to some that this attribute of God needs defending. That God is everywhere present in the totality of His person is so basic to Christian thought that most Christians will be surprised to find that it too is being attacked today.

But this should not really surprise us. When processian thinkers deny what they call the "omni" attributes of God, they mean *all* the attributes of God from omniscience to omnipresence. They are forced to this path of apostasy by their commitment to rationalism.

Once God's nature is determined solely on the basis of what is "coherent" or "rational," then God's omnipresence must go the way of all the other "omni" attributes of God. After all, who can give a "coherent" explanation of "how" and "in what way" God can be everywhere without somehow becoming everything? Do God and the world occupy the same space and time? Then how do they differ?

Or, again, if God is finite and is "in" time like man, then the fastest He can go is the speed of light. Thus to go from one end of the universe to the other means that God cannot be everywhere at the same time. Thus Whitehead and his disciples claimed that God must struggle to overcome gravity and inertia.

The Bible, however, teaches the omnipresence of God in such passages as 1 Kings 8:27; Psalm 139, Isaiah 40, Jeremiah 23:24; Acts 17:24-28, and Ephesians 1:22-23.

The rationale of prayer is based on the omnipresence of God. We can pray anywhere because God is everywhere. But the finite gods of the heathen are not omnipresent. They are limited by space as well as by time. Thus when Elijah fought his "battle of the gods" on Mount

Carmel, he mocked the pagans by reminding them that their god was not omnipresent.

> Call out with a loud voice, for he is a god; either he is occupied or gone aside, or is on a journey, or perhaps he is asleep and needs to awakened (1 Kings 18:27).

If God is not omnipresent, then He can hear our prayers only if He happens to be near us at that moment. Maybe we'll get "lucky" and choose the right moment when God is passing by. We shudder to think of all the consequences of denying the omnipresence of God.

The historic Christian view is that the God of Scripture is omnipresent in the sense that He is infinite in His presence, i.e., His existence has no limits. There is no "cutting off point" for God where we can say that He begins or ends. God does not end on the boundaries of the finite universe we live in. He is greater than the universe. It is a mere speck of dust to the Almighty.

God is also omnipresent in that all things derive their existence from Him. Thus the time-space universe exists "in" God (Acts 17:28). He is actually holding together all things (Colossians 1:17). Thus He is everywhere present (Psalm 139).

God and Anthropomorphic Language

When processians such as Clark Pinnock argue against the timelessness of God, they appeal to those passages in Scripture which speak of God in temporal terms.[1] They deny that they are anthropomorphic and claim that we must interpret these passages in a literal sense.

Genesis 11:1-9 is a classic example. Some processians argue that God was ignorant of what man was up to. So, He went down to take a quiet look. Isn't this proof that God does not know the future?

First, no *future* building projects are mentioned anywhere in the text. The story has to do with what man had *already* built. If we take it literally, then God has no knowledge of the *past* or the *present*.

Second, the passage speaks of God in spatial terms such as "coming down" or "going up." If the processians are to be consistent, then they must say God is limited by space as well as by time. This means that God is not omnipresent. But this is not acceptable to Christians.

But if they say that the spatial language is only "anthropomorphic" and that God is really "spaceless," then their sole "Biblical" argument against the timelessness of God is overthrown.

Most "evangelical" processians on this point are quite hypocritical. In private conversation they are willing to state their objections to God's omnipresence. But when we ask them to put it in writing so we can document what they are saying, they refuse to do so. They know that they would soon lose their teaching positions in evangelical institutions.

Conclusion

We can pray with confidence because the Almighty is not limited by space or time. He can answer prayer anywhere, at any time. His omnipresence means that He is everywhere present in the totality of all His infinite attributes. When we pray, we are not just touching a part of God, but we are encountering the infinite Person of the Sovereign Creator of the universe.

THE OMNISCIENCE
OF GOD

The doctrine of the omniscience of God comes naturally after God's omnipresence. If God is everywhere and is holding all things together by His power, then He knows everything about everything. His understanding is as limitless as His being.

Now this is so fundamental to the average Christian that it is hard for us to believe that some people who claim to be "evangelicals" deny the omniscience of God.

Perhaps part of the confusion is caused by their use of the old Socinian trick of redefining the word "omniscience" to mean the exact opposite of what orthodox theology has always meant by the term. Much of processian and moral government theology is nothing more than a classic example of "Humpty Dumpty-ism," in which orthodox terms are given heretical definitions in order to keep up the facade of being "Christian" as long as possible.

The Controversy in History

Jonathan Edwards, the father of the Great Awakening, faced a revival of Socinian theology in his own day that denied the foreknowledge of God. In his refutation of the idea that God cannot know the future, he began with this apology.

> One would think it wholly needless to enter on such an argument with any that profess themselves Christians: but so it is; God's certain Foreknowledge of the free acts of moral agents, is denied by some that pretend to believe the Scriptures to be the Word of God; and espe-

cially as of late. I therefore shall consider the evidence of such a prescience in the Most High.[1]

After the dust had cleared on the debate in Edwards's day, the lines
were clearly drawn. Evangelical Christians believed in the foreknowledge of God and those who denied it should leave the Christian Church
and join the Unitarians. Those who did leave are to be admired for
their honesty.

In eighteenth-century England, the famous theologian and hymnwriter, Augustus Toplady, waded into the battle against those who denied the foreknowledge of God. He pointed out that while classic Arminian theology teaches God's foreknowledge, in their haste to escape
Reformed theology, some Arminians had left their own faith and had
jumped into a form of atheism! Toplady stated:

> If you say, "God does not know what the event will be;" I give you up
> as incurable. It is less impious to deny the very existence of God, than
> to strip him of his omniscience and thereby make him (as far as in
> you lies) such an one as yourself. By pleading divine ignorance (I
> shudder at the very idea) you certainly slip out of my hands; and it is
> the only way by which you can. But your escape costs you very dear.
> In flying from Calvinism, you jump into atheism.[2]

Toplady demonstrates on pages 94, 107-08, 111, 154ff., 232, 274,
and 756 that the denial of the foreknowledge of God is not in accord
with the Reformed doctrine of the Church of England or with the theology of Wesleyan Arminianism. He labels such denials as heresy and
atheism.

It was not until the Fundamentalist/Liberal debates at the beginning
of the twentieth century that the issues of God's infinite nature and
foreknowledge surfaced once again. But this time the evangelical Christians lost and the mainline denominations and their seminaries were
taken over by liberal theologians who taught that god was a finite being
who was not omniscient, omnipotent, sovereign, immutable, or perfect.

The Unitarians rightfully complained that most mainline theologians were now "Unitarian" in everything but membership. They should
therefore in all honesty leave the Christian Church and join with them.
If they did, the Unitarian Church would become one of the biggest
denominations in the United States. But the cost in terms of money

and power prevented most liberals being honest enough to make the break.

The fall of the mainline denominations into the hands of the processians resulted in a mass exodus of those who truly loved the Christian faith. They went on to establish the fundamental and evangelical denominations that exist today. In some cases, as with Gresham Machen, the liberals actually forced conservative Christians to leave.

An Essential Attribute

Omniscience has always been viewed as an essential attribute of God in Christian theology. The conviction that God knows everything has always meant that He knows everything only as God can know it. Thus God's knowledge of everything must be defined in terms of God's *divine* nature.

Since all the attributes interrelate and define each other, this means that the *only* knowledge that God can have is an eternal, self-existent, infinite, and perfect knowledge. It does not matter if we are thinking of God's knowledge of Himself, the world, or the future. His knowledge can never be anything less than *divine* because He is GOD.

God's knowledge is as eternal as He is. What God knows now, He has always known, and will always know. We can never draw a line and say, "Here is where God's knowledge *began* because He first *learned* of it here." If God is eternal, then His knowledge has no beginning. Neither does it have an end, as if we could draw another line and say, "Here is where God's knowledge *ends*. He cannot know anything beyond this point."

Since God's knowledge is eternal, it is likewise self-existent and infinite. It is self-existent in that it is not dependent on anything, not even time. It is infinite in that His knowledge of Himself or of the universe has no limits. As the psalmist declared, "His understanding is *infinite*" (Psalm 147:5, emphasis mine).

God's knowledge is immediate and complete. It is not built up little by little each time the dice are thrown. In that it is eternal, infinite, and self-existent, it is no surprise to find the Bible saying that God is "*perfect* in knowledge" (Job 37:16, emphasis mine). Thus God's knowledge does not increase or decrease. It does not depend on the investigation of future events. He knows all things from all eternity. As Job declared, "He knows . . . and He sees . . . without investigating" (Job 11:11).

But what if we decide that God cannot know the future? We end up with a finite god who was ignorant of *all* things from *all* eternity! He did not know that he would create the world. He did not even know what he would create or what would happen to it. All his actions are strictly based on "spur of the moment" decisions and haphazard events. In short, having no foresight, this god was *blind*. Having no foreknowledge, this god was *ignorant*. Before the world was created, his mind was a dark void of emptiness. Is this god the GOD of the Bible?

Another thing to consider when thinking about the idea that God does not know the future is that this means that God cannot love people before they are born! Thus God did not love us before He made the world. Since God cannot know the free acts of men, particularly their sins, then He cannot know us as we are going to be. The implications are staggering! No one can say that Jesus loved him and died for him on the cross, because He did not know about him or his sins for they were yet future! Is this what the Bible teaches?

Biblical Passages

The Biblical support for the omniscience of God is so overwhelming that processians generally ignore the Bible and argue on the basis of their "reason" and "intuition." We prefer to argue from God's reason and intuition as revealed in Scripture.

In Acts 15, when James spoke at the Jerusalem Council on the inclusion of the Gentiles into the Church, he stated two things. First, the Old Testament prophets had foreknown and predicted that the Gentiles would come into the Church (vv. 15-17). Second, God knew from all eternity whatever He was going to do in space-time history.

> Known unto God are all His works from the beginning of the world (Acts 15:18, KJV).

God's omniscience means that God knows all of space-time history from the beginning to the end. How else can He know what He is going to do throughout time? G. V. Lechler comments,

> The meaning of the words which James adds, is the following: That which happens in our day, God knew from the beginning, and had resolved to perform; that which we live to see is simply the execution of an eternal decree of God.[3]

In his classic commentary on Acts, J. A. Alexander states,

> . . . the reception of the Gentiles into the Church was no after-
> thought or innovation, but a part of the divine plan from the begin-
> ning . . . *from eternity.*[4]

The Lutheran scholar Lenski points out that the Greek literally
reads, "known from the eon his work to God"! He comments further:

> Far more preferable is the translation of the A.V., which is also well
> supported textually. . . . James quite pertinently declares that an eon
> before the time that God would do a work he already knew what that
> work would be and thus could foretell it. . . . God is now doing a work
> which he ages ago knew he would do.[5]

Heinrich Meyer also points out that:

> *By whom* they were known from the beginning, is evident from the
> context, namely, by God who accomplishes them in the fulness of
> time. He accordingly carries into effect nothing which, has not been
> from the beginning evident to Him in His consciousness and counsel;
> how *important* and *sacred* must they consequently appear![7]

James declares that God knew all things from eternity. Before He
created the world, He knew what He was going to create. He knew of
the Fall of man into sin and guilt. It did not take the Almighty by
surprise. But He also knew that He would send His Son to die on the
cross for our sins (1 Peter 1:20; Revelation 13:8). Thus He preached the
Gospel to a fallen Adam and Eve and told them of a coming Savior
(Genesis 3:15).

The Gospel promise that a Savior would crush the head of the ser-
pent and set us free from sin is proof of the foreknowledge of God.
Salvation was not a hasty plan thrown together by God after He was
surprised by Adam's sin. The Bible speaks of salvation as something
that was known and planned by God *before* the space-time world was
created. (See Ephesians 1:4; 3:11; 2 Timothy 1:9; Titus 1:2; 1 Peter
1:20; Revelation 13:8.)

Since all things are known to God from eternity, then He knows all
things at any point of history. In Matthew 24:35, we are told that *"from
the foundation of the world"* God has prepared a kingdom for the saints

when Jesus comes back. The names of those who will enter that kingdom are known to God *"from the foundation of the world"* (Revelation
13:8; 17:8, emphasis mine).

That God would create something while not knowing what He was
creating and what would happen to it is absurd. If an earthly king is
deemed wise by Jesus in Luke 14:28-32 because he knows ahead what
he is going to do, how much more the heavenly King of the universe!
Hannah rejoiced because, "The Lord is a God of knowledge" (1 Samuel
2:3), not of ignorance.

In Psalm 139:1-6, the Psalmist claims that God knows everything
about him *before* he opens his mouth. Jeremiah 32:19 declares that
God's "eyes are open to all the ways of the sons of men." Hebrews 4:13
makes it clear that "all things are open and laid bare" before God. And
1 John 3:20 declares that God "knows all things." Can words be plainer?

The choice ultimately comes down to believing either those who
say, "God does *not* know all things," or the Word of God, which says,
"God knows *all* things."

Prayer and Omniscience

Does prayer inform God? Is He ignorant of our needs until we state
them? Or does God already know what we need *before* we ask? Does He
know what we will ask *before* we ask for it? Isaiah tells us:

> Before they call, I will answer; and while they are still speaking, I will
> hear (Isaiah 65:24).

The Lord Jesus taught His disciples,

> Your heavenly Father knows what you need, *before* you ask Him (Mat-
> thew 6:8, emphasis mine).

David even claimed that God knew what he was going to ask *before* he
asked it!

> Even *before* there is a word on my tongue, behold, O Lord, *Thou dost*
> *know it all* (Psalm 139:4, emphasis mine).

The purpose of prayer is not to inform God of what we need as if He were ignorant. No, the purpose of prayer is to deepen our trust and confidence in God. Prayer reminds us of the promises and provisions of God. It enables us to become mighty in faith.

Now the processians will complain that since God already knows what we need before we ask and knows ahead of time what we shall ask before we ask it, then prayer is useless. This is a perfect example of the stupidity of following "reason" instead of obeying revelation!

Christians delight in the fact that God knows what they need not only *all the time* but *from all eternity*. They rejoice that God will answer in accordance with *His* will, not theirs, because they assume that God knows what is best for them (Matthew 6:10; 1 John 5:14).

Do We Know More Than God?

We must also object to the argument put forth by some processians that God is not omniscient because He cannot know by experience what man knows. For example, God cannot know how watermelon or any other food tastes because He has no tastebuds! Since God does not know all that man knows then man actually has greater knowledge than God!

The psalmist did not hesitate to call such ideas "senseless" and "stupid."

> Pay heed, you senseless among the people;
> And when will you understand, stupid ones?
> He who planted the ear, does He not hear?
> He who formed the eye, does He not see (Psalm 94:8-9)?

God does not need an ear to hear, an eye to see, a tongue to taste, a nose to smell, or a finger to touch. Who do you think created all the sights, sounds, smells, colors, and textures? He who created the watermelon knows *more* about it than man, not less.

He who made this world, and made it beautiful with colors of every hue, with billions of brilliant flowers that fill the air with sweet perfume, with the songs of innumerable birds, and with the softness of a newborn baby, is not jealous of the poor, pathetic, five senses of man. God's perception and experience of the world He has made is beyond our comprehension to even express. It is too high! It is too wonderful!

God's Foreknowledge of the Future

Now that we have looked at God's omniscience in general, we need to establish that this omniscience extends to the future. By the "future," we include all the details of everything that will happen, including the free acts of men and angels. The following arguments establish this Biblical position.

The Plain Statement of Scripture

For those who are satisfied by the plain statement of Scripture, the following passages are all that are needed.

- God "foreknows" the future: Acts 2:23; Romans 8:29; 11:2; 1 Peter 1:2
- God "foresees" the future: Galatians 3:8

To these we add God's foreordination and predestination, because it is impossible to foreordain something unless you know about it.

- God "foreordains" the future: 1 Peter 1:20
- God "predestines" the future: Romans 8:29, 30; Ephesians 1:5, 11

Foreknowledge: The Chief Attribute of God

The prophet Isaiah viewed God's infallible and perfect knowledge of the future as the final proof of Jehovah's divinity. The gods of the heathen could not tell the future. But the God of Israel could foresee and foretell it in the greatest detail.

God begins with a challenge to the gods of heathendom.

> "Present your case," the Lord says.
> "Bring forward your strong arguments,"
> the King of Jacob says (Isaiah 41:21).

Now we will see who is GOD! He is GOD who knows all things including the future and can *prove* that He knows the future by infallibly foretelling it.

> Let them bring forth and declare to us
> *what is going to take place;* . . .
> Or announce to us *what is coming.*
> Declare the things *that are going to come afterward,*

That we may know that you are gods (Isaiah 41:22-23, emphasis mine).

When the pagan gods fail the test, God mocks them.

Behold, you are of no account,
And your work amounts to nothing.
He who chooses you is an abomination (Isaiah 41:24).

Then God sets forth His case for divinity.

I have aroused one from the north, . . .
And *he will come* upon rulers as upon mortar,
Even as the potter treads clay.
Who has declared this *from the beginning*, that we might know?
Or, *from former times*, that we may say, "He is right!"
    (Isaiah 41:25-26, emphasis mine).

There is no God besides Me.
And who is like me? Let him proclaim and declare it; . . .
And let them declare to them the things that *are coming*
And *the events that are going to take place*
    (Isaiah 44:6, 7, 26, 28, emphasis mine).

Ask Me about the *things to come* concerning My sons. . . .
Who has announced this *from of old*?
Who has *long since declared it*?
Is it not I, the LORD?
And there is no other God besides Me
    (Isaiah 45:11, 21, emphasis mine).

I am God, and there is no one like Me,
Declaring *the end from the beginning*
And *from ancient times* things which have been done. . . .
Truly I have spoken; truly I will *bring it to pass*.
I have planned it, surely I will do it
    (Isaiah 46:9-11, emphasis mine).

God's whole case for His deity rests on the certainty of His perfect knowledge of the future in all of its details. This is why Christian theology has always stated that any god that does not know or control the future is no God at all! The processians and moral government theologians are attacking the Godhood of God when they deny His foreknowledge.

The End from the Beginning. Notice that in Isaiah 46:10, God declares that He knows "the end from the beginning." The arrangement of the words is striking because it is the exact opposite of the way *man* knows history.

Because man is limited by space-time, he must always learn about things as they unfold in time, i.e., from the beginning to the end. The "end" is not known to us. We must gradually work our way toward the end. Thus human knowledge is gradual and accumulative. It is always from "the beginning to the end."

But God tells us that He knows the end *before* the beginning. Thus when the world began, He already knew all of history "from the end to the beginning." Thus His knowledge is not gradual or cumulative like man's. It is eternal, infinite, perfect, and *timeless.*

Many Examples of God's Foreknowledge

All that is needed to refute the Socinian idea that God does not know the future acts of men is to find just *one* passage which plainly states that God foreknew what a certain man would do before he did it. If just *one* free act of man is foreknown and the man is still held accountable for that act, then *all* the acts of men can be foreknown without affecting human accountability in any sense.

In *hundreds* of Biblical passages God foreknows what people were going to do before they existed, were born, grew up, or thought or planned about doing anything. But we will limit ourselves to just a few sample passages.

Abraham, the Exodus, and Foreknowledge. God told Abraham that his descendants would become slaves in Egypt for four hundred years, but after that God would liberate them. And God said to Abraham:

> Know for certain that your descendants will be strangers in a land that is not theirs, where they will be enslaved and oppressed four hundred years. But I will also judge the nation whom they will serve; and afterward they will come out with many possessions (Genesis 15:13-14).

The passage is remarkable for several reasons. First, it refutes the claims of those who say that Biblical prophecies are not "certain," i.e., infallible. Notice that God says what He foreknows and foretells will happen "*for certain.*"

Second, the certainty of God's foreknowledge refutes the processian idea that "chance" controls the future. God determines the future according to this passage.

Third, notice clearly that although the future oppression of the Jews at the hands of the Egyptians is declared to be *certain* because it is *foreknown* and *foretold* by God, this did not negate the *accountability* of the Egyptians. Thus God will judge them for their sins. This at once forever refutes the argument that if God has an infallible and perfect knowledge of the future, this means that man is not accountable for his acts. Were the rebellious attitudes and actions of Pharaoh in refusing to let the Jews go foreknown and foretold by God (Exodus 3:19; 7:14; 9:30; 11:9)? Yet, he was still held accountable to his Maker.

Foreknowledge of Future Acts. The free acts of a king yet to be born three hundred years in the future were foreknown and predicted in 1 Kings 13:1-6. Let processians here note that prophecies are infallible, "the thing shall *surely* come to pass" (v. 32).

The future acts of Ahab (1 Kings 21:20-22), Hazael (2 Kings 8:12), Cyrus (Isaiah 44:28) were foreknown and foretold by God. Daniel even foretold the future empires of the world: Babylonian, Medo-Persian, Greek, and Roman.

The Messianic Prophecies. Perhaps the greatest proofs of the foreknowledge of God are the hundreds of Messianic prophecies in which God reveals in minute detail what Jesus and those around Him will do in the future. The signs and place of His birth, the slaughter of the infants, His flight into Egypt, the coming of John the Baptist, the cleansing of the Temple, the triumphant entry on an ass, the betrayal by Judas, the plucking of the beard, the death on the cross, and the empty tomb, all bear eloquent witness to the omniscient eye of the Almighty.

The Foreknowledge of Jesus. As incarnate Deity, Jesus knew and predicted the future free acts of men. He knew that Judas would betray Him from the very beginning (John 6:64). He knew all the details of Peter's life, including his denial in the courtyard, his repentance, ministry, old age, and final death (Mark 14:30; John 21:18, 19). He described in great detail how the Temple and Jerusalem would be destroyed some thirty-seven years before it took place (Matthew 24:2).

Human History is His-story. Just as Genesis tells of the beginning of human history, the Book of Revelation tells us how it will end. The Bible maps out human history from beginning to end in terms of being His-story. He is the Lord of History, and nations rise and fall under His decrees. History is traveling along a predetermined path toward a predetermined victory over evil.

Prophecy Impossible Without Foreknowledge

The reliability of Biblical prophecy is based on the fact that God is said to tell us what He *knows* will happen in the future. Thus God told Jeremiah that He knew all about him before he was even born (Jeremiah 1:5). When God promised Abraham that he would become the father of many nations, He was, "calling those things which are not [yet] as though they were" (Romans 4:17).

Biblical prophecy is never presented as "guesswork" or "a shot in the dark" on God's part as if its future fulfillment depended on the "roll of the dice." The prophets declare what *will* infallibly come to pass.

No Passages to the Contrary

Do any passages clearly state that God is *not* all-knowing? No! Do any passages state in clear language that God is ignorant of the future? No! Do any passages teach that God is ignorant by nature? No! Are there any passages which teach that foreknowledge is impossible? No!

Then what do "evangelical" processians do when they want to give a Biblical argument against God's foreknowledge of the future? They argue that several Biblical passages suggest that God learned something *new* that He did not know beforehand.

"Didn't God *ask* Adam where he was? Doesn't this mean He did *not* know where Adam was hiding? Didn't God have to investigate the Tower of Babel to learn what man was doing? Didn't God learn something new about Abraham when he was willing to kill his son?" Such arguments are the typical "Biblical" evidences given by processians to prove that God cannot know the future. But in every case the passage concerns God's *present* knowledge of man and actually has nothing to do with the future.

When God called out to Adam, "Where are you?", He was asking about the *present* whereabouts of Adam (Genesis 3:9). It had nothing to do with the future. He did not say, "Where will you be tomorrow?" If the processian argument were valid, then God would not know the *present location of anyone*. It doesn't take much to see the absurdity of that line of reasoning.

The same can be said of Genesis 11, where God "came down" to see what man was doing. The knowledge that God sought had nothing to do with the future. If we take this passage literally, then God does not have any *present* knowledge of what people are doing.

When the angel told Abraham on the mountain where Isaac was almost sacrificed that, "now I know that you fear God," he was referring to the *present spiritual* condition of Abraham's heart. The issue has nothing to do with future events. It concerns the attitude of Abraham's heart. If this passage is to be taken literally, then what do we do with the dozens of passages that plainly teach that God knows the hearts of all men (Jeremiah 17:10; Hebrews 4:12-13)?

Christian theologians have always interpreted the above passages as being anthropomorphic in nature, i.e., God is described in human terms in a figurative way. Thus whenever the Bible talks about God's going from place to place, looking at this or that, having hands, eyes, or ears, none of these should be taken literally any more than when God is described as having the wings of a bird! Thus Adam was asked the question for *his* benefit, not God's. It was *Abraham* who needed to know the condition of his heart, not God.

In terms of hermeneutics, if we must choose between a didactic passage in Scripture where God's foreknowledge is clearly taught and a historical narrative where figurative language is used, the didactic passages must be given the dominance.

Conclusion

The Scriptures clearly teach that God as GOD knows all things. This means His understanding of Himself is perfect and complete. He knows all about the past, present, and future of the universe which He made out of nothing. And He knows about everything and everyone in it. Nothing is hid from the eyes of Him with whom we have to do.

TWENTY-THREE

THE OMNIPOTENCE
OF GOD

This is one of the most misunderstood and the most maligned attributes of God. Yet, it is an essential attribute that makes God GOD. Perhaps the best way to start our study of this attribute is to point out what we do *not* mean when we say that God is omnipotent.

The attribute of omnipotence does not mean that God has absolute freedom to do or be anything at all even if it contradicts His nature. While God is free to be GOD in all the fullness of His divine nature, He is not free to become non-God or act in a manner inconsistent with His immutable, perfect, good, and holy nature.

This at once dismisses one Greek riddle which freshman philosophy students love to discuss: Can God make a rock so big He can't move it? Now, in order for this riddle to work it must be assumed that God can do absolutely *anything* in the Greek sense of an open-ended chance-based universe. Once this assumption is granted, the riddle takes on the character of a complicated question in logic which means that more than one question is being asked at the same time.

The first question is, Can God do *absolutely* anything He wants?

The second question assumes the first question was answered in the affirmative: Well, if God can do *anything*, then can He do something which is non-Godlike? Can God contradict Himself by making something more powerful and Godlike than Himself? Namely, can He make a rock which is *more* powerful than Himself? If not, then God cannot do absolutely anything. But if so, then He is not all-powerful.

Those who hold to an "open" view of God, such as Rice, have no answer to the riddle. But orthodox Christians do. We disagree with the first basic assumption because Scripture states that God "*cannot* deny

Himself" (2 Timothy 2:13, emphasis mine). Thus God cannot lie or do anything that is inconsistent with His divine nature.

The Meaning of Omnipotence

Omnipotence means that God is an infinite Power who can never be depleted, drained, or exhausted. He is infinitely perfect in that He is limitless, eternal, and self-existent. God does not need to draw on any source of power outside Himself for anything.

Thus the omnipotence of God speaks of the infinite reservoir of power resident within God, at His disposal whenever He cares to exercise it in accordance with His nature.

It is in this sense that God is given the name the "Almighty" or "All-Powerful One" in Scripture no fewer than fifty-six times! God is called the "Almighty" in the Law, the Writings, and the Prophets. From the book of Genesis to the book of Revelation, God reveals Himself as the Omnipotent God.

Since the only limitations to omnipotence are those that arise out of the nature of God, once God sets out to do something, nothing and no one outside of Himself can defeat Him. Thus nothing that does not contradict His nature is *impossible* for God to do. Nothing outside Him can limit His power. (See Genesis 18:14; Job 42:2; Psalm 115:3; Jeremiah 32:17, 27; Daniel 4:35; Zechariah 8:6; Matthew 19:26; Luke 1:37.)

Has anyone shown how and in what way the nature of God prevents His knowing the future? No! Is knowing the future too difficult for God? Of course not! Time is only an aspect of the world which He made. No one has ever shown how God's *nature* is contradicted by His knowledge of the future.

The omnipotence of God is essential for all the other attributes of God. If He is not omnipotent, how can He be self-existent? If His power is anything less than infinite, then how can it be eternal? How can God be omnipresent or omniscient if He is not the Almighty? How can He be the Creator and Sustainer of all things unless His power knows no beginning or end?

Divine Sovereignty or Providence

It may come as a surprise to some evangelicals but God's sovereignty or providence has always been viewed as one of the attributes of God by the Christian Church. It follows naturally from and is based upon God's omnipotence. Indeed, as we shall see, it was viewed as an essential attribute of God by the early Church and anyone who dared to deny it was called an atheist. Divine providence was thus not viewed as something that God could jettison and still remain GOD. It is an essential part of historic Christian theism.

Divine sovereignty means that God is in control of this universe and that there is no such thing as chance or luck. Everything has a divine purpose and fits in with God's plan of the ages which we call "history" or "His-story." It means that He is the King of kings and the Lord of lords and that nothing happens in this world but must first pass through His will.

Since God is the Creator of all things, He has the moral right to do whatever He wants with what He has made. This is Paul's argument in Romans 9. God is the Potter and we are the clay. Thus He can do with us as He pleases.

When someone asks us, "Do you believe in free will?" we usually reply, "Yes, God has a free will and He can do with you as He pleases." This usually provokes the rather frantic response, "I don't mean God's free will. I mean *man's* free will!"

This highlights the main problem that afflicts most discussions of God's sovereignty and man's will. The humanist will always begin with *man* and will strive to establish that *man's will* is ultimate in a universe ruled by chance, while theists will begin with God and will strive to establish that *God's will* is ultimate in His creation.

We believe with the Apostle Paul that if the choice comes down to either exalting God or man, God is to be given the preeminence in all things (Romans 3:4).

Should We Begin with Man or with God?

Where should we begin when studying God's sovereignty and man's responsibility? Should we begin with man and establish his free will and then define divine sovereignty in such a way that it does not conflict with man? Or, should we begin with God and His free will and then develop our understanding of man from that viewpoint?

For Bible-believing Christians, only one answer is possible. We must begin where Scripture begins. And when we open the Bible, what do we find? The Bible begins with GOD, not man!

This forever establishes that we must begin with GOD and not man. Since GOD is the "measure of all things" and the Origin of meaning, man and his will have no meaning unless we first begin with God. Thus before we can understand what man is, we must first understand what God is.

If Genesis 1:1 teaches us anything, it teaches us that God is sovereign because He created what He wanted, when He wanted, and where He wanted. In His act of creation He was absolutely unlimited by anything other than His own nature. He was and remains sovereign over all that He has made. It is by His sovereign power that the universe is now being held together (Colossians 1:17). Everything is being worked together by God according to His sovereign will (Romans 8:28; Ephesians 1:11). Everything that happens, happens according to His free will (Romans 11:36).

The Scriptures always describe God as actively controlling and guiding the entire creation (Psalm 103:19). It is never viewed as bare potential. It does not matter if we consider such things as the wind, the rain, the grass, or the trees, God controls them all (Psalm 104:5-17). Even the brute beasts of the field gladly obey His sovereign will (Psalm 104:14-30).

But What About Man?

And what shall we say about mankind? Does God rule over the realm of mankiind? Both the Old and New Testaments clearly teach that God is the blessed Controller of all things including mankind (1 Samuel 2:3-10; Acts 17:26). As the book of Daniel declares, "The Most High is ruler over the realm of mankind" (Daniel 4:25, 34-37).

The only people pictured in the Bible as rebelling against God's sovereign control of all things are the wicked (Psalm 2:1-4; Daniel 4). As a matter of record, no one has ever found a single passage in Scripture which says that God is *not* sovereign, or in which one of the prophets or apostles rebelled against divine sovereignty as a false teaching. God's control over all things was viewed as a necessary truth by which the saints lived their daily lives (Job 42:2; James 4:13-15).

Does God's sovereignty mean that man is not accountable for his sin? No! Does this mean that man is a robot? No! Does this mean fatalism? No! It is actually the other way around. Because God is sovereign, He has the *right* to hold man responsible for his words and deeds. Because God is sovereign, there *will* be a Day of Judgment. Because He is sovereign, He imposes His law on man regardless if man wants it, and will hold him responsible to keep it even when man rejects it!

Conclusion

We stand in amazement before the God who has revealed Himself in Scripture. He is infinitely perfect in all His being and power, and wondrous in all His mighty deeds. So all-powerful, all-wise, and all-knowing is the Lord of Glory! He is the great I AM, the Alpha and the Omega, the Beginning and the End.

> Now unto The King eternal, immortal, invisible, the only wise God, be honor and glory forever and ever. Amen (1 Timothy 1:17).

PART FOUR

THE GOD OF CHRISTIAN THEOLOGY

TWENTY - FOUR

THE TESTIMONY OF THE CHURCH FATHERS

A s the Apostles went forth in the power of the Spirit, they preached the good news that there is only one true living God who is the Creator and Sustainer of all things. They called upon all men to bow before this God and to accept His Son as their Savior.

What kind of God did they preach? How were they understood by the people of their day and the immediate generations to follow? Did they bare their breasts to the sword for an infinite God or a finite god? Were they willing to be devoured by lions for the sake of a finite god who did not know that this would happen? Or did they face a thousand deaths with the confidence that God was sovereign as well as omniscient?

Questions such as these deserve an answer. The following readings focus on those aspects of the Divine Nature that have been problematic to philosophers and heretics from the very beginning.

Modern "evangelical" processians try to give the impression that their finite god who does not know the future was the God of the Early Church and that orthodox theology is Greek philosophy. In order to remove any doubt as to who represents the early Church, the following readings are given. All references are to *The Ante-Nicene Fathers*, hereafter ANF (Grand Rapids: Eerdmans, rep. 1981).

As one surveys the writings of the early Church it will become abundantly clear that truly "nothing is new under the sun" (Ecclesiastes 1:9). The arguments raised by heretics and pagan philosophers against the Christian God in the first century are the same ones repeated by modern processians and the moral government people!

Self-Existent

The God of the early Church did not *need* the world for His own existence. He was self-sufficient in Himself and was not a finite, dependent being in need of anything outside of Himself. He existed prior to, independent of, and apart from the world which He made out of nothing for His own glory. God was a self-existent Being.

God was thus *qualitatively* distinct from the world in that He was divine and the world was *not* divine. The world did not partake of, share in, participate in, flow out of, or evolve from God's Divine Essense or Being in any sense.

This meant, in contrast to the Gnostics, that man was not divine. He did not have a "spark of divinity" within him. He was not a god and could never become one. It was a lie of the Devil that man could become a god. God and man did not share the same kind of existence. Man was a finite, dependent being who existed totally due to the power and will of the Creator who upholds all things.

Irenaeus Against Heresies

> God . . . is Himself uncreated, both without beginning and end, and lacking nothing. He is Himself sufficient for Himself; and still further, He grants to all others this very thing, existence . . . so that He indeed who made all things can alone, together with His Word, properly be termed God and Lord; but the things which have been made cannot have this term applied to them, neither should they justly assume that appellation which belongs to the Creator (ANF 1:422).

Athenagoras' Plea for the Christians

> God is Himself everything to Himself (ANF 2:136).

Incomprehensible

The early Christians took the Bible seriously when it states that it contains many things that "surpass all understanding" (Ephesians 3:19). They assumed that revelation would of necessity contain many mysteries because man's intellectual capacity was finite. They used every word possible in Greek and Latin so as not to be misunderstood. Thus the God revealed in Scripture was: "incomprehensible," "ineffable," "inde-

scribable," "unfathomable," "inconceivable," "incomparable," "inimitable," "unutterable," etc.

But they did not fall into the trap of Greek dichotomies such as
that God must either be completely known by man or absolutely unknown to man. They taught that God was both known *and* unknown.
He was "unknown" in the sense that our puny minds will never fully
grasp Him. But He was "known" because He has revealed Himself.

The First Epistle of Clement

His incomprehensible wisdom (ANF 1:13).

Address of Tatian to the Greeks

He who is not visible to human eyes, nor comes within the compass
of human art (i.e., philosophy) (ANF 2:66).

Theophilus to Autolycus

The appearance of God is ineffable and indescribable, and cannot be
seen by eyes of flesh. For in glory He is incomprehensible, in greatness
unfathomable, in height inconceivable, in power incomparable, in
wisdom unrivalled, in goodness inimitable, in kindness unutterable
(ANF II:89-90).

The Stromata of Clement of Alexandria

God is . . . beyond expression by words . . . the impossibility of expressing God . . . what is divine is unutterable by human power . . . in-
effableness the bosom of God (ANF 2:463).

The Apology of Tertullian

[God] is incomprehensible, though in grace He is manifested. He is
beyond our utmost thought, though our human faculties conceive of
Him. He is therefore equally real and great. But that which, in the
ordinary sense, can be seen and handled and conceived, is inferior to
the eyes by which it is taken in, and the hands by which it is tainted,
and the faculties by which it is discovered; but that which is infinite is
known only to itself. This it is which gives some notion of God, while
yet beyond all our conceptions—our very incapacity of fully grasping
Him affords us the idea of what He really is. He is presented to our

minds in His transcendent greatness, as at once known and unknown. . . . God has added a written revelation for the behoof of
every one whose heart is set on seeking Him, that seeking he may
find, and finding believe, and believing obey (ANF 3:31-32).

Tertullian Against Marcion

Isaiah even so early, with the clearness of an apostle, foreseeing the
thoughts of heretical hearts, asked, "Who hath known the mind of
the Lord? . . ." With whom the apostle agreeing exclaims, . . . "His
judgments unsearchable," as being those of God the Judge; and "His
ways past finding out," as comprising an understanding and knowledge
which no man has ever shown to Him, except it may be those critics
of the Divine Being, who say, God ought not to have been this, and
He ought rather to have been that; as if any one knew what is in
God, except the Spirit of God. Moreover, having the spirit of the
world, and "in the wisdom of God by wisdom knowing not God," they
seem to themselves to be wiser than God; because, as the wisdom of
the world is foolishness with God, so also the wisdom of God is folly
in the world's esteem. We, however, know that "the foolishness of
God is wiser than men, and the weakness of God is stronger than
men" (ANF 3:298).

The Octavius of Minucius Felix

He can neither be seen—He is brighter than light; nor can be grasped—
He is purer than touch; nor estimated; He is greater than all perceptions; infinite, immense, and how great is known to Himself alone.
But our heart is too limited to understand Him, and therefore we are
then worthily estimating Him when we say that He is beyond estima-
tion. I will speak out in what manner I feel. He who thinks that he
knows the magnitude of God, is diminishing it; he who desires not to
lessen it, knows it not (ANF 4:183).

Infinite

God is incomprehensible because He is infinite, i.e. not limited or
contained, in His nature and attributes. Since man is finite, he is not
capable of an infinite comprehension of anything, much less God. Man
must rest content with a finite but true comprehension of the God who
has revealed Himself in Scripture.

The First Epistle of Clement

The Creator and Lord of all . . . by His infinitely great power . . . established the heavens (ANF 1:13).

Irenaeus Against Heresies

There is nothing either above Him or after Him . . . alone containing all things, and Himself commanding all things into existence . . . should contain all things in His immensity, and should be contained [i.e. limited] by no one (ANF 1:359).

[They are] malignantly asserting that . . . He sits after the fashion of a man, and is contained [i.e., limited] within bounds (ANF 1:465).

The Pastor of Hermas

There is one God who created and finished all things, and made all things out of nothing. He alone is able to contain the whole, but Himself cannot be contained [i.e., limited] (ANF 2:20). Note: The word translated "contained" is *apeiros* in the Greek text and *immensus* in the Latin. It means that God cannot be limited or placed within bounds for He is infinite.

The Stromata of Clement of Alexandria

God . . . [is] boundless (i.e., limitless) (ANF 2:463).

Apology of Tertullian

That which is infinite is known only to itself. This it is which gives some notion of God (ANF 3:32).

The Octavius of Minucius Felix

He is greater than all perceptions; infinite, immense, and how great is known only to Himself (ANF 4:183).

Perfect

Being infinite, God is not defective in His nature or in any of His attributes. He is thus not "lacking," "in need of completion," or "evolving toward perfection," for He has always been perfect, is now perfect, and will always be perfect. God is therefore "perfect" according to the Fathers. He is not impotent or ignorant as if He were lacking in power or knowledge.

Because God is uncreated, He is not in the process of growing or learning like man. Marcion's idea that god was not perfect but growing or learning was viewed as heresy by the early Church. Such a god was indigent or defective. He made the world because he needed it. In opposition to such a processian deity, the Fathers taught that God is the eternal Uncreated One who is perfect, complete, and lacking in nothing.

Irenaeus Against Heresies

> For He is Himself uncreated . . . without beginning and end . . . lacking nothing (ANF 1:422).

> For the Uncreated is perfect, that is, God. Now it was necessary that man should in the first instance be created; and having been created, should receive growth; and having received growth, should be strengthened; and having been strengthened, should abound; and having abounded, should recover (from the disease of sin). . . . Irrational, therefore, in every respect, are they who . . . ascribe to God the infirmity of their nature. Such persons know neither God, nor themselves, being insatiable and ungrateful, unwilling to be at the outset what they have also been created—men subject to passions; but go beyond the law of the human race, and before that they become men, they wish to be even now like God their Creator, and they who are more destitute of reason than dumb animals (insist) that there is no distinction between the uncreated God and man, a creature of today . . . for (we) cast blame upon Him, because we have not been made gods from the beginning (ANF 1:522).

Address of Tatian to the Greeks

> He who is in want of nothing is not to be misrepresented by us as though He were indigent (ANF 2:66).

> . . . the perfect God (ANF 2:70).

Theophilus to Autolycus

God made all things out of nothing; for nothing was coeval with God: but He being His own place, and wanting nothing, and existing before the ages, willed to make man. . . . For he that is created is also needy; but he that is uncreated stands in need of nothing (ANF 2:98).

Athenagoras' Plea for the Christians

The world was not created because God needed it; for God is Himself everything to Himself (ANF 2:136).

God, being perfectly good . . . (ANF 2:143).

The Stromata of Clement of Alexandria

. . . the Divinity needs nothing (ANF 2:526).[1]

God, who, needing nothing, supplies all men with all things. . . . The Deity neither is, then in want of aught (ANF 2:526-27).

How can He . . . need anything? (ANF 2:530).

Tertullian Against Marcion

God is . . . perfect in all things. . . . Prove, then, that the goodness of your god is a perfect one. That it is indeed *imperfect* has been already sufficiently shown. . . . It is not simply imperfect, but actually feeble, weak, and exhausted (ANF 3:289).

. . . the One only perfect Divinity (ANF 3:297).

Transcendent

Regarding God as infinite and perfect, the Fathers spoke of Him as being "above" all things. Thus He alone is transcendent in the sense that nothing stands "over" God to limit or control Him, "under" God as the "ground" of His existence, or "alongside" God to rival and frustrate Him. Nothing could limit the Almighty because anything that could limit God would be a greater God than God.

Irenaeus Against Heresies

The Creator . . . [is not] the fruit of a defect, . . . there is nothing either above Him, or after Him. . . . For how can there be any other Fulness, or Principle, or Power, or God, above Him . . . ? But if there is anything beyond Him, He is not then the Pleroma of all, nor does He contain all. . . . In such a case, He would have both beginning, middle, and end . . . and should be held in, bounded [limited], and enclosed by those existences that are outside of Him . . . the good God of Marcion, is established and enclosed in some other, and is surrounded from without by another mighty Being, who must of necessity be greater, inasmuch as that which contains is greater than that which is contained (ANF 1:359-60).

Theophilus to Autolycus

He is . . . the Highest because of His being above all (ANF 2:90).

Athenagoras' Plea for the Christians

He that made the world is above the things created. . . . The Creator of the world is above the things created, managing that by His providential care.., what place is there for the second god, or for the other gods? For He is not in the world . . . nor about the world, for God the Maker of the world is above it (ANF 2:132).

Apology of Tertullian

He is presented to our minds in His transcendent greatness (ANF 3:32).

Immutable

That God was perfect meant that He was immutable, unalterable, and unchanging in His nature and attributes.

The First Epistle of Clement

By His infinitely great power He established the heavens . . . and fixed it upon the immoveable foundation of His own will (ANF 1:13).

Irenaeus Against Heresies

(We are not to suppose that the true God can be changed.) When the fashion of this world passes away, not only shall God remain, but His servants also (ANF 1:465).

Theophilus to Autolycus

He is without beginning, because He is unbegotten; and He is unchangable, because He is immortal (ANF 21:90).

God, because He is uncreated, is also unalterable. . . . That which is created is mutable and alterable, but that which is uncreated is immutable and unalterable (ANF 2:95).

The Stromata of Clement of Alexandria

He is the only true God, who exists in the invariableness of righteous goodness (ANF 2:527).

Omniscient

The God of our Fathers was an all-knowing God. The idea of the Gnostics, Manichaeans, and Marcionites that God was ignorant or defective in His knowledge was viewed with horror and labeled heretical. God knew all things. Thus He was not ignorant of anything, not even the future.

The First Epistle of Clement

The Creator . . . is all-seeing and . . . omnipresent.[2]

The omnipotent and omniscient God . . . all things are nigh unto Him. . . . All things are open before Him, and nothing can be hidden from His counsel. . . . Since then all things are seen and heard (by God), let us fear Him (ANF 1:12).

God . . . seeth all things (ANF I:21).

Justin's Dialogue With Trypho

The ineffable Father . . . sees all things, and knows all things (ANF 1:263).

Justin on the Sole Government of God

Him who knows all things (ANF 1:290).

Irenaeus Against Heresies

I apply against the heretics at large . . . (who) blaspheme . . . to ascribe His origin to defect and ignorance (ANF 1:407).

The Stromata of Clement of Alexandria

God knows and perceives all things—not the words only, but also the thought. . . . God is all ear and eye, if we may be permitted to use these expressions (ANF 2:533).

Eternity and Time

The early Christians believed that the first point of revelation and theology is that God created *all* things. Nothing is uncreated and, therefore, eternal alongside of or over God. Thus both time and space were created out of nothing. God was timeless because He was time's Creator. Since the Creator is greater than what He creates, He is not bound by time or space.

As a created thing, the space-time universe is open and present to God in its entirety. How this was accomplished, or how it could be comprehended or explained, the Fathers did not pretend to understand. It was enough that the Scriptures clearly taught that only God was eternal and that the time-space universe was created by Him out of nothing.

The Apostolic view was in direct conflict with all the pagan religions around them. They all taught that time was not created but eternal. Thus they believed in "endless time." Time was, therefore, "over" the gods and was a god named Kronos.

The Fathers saw that if time was not created by God, then God was created by Time. There is room in this universe for only *one* Creator God. But since God is the Creator of *all* things, time is only a finite aspect of the creation and not a rival god.

The Epistle of St. Ignatius to Polycarp

Await Him that is above every season, the Eternal, the Invisible.[3]

Lightfoot comments that the phrase "above every season" should be translated, "to whom all seasons are alike." The word for "eternal" in the Greek is *achronon* which means, "transcending the limits of time."[4]

The Syriac text reads in this place, "Him who is above the times, Him to whom there are no times, Him who is unseen."[5] This wording is also found in a later quotation.[6]

Justin's Dialogue With Trypho

There will be no other God, O Trypho, nor was there from eternity any other existing (ANF 1:199).

Justin to the Greeks

Time was created along with the heavens. . . . the creation of time had received its original constitution from days and months and years (ANF 1:287).

Address of Tatian to the Greeks

Our God did not begin to be in time; He alone is without beginning, and He himself is the beginning of all things (ANF 2:66).

Time remains present as long as the Creator wills it to exist (ANF 2:76).

The Instructor (Clement of Alexandria)

(He is) Lord of all time and space (ANF 2:296).

Tertullian Against Marcion

What new god is there, except a false one? Not even Saturn will be proved to be a god by all his ancient fame, because it was a novel pretence which some time or other produced even him, when it first gave him godship. On the contrary, living and perfect Deity has its origin neither in novelty nor in antiquity, but in its own true nature. Eternity has no time. . . . God, moreover, is as independent of beginning and end as He is of time, which is only the arbiter and measurer of a beginning and an end (ANF 3:276).

Future events are sometimes announced as if they were already passed. For . . . there is no difference of time with that Being in whom eternity itself directs a uniform condition of seasons (ANF 3:324).

Foreknowledge

The Christian Church from the very beginning believed in an Omniscient God who not only knew the future but also ordained it from beginning to end. Some of the Fathers such as Tatian and Theophilus became Christians because the God of the Bible proved His divinity by His foreknowledge and prediction of the future.

The Marcionites, Gnostics, Manichaeans, and Valentinians argued that if God knew the future, He would be the Author of evil. In order to avoid this, the heretics claimed that God was neither omniscient nor omnipotent.

Justin's First Apology

He foreknows [the future] . . . the prophets of God . . . published beforehand things that were to come to pass, ere ever they happened (ANF 1:172-73).

He declares things that are to come to pass, in the manner of one who foretells the future. . . . The Spirit of prophecy speaks as predicting things that are to come to pass (ANF 1:175).

The Spirit of prophecy speaks of things that are about to come to pass as if they had already taken place. . . . The things which he absolutely knows will take place, He predicts as if already they had taken place (ANF 1:176-77).

Future events being foretold . . . God, foreknowing all that shall be done by men . . . He foretells by the Spirit of prophecy (ANF 1:177).

Until the number of those who are foreknown by Him . . . is complete (ANF 1:178).

It was foreknown that these infamous things should be uttered against those who confessed Christ, and that those who slandered Him, and said that it was well to preserve the ancient customs, should be miserable (ANF 1:179).

All things which have already happened had been predicted by the prophets before they came to pass. . . . those things which are in like manner predicted, but are yet to come to pass, shall certainly happen. For as the things which have already taken place came to pass when foretold, and even though unknown, so shall the things that remain, even though they be unknown and disbelieved, yet come to pass (ANF 1:180).

Justin's Dialogue With Trypho

We know that He foreknew all that would happen (ANF 1:240).

But lest anyone should say, He did not know then that He had to suffer, He adds immediately in the Psalm, "And it is not for want of understanding in me." Even as there was no ignorance on God's part when He asked Adam where he was, or asked Cain where Abel was; but (it was done) to convince each what kind of man he was, and in order that through the record (of Scripture) we might have a knowledge of all: so likewise Christ declared that ignorance was not on His side, but on theirs (ANF 1:248).

God foreknowing this would happen, had thus spoken. (ANF 1:251)

God, foreknowing before that you would do such things, pronounced this curse upon you (ANF 1:266).

But if the word of God foretells that some angels and men shall be certainly punished, it did so because it foreknew that they would be unchangeably (wicked) (ANF 1:270).

Irenaeus Against Heresies

God, knowing the number of those who will not believe, since He foreknows all things, has given them over to unbelief, and turned away His face from men of this stamp, leaving them in the darkness which they have chosen for themselves (ANF 1:502).

At the same time by His prescience He knew the infirmity of human beings, and the consequences which would flow from it (ANF 1:522).

The Pastor of Hermas

The Lord . . . foreknowing all things (ANF 2:22).

Address of Tatian to the Greeks

I happened to meet with certain barbaric writings [i.e., the Scriptures]. . . . I was led to put faith in these by . . . the foreknowledge displayed of future events (ANF 2:77).

Theophilus to Autolycus

I met with the sacred Scriptures of the holy prophets, who by the Spirit of God foretold the things that have already happened, just as they came to pass, and the things now occurring as they are happening, and things future in the order in which they shall be accomplished. (ANF 2:93)

The divine wisdom foreknew that some would trifle and name a multitude of gods that do not exist (ANF 2:98).

The Instructor (Clement of Alexandria)

He shows . . . His divinity in His foreknowledge of what would take place (ANF 2:228).

The Stromata of Clement of Alexandria

The Omnipotent God . . . foreknew all things (ANF 2:493).

The truly kingly man . . . is convinced that God knows and perceives all things . . . knows the elect already, even before his birth, knows what is to be as already existent (ANF 2:533).

Tertullian Against Marcion

So certain and united were the early Christians in their faith in the foreknowledge of God that they called anyone who denied it a "heretic" and a "dog." The "evangelical" processians such as Clark Pinnock and moral government people such as H. Roy Elseth would have been denounced as such by the early Church.

> Not as if He were ignorant . . . until He saw it (ANF 3:300).

> Now then, ye dogs, whom the apostle puts outside, and who yelp at the God of truth, let us come to your various questions. These are the bones of contention, which you are perpetually gnawing! If God is good, and prescient of the future, and able to avert evil, why did He permit man . . . to be deceived by the devil, and fall from obedience of the law unto death? For if He had been good, and so unwilling that such a catastrophe should happen, and prescient, so as not to be ignorant of what was to come to pass, and powerful enough to hinder its occurrence, that issue would never have come about, which should be impossible under these three conditions of the divine greatness. Since, however, it has occurred, the contrary proposition is most certainly true, that God must be deemed neither good, nor prescient, nor powerful. For *as* no such issue could have happened had God been such as He is reputed—good, and prescient, and mighty—*so* has this issue actually happened, because He is not such a God. In reply, we must first vindicate those attributes in the Creator which are called into question—namely, His goodness and foreknowledge, and power. . . . The Creator's works testify at once to His goodness . . . and to His power. . . . In short, both they are great because they are good; and God is likewise mighty, because all things are His own, whence He is almighty. But what shall I say of His prescience, which has for its witnesses as many prophets as it inspired? After all, what title to prescience do we look for in the Author of the universe, since it was by this very attribute that He foreknew all things when He appointed them their places, and appointed them their places when He foreknew them? There is sin itself. If He had not foreknown this, He would not have proclaimed a caution against it under the penalty of death. . . . let us consider man's condition also—whether *it* were not, in fact, rather the cause why that [i.e. sin] came to pass . . . what happened to him should be laid to his own charge, and not to God's (ANF 3:300-01).

> . . . for even this [i.e., the Fall] God, of course, foresaw (ANF 3:302).

Divine Sovereignty or Providence

The early Christians saw any denial of God's sovereign rule of the universe as atheism. Sovereignty to them meant that God, in fact, was ruling the world. They rejected the Greek gods of time, fate, and chance.

But, at the same time, they did not make God the Author or cause of evil. They simply accepted the plain teaching of Scripture that God's sovereignty and human responsibilty were *both* true. How and in what way this could be, they left in the hands of the Almighty. Only pagan philosophers and heretics such as Marcion denied Providence.

The First Epistle of Clement

> The heavens, revolving under His government, are subject to Him in peace. Day and night run the course appointed by Him, in no wise hindering each other. The sun and moon, with the companies of the stars, roll on in harmony according to His command, within their prescribed limits, and without any deviation. The fruitful earth, according to His will, brings forth food in abundance, at the proper seasons, for man and beast and all the living beings upon it, never hesitating, nor changing any of the ordinances which He has fixed (ANF 1:10).

> For by His infinitely great power He established the heavens, and by His incomprehensible wisdom He adorned them. He also divided the earth from the water which surrounds it, and fixed it upon the immoveable foundation of His own will (ANF 1:13).

> God, who seeth all things, and who is the Ruler of all spirits and the Lord of all flesh (ANF 1:21).

Irenaeus Against Heresies

> We have learned from the Scriptures that God holds the supremacy over all things. But whence or in what way He produced it, neither has Scripture anywhere declared; now does it become us to conjecture, so as, in accordance with our own opinions, to form endless conjectures concerning God, but we should leave such knowledge in the hands of God Himself.

In like manner, also, we must leave the cause why, while all things were made by God, certain of His creatures sinned and revolted from a state of submission to God. . . . Since, therefore, we know but in part, we ought to leave all sorts of (difficult) questions in the hands of Him.

That eternal fire, is prepared for sinners . . . the Scriptures demonstrate. And that God foreknew that this would happen, the Scriptures do in like manner demonstrate. . . . But the cause itself of the nature of such transgressors neither has any Scripture informed us, nor has an apostle told us, nor has the Lord taught us. It becomes us, therefore, to leave the knowledge of this matter to God. . . . When we investigate points which are above us . . . we should display such an extreme of presumption as to lay open God . . . as if already we had found out, by the vain talk . . . to assert that He derived His substance from apostasy and ignorance, so as to frame an impious hypothesis in opposition to God (ANF 1:401).

God the Father ruling over all (ANF 1:418).

God does, however, exercise a providence over all things. . . . by His providence . . . the Maker of this universe . . . exercises a providence over all things, and arranges the affairs of our world (ANF 1:459).

The Pastor of Hermas

God . . . rules over all things (ANF 2:51).

Address of Tatian to the Greeks

What noble thing have you produced by your pursuit of philosophy?. . . . Aristotle, who absurdly placed a limit to Providence and made happiness to consist in the things which give pleasure (ANF 2:65).

Theophilus to Autolycus

His sovereignty. . . . Providence. . . . He is Lord because He rules over all things. . . . He Himself rules and embraces all. . . . God is the governor (lit.,*pilot*) of the whole universe (ANF 2:90).

Some of the philosophers . . . have dared to give out that there is no providence of God at all (ANF 2:95).

Sophocles . . . denied Providence. . . . Euripides [too] (ANF 2:97).

They say that the gods have no more power than men. . . . How many atheistic opinions Clitmachus the academician introduced . . . demolishing providence. . . . Euhemerus, and Epicurus, and Pythagoras . . . abolish providence . . . some have absolutely canceled God and providence. . . . Now we also confess that God exists, but that He is one, the creator, and maker, and fashioner of this universe; and we know that all things are arranged by His providence, but by Him alone (ANF 2:113).

Athenagoras' Plea for the Christians

Providence . . . over the things created and ordered by Him; so that God may have the universal and general providence of the whole. . . . (but) the poets and philosophers have denied a divine providence. . . . The same thing led Aristotle to say that the things below the heaven are not under the care of Providence. . . . Some . . . have therefore thought that this universe is constituted without any definite order, and is driven hither and thither by an irrational chance. But they do not understand (ANF 2:142).

The Stromata of Clement of Alexandria

Providence . . . by Basilides, is done away with (ANF 2:424).

He is in no respect whatever the cause of evil. For all things are arranged with a view to . . . salvation . . . by the Lord of the universe, both generally and particularly (ANF 2:526).

. . . (those) who, falling into licentiousness in pleasures, and grievous pains, and unlooked-for accidents, and bidding defiance to events, say that there is no God, or that, although existing, He does not oversee all things (ANF 2:527).

The Octavius of Minucius Felix

He orders everything, whatever it is, by a word; arranges it by His wisdom; perfects it by His power (ANF 4:183).

The world is governed by providence and directed by the will of one God (ANF 4:184).

The Fathers and the Philosophers

The early Christians who received the God revealed in Scripture believed in an infinite/personal God who was all-seeing and all-powerful. They rejected the finite gods of the philosophers and of the heretics because such gods did not even know the future.

The Fathers rested in the security of the sovereign providence of God and had no sympathy for the chance-produced universe of the Greeks with their knee-jerk deities. God was immutably perfect, wise, holy, just, and good. He was not responsible for evil—man was.

But what about the accusation that one hears today that the Church's concept of God came from Greek philosophy? What was the attitude of the Apostolic Fathers toward such men as Plato?

The evidence from the writings of the early Fathers reveals that they believed that it was impossible to discover the nature of God on the basis of human reason or experience. Neither could truth, justice, morals, or beauty be found solely on the basis of man's reason.

In the eyes of the Fathers, the philosophers totally failed to come up with any truth whatsoever on their own. The few times they hit on an idea that was true, they stole it from the Bible.

The philosophers were atheistic, ignorant, conceited, argumentative, deceitful, and wicked. Their vain speculations and continual harping on the problem of evil have led to nothing but damnable heresies. They never solved anything or helped anyone on to God and salvation.[7]

The early Church's answer to humanism was to submit to the infallible and perfect Word of God; to rest in its inspiration and not to go beyond its declaration, to be satisfied that if a question is not answered in Scripture, it must not be important for us to know or it is beyond our capacity to understand.

Conclusion

The faith of the early Church was clearly centered on an infinite God who is perfect and immutable in all things. Those who worship a finite god do not worship the Christian God.

THE TESTIMONY OF THE CREEDS OF THE CHURCH

Having seen that the God revealed in Scripture is the God received by the early Christian fathers, it should come as no surprise that this same God is confessed in the historic creeds of the Christian Church. Those who wish to bear the name "Christian" *must* believe in the Christian faith as revealed in the Scriptures and confessed by the Church for nearly two thousand years. Otherwise, the word *Christian* has lost all meaning.

Early Creedal Statements

The first creedal statements in the Church were composed originally as confessions of faith uttered at baptism. This followed the example of Philip, who had the Eunuch confess his faith before being baptized (Acts 8:29-39). These baptismal confessions were so succinct and powerful that they became popular in both private and public worship.

All the early Greek and Latin creeds describe God as "Almighty." The Latin or Greek words such as *omnipotens* reveal that the omnipotence of God was viewed as essential to the Christian concept of God. A God who was anything less than absolutely omnipotent could not be the God of Scripture. For this reason, the first or second attribute of God always confessed was His omnipotence.

That God was sovereign over all things was taken for granted once His omnipotence was accepted. The idea of a god who was tossed this way and that by the winds of chance was viewed as heresy. God's providential rule over the world was viewed as an essential part of the Christian God.

God was viewed as being infinite in all His attributes. He was transcendent and immutably perfect in all things. He was "over" time as well as space, seeing He was eternal.

The Classic Creeds of the Church

The Christian Church has from the beginning set forth its faith in creeds and confessions. What "Christians" believe is thus a matter of historical record and not subjective feelings. If someone does not believe in the historic Christian faith as outlined in the great creeds of the Church, he is not to be viewed as Christian but as an heretic or pagan. Love for God, His Word, and our neighbor demand such a judgment.

We will restrict our citation of the creeds to their statements concerning the nature of God.

The Apostles' Creed (A.D. 200)

> I Believe in God the Father *Almighty*,
> *Maker* of heaven and earth.[1]

In this historic creed, which is used today in Protestant as well as Catholic churches, the omnipotence of God is confessed as an essential part of the Christian faith. The doctrine that God is the Creator of all things including time is also viewed as an essential part of the Christian faith. Monism with its eternal time is a pagan idea repugnant to Christians.

The Nicene Creed (A.D. 381)

> We believe in *one* God the Father *Almighty*,
> *Maker* of heaven and earth,
> And of *all things visible and invisible.*
> And in *one* Lord Jesus Christ, . . .
>   begotten of the Father *before all worlds* (aeons), . . .
> By whom *all things were made.*[2]

In this beautiful creed, which exalts the deity of Christ, the unity and the omnipotence of God are proclaimed. When the creed states that God is the Creator of "all things," it includes time as well as space.

Christ was "begotten of the Father" *before* the aeons, i.e., *before* time itself was created.

The Constantinopolitan Creed (A.D. 381)

> We believe in *one* God the Father *Almighty*,
> *Maker* of heaven and earth,
>   and of *all things visible and invisible*.
> And in one Lord Jesus Christ, . . .
> Begotten of the Father *before all worlds* (aeons). . . .[3]

This creed joins in the same confession of the Faith as the Nicene creed. The unity, omnipotence, Creatorhood, and eternity of God are confessed.

The Creed of Chalcedon (A.D. 451)

> We, then, following the holy Fathers, all with one consent, teach men to confess one and the same Son, our Lord Jesus Christ, the same *perfect* in Godhead . . . to be acknowledged in two natures, inconfusedly, *unchangeably*, indivisibly, inseparably. . . .[4]

The Chalcedon Creed proclaims the perfection and immutability of Christ as God. The Greek text is quite emphatic that Christ as God is "without change," i.e., immutable. This follows from the fact that He is "perfect in Godhead."

The Athanasian Creed (A.D. 490)

> We worship *one* God in Trinity, and Trinity in Unity; . . . the Father *incomprehensible* (lit., "infinite"): the Son *incomprehensible* (lit., "infinite"): and the Holy Ghost *incomprehensible* (lit., "infinite"). . . . There are not three uncreated: nor three *incomprehensibles* (lit., "infinites"), but *one uncreated*: and *one incomprehensible* (lit., "infinite"). So likewise the Father is *Almighty* (lit., "Omnipotent"): the Son *Almighty* (lit., "Omnipotent"): and the Holy Ghost *Almighty* (lit., "Omnipotent"). . . .the Son of God, is God and Man; . . . begotten *before the worlds* (*ante secula genitus*); . . . *Perfect* God (*Perfectus Deus*).[5]

The Athanasian Creed held great authority not only throughout the Middle Ages but also during the Reformation. The Protestant

Churches confessed this creed just as they did the Apostles' Creed. Lutheran and Reformed churches all accepted this creed as expressing the universal or catholic faith of all those who are "Christians."

Belief in the unity and Trinity of God is confessed as essential for salvation. This creed is the greatest statement on the deity of Christ that the Christian Church ever produced.

The word "incomprehensible" was based on an inaccurate Greek text of the creed. Subsequent research has established that the text actually reads *immensus* in the Latin and *apeiros* in the Greek. The Triune God is confessed as "infinite" in nature.[6]

The word *Almighty* is *omnipotens* in the Latin and means that the triune God is Omnipotent in nature. The Son was begotten of the Father "before the worlds," i.e., before time was created. The perfection of God is an essential aspect of the deity of Christ. Any denial of the perfection of God is an attack on the Trinity.

Denominational Creeds

The task of going through all the creeds of all the different Christian churches is far beyond the scope of this work. That Philip Schaff wrote three large volumes on this subject is an indication of the immense amount of material to be covered. The most that we can do is to give a summary of the creeds and confessions that Schaff collected in his day and hope that someone else will have the opportunity to bring the material up to date.

The Christian Church is often viewed in terms of such divisions as Eastern and Western, Roman and Protestant, Lutheran and Anglican, Reformed and Arminian, Anabaptist and Evangelical, Mainline and Fundamental. They are all considered parts of Christendom in that they share the essential Christian doctrine of God: only one Triune God of Father, Son, and Holy Spirit, Maker of heaven and earth, as eternal spirit, is infinite, perfect, immutable, omniscient, omnipotent, omnipresent, invisible, holy, and true.

The creeds, confessions, and catechisms of *all* Christian denominations that we have been able to secure express faith in this historic Christian conception of God. The only creeds that deny the perfection, immutability, omniscience, omnipotence, omnipresence, and Providence of God are *cultic* groups such as the Jehovah's Witnesses. The finite god of the processians thus cannot be considered as part of the historic Christian conception of God.

Wesleyan Arminian Theology

As a matter of historical record, we could not find a single Arminian denomination, which, in its confessions or creeds, denies that God knows the future. Almost without exception Arminians have always argued that election and predestination are based on God's *foreknowledge* of man's faith.

All the Wesleyan confessions clearly state that God is infinite, perfect, eternal, all-knowing, and all-powerful. Such theologians as Watson, Wakefield, Raymond, Ralston, Miley, and Wiley all defend the omniscience and omnipotence of God.[7]

Thus those modern thinkers who claim to be Arminian in theology and who deny the foreknowledge of God have actually denied the historic Arminian faith.

The same can be said of the statements of faith given by Reformed, Lutheran, Anglican, Presbyterian, Congregational, Ana-baptist, Baptist, Pentecostal, Methodist, Evangelical, Charismatic, Independent, nondenominational, and Fundamentalist Churches. The historic Christian conception of God is an essential feature of their creeds. Those who deny this conception of God have therefore placed themselves *outside* of the Christian Church.

Conclusion

While this may seem harsh to those corrupted by relativism, the Christian Church has always taught that any doctrine which denies the faith should not be called "Christian." While we cannot judge someone's heart to see if he is "saved," we can judge whether or not his doctrines are Christian.

THE TESTIMONY OF EVANGELICAL THEOLOGY

A s we have seen, the idea of a limited, finite god is totally foreign to the Church fathers and to the creeds of Christendom. In this chapter we shall briefly survey the writings of evangelical theologians, to show once again that nobody in the Christian Church has ever held to this grotesque idea.

In British evangelical theology, the fullest refutation of the idea that God does not know the future was given by the greatest of all Puritan divines, Dr. John Owen. In 1654, the Church of England asked Owen to write a refutation of Socinianism. He entitled the subsequent work, *Vindiciae Evangelicae; The Mystery of the Gospel Vindicated and Socinianism Examined.* This landmark work is found in Volume 12 of *The Works of John Owen* (London, Banner of Truth Trust, 1966), and is still worthy of careful study.

The greatest evangelical theologian the United States ever produced was Jonathan Edwards. His detailed refutation of the denial of God's foreknowledge is given in a work entitled, *On the Freedom of the Will.* It can be found in *The Works of Jonathan Edwards* (Edinburgh: The Banner of Truth Trust, 1974), volume 1, pp. 30f. It has never been successfully refuted.

Timothy Dwight, a grandson of Edwards and president of Yale, clearly saw where the liberal theology of his day was headed with its denial of the immutability and foreknowledge of God. He pointed out the consequences of the idea that God was *changing*. His words equally apply to modern processians.

Were God, contrary to this glorious character, to begin to change, what a mighty difference would be introduced into his being, his attributes, and his conduct! . . . God must, in the case supposed, become less powerful, less knowing, or less good. How fearful to all virtuous beings in the Universe, must such a change be! Were he a mutable God, it would be impossible for us to know, that what was his pleasure yesterday, would be his pleasure today; and what he had required yesterday, he would not prohibit today; or that what he promised yesterday, he would be willing to perform at any future period.

What he now loved, he might hereafter hate: what he now approved, he might hereafter condemn: what he now rewarded, he might hereafter punish. Of course, virtuous beings, now loved, approved, and rewarded, by him, might one day be hated, condemned, and punished. Wicked beings, on the contrary, now the objects of his hatred, and declared to be hereafter the objects of his punishment, might one day become the objects of his friendship and favour; and triumph over the good in a manner equally unreasonable and dreadful.[1]

The Fundamentalist/Liberal Debates

During the 1920s, the debate between Christianity and liberalism focused on the nature of God. The liberals denied the historic Christian concept of an infinite, all-knowing, all-wise, and all-powerful God. In its place, they put forth the idea of a finite god who did not know the future. This god had to struggle like man to get anything done because he was as limited as man. All of the attributes of God were either rejected outright or radically redefined to mean the opposite of what they had always historically meant.

The Fundamentalist/Modernist controversy was but the culmination of trends that had arisen during the two previous centuries. Christian scholars had never taken these attacks on God lightly. They knew that the Christian system rested on its concept of God. If its foundation be destroyed, Christianity cannot survive. All orthodox systematic theologies contained refutations of the liberal denial of the omniscience and omnipotence of God. *All* evangelical theologians, regardless if they were Presbyterians or Baptists, Calvinists or Arminians, were united in their opposition to the liberal attempt to reduce God's knowledge and power:

- C. Hodge, *Systematic Theology* [1871], 1:400ff. Northern Presbyterian.
- J. Dagg, *Manual Of Theology and Church Order* [1857], pp. 71ff. Baptist.
- R. Dabney, *Lectures In Systematic Theology* [1878], pp. 156ff. Southern Presbyterian.
- A. Hodge, *Outlines of Theology* [1879], pp. 146ff. Northern Presbyterian.
- J. Boyce, *Abstract of Systematic Theology* [1887], pp. 87ff. Baptist.
- A. Strong, *Systematic Theology* [1907], pp. 284ff. Baptist.
- L. Chafer, *Systematic Theology* [1964], 1:192-96. Dispensationalist.
- R. Watson, *Theological Institutes* [1974], 1:376-77. Methodist.

For example, the Baptist theologian Augustus Hopkins Strong documents in his *Systematic Theology* that the denial of the omniscience of God comes from Greek philosophy, particularly Aristotle. The denial of the omniscience of God is thus a philosophical perversion and not a scriptural idea. He quotes Martineau, who stated:

> The belief in the divine foreknowledge of our future has no basis in philosophy. We no longer deem it true that even God knows the moment of my moral life that is coming next. Even he does not know whether I shall yield to the secret temptation at midday. To him life is a drama of which he knows not the conclusion (p. 285).

Martineau at least was honest enough to admit that his god did not know if he or the Devil will win in the end.

In his response, Strong quotes Dr. A. J. Gordon, a noted theologian, expositor, hymnwriter, and author of the nineteenth-century, who beautifully lampooned the idea of a finite deity who did not know the future.

> There is nothing so dreary and dreadful as to be living under the direction of such a God. The universe is rushing on like an express-train in the darkness without headlights or engineer; at any moment we may be plunged into the abyss (p. 285).

Strong points out that in Isaiah 41:21-22:

> God makes his foreknowledge the test of his Godhood in the controversy with idols (p. 285).

After reviewing the Biblical basis of God's prescience, he admits that although the Bible clearly teaches the omniscience of God, we are not told "how" and "in what way" God foreknows the future.

> How God foreknows free human decisions we may not be able to say, but then the method of God's knowledge in many other respects is unknown to us (p. 285).

Man's reason must bow in humility before revelation. God knows all things from eternity, and man is accountable to his Creator for his actions. God's foreknowledge and man's accountability do not need to be reconciled. They are two truths revealed in Scripture, that surpass the puny mind of man to comprehend.

This same position was taken by the standard reference works used by Bible-believing Christians. They *all* rejected the Socinian idea that God was ignorant of the future. This included such Methodist reference works as McClintock and Strong, *Cyclopedia of Biblical, Theological, and Ecclesiastical Literature* (vol. VIII, pp. 555ff.).

The same is true for such classic works as *The International Standard Bible Encyclopedia* (vol. II, pp. 1128ff.).

The same position is maintained by such present-day standard evangelical works as *Baker's Dictionary of Theology* (p. 225), *The Zondervan Pictorial Bible Dictionary*, (pp. 316ff.), etc.

Indeed, all the modern-day evangelical and Reformed systematic theology texts defend the historic Christian conception of God.

- H. Theissen, *Lectures In Systematic Theology* [1949], pp. 124ff. Baptist.
- L. Berkhof, *Systematic Theology* [1941], pp. 67ff. Christian Reformed.

We do not consider any writer an "evangelical" if he denies the orthodox view of the inspiration, inerrancy, and absolute authority of Scripture. That some liberal thinkers are today trying to pass themselves off as "evangelicals" is a fulfillment of Jesus' warning to beware of ravenous wolves in sheep's clothing. Their condemnation is just.

The Fundamentalist versus Liberal debate over these issues filled the theological journals of the day. Charles W. Hodge,[2] William Johnson,[3] Clarence Bouma,[4] and David Clark[5] wrote articles that refuted the idea that God was limited in power and knowledge. They viewed the finite god idea as pagan philosophy and as the end-product of the theory of evolution.

Now that the same issues are being raised all over again today, modern Christians must object to the "evolutionizing" and "relativizing" of God.

Carl F. H. Henry

The most outstanding evangelical scholar of the twentieth century, Dr. Henry has for several decades repeatedly warned Christians that modern theologians believe in false gods. In the early 1960s, in an article on modern theology, Henry predicted that, in a "battle of the gods," the Christian God of the Bible would be pitted against the false gods of Western philosophy and Eastern religions. His prophetic words have come true.

> Today the God of the Bible is ranged in fresh battle against the ancient gods of resurgent Oriental religions, against the modern gods of Occidental cults, against the speculative gods of liberal theologians . . . all previous traditions now seem to be converging for one mighty, final struggle to the death.[6]

Dr. Henry felt so strongly about the ensuing "battle of the gods," that, beginning in the late 1970s, he produced a series of volumes entitled *God, Revelation and Authority*, which the *New York Times* describes as "the most important work of evangelical theology in modern times."[7]

In this series, Henry documents and refutes such false gods as the processian deities. He demonstrates in minute detail that all the attacks on the transcendent omniscience and omnipotence of God are rooted in pagan philosophic assumptions. The attack on the timelessness of God and His knowledge of the future is revealed as nothing more than an attempt to revive the gods of ancient Greece. He does not compromise with the forces of liberalism or spare apostate evangelicals from his searching critique. In Volume 5 of the series, Henry points out:

> One point is all too seldom recognized: when professioanl philosophers and systematic theologians project modern theories that eliminate timelessness from the nature of God they do more than simply reconstruct a particular perfection of the biblical God; what they do is substitute a deity very different from the God of orthodox theism (p. 253).

Both the Old and New Testaments teach that God foreknows the future, that he is prescient of the events and circumstances of the created temporal world. This foreknowledge of the future distinguishes the Living God from idols and false gods (p. 278).

Christian theology has affirmed both God's essential timelessness and his essential changelessness (p. 288).

Advocacy of a changing God is but a confusing declaration that Change is god. . . . But a divinity whose name is Change cannot be the guarantor even of the continually changing (p. 306).

Gordon Clark

Gordon Clark was without a doubt one of the greatest Christian philosophers who ever lived. In his work entitled, *Religion, Reason, and Revelation,* he used his skill in logic to devastate humanistic philosophy, including the idea of a finite god who did not know the future.

Today, then, as in the past, the existence of evil is a crucial question, and the answer frequently includes the idea of a limited deity. Many modern philosophers, such as John Stuart Mill, William Pepperell Montague, and Georgia Harkness, as well as the ancient Zoroaster and Plato, accept a finite god. But it must be clearly understood that this idea is incompatible with Christianity. The Bible presents God as omnipotent, and only on this basis can a Christian view of evil be worked out.[8]

Royce Gordon Gruenler

Dr. Gruenler was at one time a processian who believed that god did not know the future. In his book, *The Inexhaustible God,* which is part autobiographical as well as theological, he bears eloquent testimony to the sovereign grace of an omnipotent and omniscient God who was pleased to open his eyes to the heretical nature of processianism and to lead him to back to the Christian faith.[9]

He traces his apostasy into processianism as,

The . . . effect of my shifting my focus of authority from Scripture to the philosophical canons of process theism.[10]

As one who was personally and professionally involved in the heresy of processianism, Gruenler's conclusions concerning it cannot be dismissed lightly.

> The school (of processianism) has ancient origins. Heraclitus and Protagoras, repudiating their opponents' view that what is really real is the eternal and the changeless, long ago exalted time and space and man as the measure of all things. In our own day, Alfred North Whitehead and Charles Hartshorne have attempted to fuse these two poles together, but in point of fact they have come down on Heraclitus' side. In an age of change they have made relativity and timespace a given, even for God.[11]

> The limited deity of process theology is rather like the demiurge of Plato's *Timaeus*, or Ahura Mazda in Zoroastrianism, or the principle of light in Manicheism.[12]

> . . . the limitation of God to time and space has to be considered a modern idolatry.[13]

Gruenler deals pointedly with Richard Rice, a Seventh-day Adventist who has introduced processianism into the Seventh-day Adventist Church. He faults him for always assuming humanistic definitions of such key terms as "freedom" and for framing his questions and arguments in the "either/or" dichotomies of pagan philosophy.[14] Rice never bothers to exegete the word *free* as found in Scripture. He simply assumes the Greek view of absolute pure chance as the meaning of "true" freedom.

Ronald H. Nash

Dr. Nash's stand against the liberal inroads into the evangelical community is well known. In a recent book on the concept of God, Nash points out the differences between the Biblical and historic Christian concept of God and the finite god of the processians, who does not know the future. He states:

> Process theologians make it clear that their God is neither omnipotent nor omniscient.[15]

Nash goes on to list eleven key concepts found in processianism that contradict the God of the Bible. Nash correctly identifies processianism as a veiled form of pantheism and calls it by that name.

In his refutation of processianism, Nash traces its origins to Greek philosophy[16] and points out that process theology leads to a denial of all orthodox doctrines such as the Trinity, the deity of Christ, the incarnation, the bodily resurrection, and the atonement.[17] If God is constantly changing, as the processians claim:

> What reason then have Christians today to believe that the God they worship is the the *same* God worshiped by Moses and revealed by Jesus Christ?[18]

In a recent symposium on process thought, Nash concludes with these sober words:

> A being who is not essentially omnipotent or omniscient, who is not the sovereign and independent Creator, is neither worthy to receive our worship nor to bear the title "God."[19]

Conclusion

Enough evidence has been presented to demonstrate that evangelical theology confesses faith in a God who is infinite in all His attributes. No other God was thought worthy of worship. Those who worship a finite god who is ignorant of the future and powerless before chance and time, should not call themselves "evangelical."

THE TESTIMONY
OF SCRIPTURE

Since the god of the processians cannot know or control the future because it is chance-directed and not predetermined by him, his actions are always "spur-of-the-moment" decisions. For example, since god did not know that Adam would sin, he did not already have a plan of salvation worked out.

This also means that god has to change his plans constantly as new developments unfold. Since he cannot know the future with any certainty, seeing it is chance-driven, then James 4:13-15 must be rewritten to apply to god!

The same holds for god's promises. Since he does not know the future, he can only say, "In the light of what I *presently* know I promise to do this or that. But tomorrow is a new day and things may not work out the way I hoped. Since I don't know what is going to happen tomorrow, none of my promises are ironclad. I may or may not keep my word."

The reader may think that surely no "evangelical" would ever suggest such an idea. In a book which at this time is published and distributed by YWAM, Roy Elseth states, "God often changes His mind and does not do the things He says He will."[1]

When we stop and think about what Elseth is saying, then even God's promise of salvation is no longer sure or certain! The implications of what the processians and moral government people are saying lead us to ask, Does God act according to some predetermined plan or purpose, or are His actions based on "spur-of-the-moment" decisions dictated by pure chance? Do His actions reflect a plan or are they totally random, being determined by pure coincidence? Is God capricious or does He do things on purpose?

These questions can be answered in only two ways. We can accept what God has said in the Bible or we can go the route of idolatry and make a god in our own image.

When we turn to the Bible, we find that God's actions are never spoken of as being random, chance-caused, without purpose or reason. Neither is God ever said to be "lucky" or "unlucky" as if mere coincidence determined His ways. What He does, He does on *purpose* according to the *counsel* of His own *will*. God's purpose, counsel, and will constitute His *plan* for the universe of men and things which He created for His own Glory.

The Plan of God

The entire Bible from Genesis to Revelation describes God as acting according to a predetermined plan and not by a "spur-of-the-moment" decision. He is never "surprised" by the turn of events or thrown into panic by unforeseen events. The future is not something unknown and unplanned to God. History flows along a predetermined path appointed by the Creator of heaven and earth. (See 2 Chronicles 25:14-23; Psalms 33:6-12; Isaiah 14:24-27; 23:1-9; Jeremiah 49:20-22; 50:45-46; Acts 2:23.)

But if God does not know the future, all His actions are merely reactions to an everchanging swirl of events spun out of chance. He cannot really plan anything, because to plan ahead requires foresight. But if the future is unknown to God, He must await the "roll of the dice" before He can react. The only way to decide if this is true is to turn to God's Word for the answer.

The Counsel of the Lord

Does the Triune God take counsel or think through what He is going to do before He does it? Does He act according to a predetermined counsel or does He act in ignorance? Does He take a "leap in the dark" and act without foresight? Is the future unknown and unplanned by God?

Once again, the only way for us to answer these questions with certainty is to examine the Scriptures to see what they say. (See Psalms 33:10-11; Jeremiah 32:16-20; Ephesians 1:11-12.)

The Will of God

Are God's plan and counsel determined by anything outside God, or do they flow out of His sovereign *will?* In Ephesians 1:11, Paul uses the genitive of origin when he says, God "works all things the counsel *which flows out and has its origin in His will."*

All things are "worked" (lit., "energized") by God according to a predetermined plan and purpose that flow out of His will. But does God's will limit the will of man? Or, does man's will limit God's will? When the will and plan of God are contradicted by the will and plan of man, who wins? Should we believe, "Thy will be done on earth as it is in heaven"? Or, should we believe that man's will is ultimate? The Bible clearly answers these questions. (See Daniel 4:24-37; John 6:38-40; Romans 9:9-21; 1 Corinthians 1:1; 2 Corinthians 1:1; Ephesians 1:1; Colossians 1:1; 2 Timothy 1:1; Ephesians 1:5, 11; Acts 18:21; Romans 1:10; 15:32; 1 Corinthians 4:19; James 4:13-16.)

The Biblical authors do not hesitate to speak of God's plan as standing forever because it is rooted in God's mind, heart, and will.

As we have demonstrated already, God is omniscient and is not ignorant of the future or anything else for that matter. To every and any issue that perplexes our minds we can say with Scripture, "God *knoweth!*" (2 Corinthians 11:11, emphasis mine).

Does God Foresee the Future?

But can we really say that God "foresees" the future? What does the Word of God say?

> And the Scripture, *foreseeing* that God would justify the Gentiles by faith, preached the gospel beforehand to Abraham, saying, "All the nations shall be blessed in you" (Galatians 3:8-9, emphasis mine).

As is the habit with the authors of Scripture, they sometimes speak of Scripture as doing what God does. Thus Scripture or God is here said to "foresee" all that happens in the future. The Gospel promises in the Old Testament were based on His "foreseeing that the Gentiles would be justified by faith."

The word *foresee* cannot be ignored. What God says, Scripture says. The foresight of the inclusion of the Gentiles into the covenant is stated without apology or limitation. There was no need for controversy on this point, for both Jew and Christian believed in the Eternal God who knows the future as well as the past and the present.

God Foreknows the Future

God's foresight of the future means that God *foreknows* the future. This foreknowledge is not uncertain or mutable. It is both certain and immutable. It is true knowledge and not a lie. It is infallible knowledge and cannot be overthrown by chance or luck. As Peter said:

> This Man, delivered up by the predetermined plan and *foreknowledge of God*, you nailed to a cross by the hands of godless men and put Him to death (Acts 2:23, emphasis mine).

Christ's death was not a rude surprise to God. That Judas, Herod, Pilate, the Jews, and the Romans conspired together to murder the Son of God did not shock God. That Jesus would be whipped, tortured, and nailed to a cross was known to God *before* it happened. Thus Peter tells us that God "foreknew" all the events which culminated in the death of Christ.

That God foreknew what these evil men would do to Jesus did not negate or lessen their responsibility in the least. Divine foreknowledge and human responsibility are placed together in this passage without any apologies.

The Apostle Paul spoke of God's "foreknowing," "predestining," "electing," "justifying," and "glorifying" sinners, without apologizing for God's actions (Romans 8:29-30). He viewed such things as "spiritual blessings" from God the Father on the basis of the work of Christ (Ephesians 1:3-11).

While the word *foreknow* means *much more* than bare pre-knowledge in Romans 8:29, it cannot mean anything *less*. The use of the word *whom* instead of *what*, means that it is not faith that is foreknown but the people of God, the elect.

To Peter, election arose out of and necessarily required God's foreknowing the future. We can be said to choose something only if we know what we are choosing as opposed to what we aren't choosing. Salvation is not a "grab bag," for God's people are chosen deliberately (1 Peter 1:1-2).

In 1 Peter 1:18-20, Peter also states that Christ's death was "foreknown before the foundation of the world." To say that Christ's death was not known by God means that it was not planned by God. It means that Christ did not die on purpose according to a predetermined plan of God. His death would have to be viewed as the greatest accident or "bad luck" to ever occur. But this passage forever establishes the truth that God knows the future acts of man and Christ in several ways.

First, God foreknew Christ's death before the Creation was spoken into being. Thus God knew about the Fall of man into sin which would bring about the need of salvation. He knew about all our sins before the world was created.

That God knew all our sins before He created us will not surprise a Christian because he knows that Christ knew all about our sins when He died on the cross. The simplest Christian knows that the Gospel declares that Christ died on the cross for all our sins even though they were *all future* (1 Corinthians 15:3-4).

If it be granted that Christ on the cross died for our sins by God's placing them on His record and punishing Him in our place, then our sins were foreseen and foreknown. To argue that, if the future acts of man are foreknown by God, this destroys human responsibility is as absurd as saying that if Christ knowingly died for our future sins, they were no longer sins!

The Socinian idea that God does not know the future was one of the chief reasons that group rejected the doctrine of Christ's atonement on the cross. Let moral government leaders take note of where process theology will take them.

Second, if God does not know the future good and evil acts of man, Christ could not have died for our sins on the cross because He did not know of them. His atonement could only cover the past sins of His people.

As a matter of fact, if the future is really "closed" to the knowledge and power of God, as is claimed by the processians, the entire concept of a substitutionary atonement falls to the ground. If God does not know the future, then Christ did not die for our sins on the cross.

Third, the word *foreknew* in this text obviously means *more* than mere preknowledge of an event before it happens. All exegetes and commentators have pointed out that Christ's death was *foreknown* because it was *foreordained*. This is why modern translations render 1 Peter 1:20, "*foreordained* before the foundation of the world." Christ's death was a *planned* event. It was decreed and ordained from all eternity.

The only alternative is to teach that Christ's death was a mistake of cosmic proportion. This would reduce the atonement to a gigantic hoax played by chance on God!

God's Immutable Purpose

Do we live from accident to accident with chance and luck determining the outcome of all things? Do things happen "on purpose"? Or, is life without any purpose, rhyme, or reason?

Scripture plainly tells us that nothing happens without some divine purpose behind it. God rules His creation and "works all things together for the good" (Romans 8:28). (See Job 42:1-2; Proverbs 16:4; Isaiah 19:12, 17; Isaiah 46:8-13; Jeremiah 4:27-30; Acts 4:28; Romans 8:28; Romans 9:10-13.)

Since God's purpose is "eternal" (Ephesians 3:11), can we go on to say that it is "immutable" and "unchangeable"? The answer to this question is not left to vain speculation. Hebrews 6:17 explains that God's purpose is "unchangeable." The immutability of God's purpose is backed up by the infallibility, perfection, and veracity of God, for "God cannot lie" (v. 18).

The only way God's purpose can become fallible or mutable is for us to claim that God can lie. While some pagan thinkers have dared to utter such blasphemy, the Scripture remains unbroken.

The Future Is "Open" to God's Knowledge and Control

We have demonstrated that the Scriptures clearly teach that God foresees and foreknows the future. But this can be true only if the future is certain and not contingent, for what God infallibly foreknows must infallibly come to pass.

The future is thus "open" to the omniscient and omnipotent mind and will of the Almighty. He can intervene in future history. This is exactly what He did when He planned, decreed, and determined before the foundation of the world that His Son should die for sinners (Revelation 13:8).

With modern day processians, while the universe is "open" to chance and choice, it is "closed" to God! When they made God "open" to the world, they "closed" the world to God!

When it could no longer be pretended that God was ignorant of the future, another old pagan idea resurfaced. What if God decided not to exercise His will? What if He chose not to ordain the future?

This crude trick was invented by the Stoic Epicurus at the beginning of humanistic philosophy. At first, it was claimed that God *chose* not to govern His creation. He simply let it go, like someone who would start a car, put it in gear, and then leap out as the car began to move, leaving it without any driver at the wheel! How this scheme solves the problem of evil has yet to be explained!

The issue boils down to this question: Has God willed, chosen, ordered, ordained, predestined, or foreordained the future of His creation? Or is the universe being jerked in one direction and then another by chance, forward and backward, possibly toward oblivion, like a driverless car which has all its doors and windows locked to shut God out?

God Determines the Future

Does the Bible speak of God's determining future events? Does Scripture speak of God's foreordering, predestining, or decreeing what shall come to pass? What does Scripture say to us on this issue?

1. God orders and directs (Proverbs 16:1, 9; 19:21; 20:24; Jeremiah 10:23; Daniel 5:23). In the above passages, we are told that although we may make all sorts of plans for the future, God is the one who has already determined what will happen. His counsel will stand. Thus man may plan his ways but the Lord will order and direct his steps (Proverbs 16:9). We may have many plans but none of them will overturn God's counsel, for it shall stand (Proverbs 19:21). Our "steps are ordained by the Lord" (Proverbs 20:24). Our ways are in God's hands (Daniel 5:23).

Most Christians understand that "man proposes but God disposes," which is a good paraphrase of Proverbs 16:9. What they must also recognize is that "a man's way is not in himself; nor is it in a man who walks to direct his steps" (Jeremiah 10:23).

Jeremiah says that man does not determine his future "ways" or "steps." This ability is "not in himself." There is no ability "in a man . . . to direct his steps." What man proposes, God will dispose as He sees fit.

The only alternative is to believe as do the heathen that "God proposes but man disposes"! They thus turn Scripture upside down and twist it to their own destruction! Man does not determine *his* future or God's future. He does not dispose of God's plans!

It is clear that heathen philosophies have championed the exact opposite position of what Scripture teaches. Who guides and directs the future steps and ways of man? While the Bible says that God does, the philosophers say man does. The contrast between revealed Truth and the vain babbling of the philosophers could not be stronger.

2. *God appoints and sets up (Daniel 5:17-31; Acts 13:48; Hebrews 9:27; 1 Peter 2:7-8)*. Is anything in the future already determined by the Lord? Does His hand reach into the future or is it too short? Does God have any defect that prevents the Almighty from determining and decreeing the future of the Creation He made? The simplest answer is to observe that all the terms that indicate God determines the future are found throughout the Scriptures.

3. *God determines and decrees*. If we accept the plain statement of Scripture, God does determine and decree that which comes to pass. As Job said, "Since his [man's] days are *determined*, the number of his months is with Thee, and his limits *Thou hast set* so that he *cannot* pass" (Job 14:5, emphasis mine).

The number of our days and months has been "determined" by the Lord and we are immortal until our "time" comes. Thus our death will not be a rude surprise to God. His plans are not frustrated because someone surprised Him by dying (Psalm 116:15).

This was even true of the Lord Jesus. He spoke of His death as being determined by God. He could not die or be murdered before His "time" (Matthew 26:18; John 7:6).

Seventy weeks have been *decreed* for your people and your holy city. . . . So you are to know and discern that from the issuing of a decree to restore and rebuild Jerusalem *until* Messiah the Prince there will be seven weeks and sixty-two weeks . . . Then *after* the sixty-two weeks the *Messiah will be cut off* . . . until a complete destruction, one that is *decreed*, is poured out on the one who makes desolate (Daniel 9:24-27, emphasis mine).

The coming of the Messiah was not a chance happening. It was not a "lucky break" for us that Christ just happened to flip a coin one day and decide to come to earth. According to Daniel, the exact time of the coming of the Messiah has "been decreed" (v. 24).

Daniel was told that he could count the number of years to the coming of the Messiah from the start of the rebuilding of Jerusalem (v. 25). It had already "been determined" when the Messiah would die and what He would accomplish by His death (v. 26). The destruction that would come was "one that is decreed" by God (v. 27).

The passage cannot be interpreted in any other way. Scripture cannot be plainer. This is a prophecy that requires not only the foreknowledge of God but also His foreordination. "That which is decreed shall be done" (Daniel 11:36).

Daniel had to deal with manmade gods and religions in his own day. These finite gods were limited in knowledge and power. Thus their plans for the future were mutable and fallible. But Daniel's God was the Most High Creator and Sovereign Ruler of all things (Daniel 4:25, 32). God's decrees were not mutable or fallible, for "that which is decreed will be done" (Daniel 11:36). No one in heaven or on earth can resist His decrees (Daniel 4:35).

> The Son of Man is going as it has been *determined*; but woe to that man through whom He is betrayed (Luke 22:22, emphasis mine).

If God has "determined" all things, then this would mean that even the evil acts of men, such as Judas's betrayal of Jesus, were determined. Is that what Scripture teaches?

The betrayal of Jesus was indeed a wicked deed. Judas is condemned in Scripture and he will one day stand before the Lord whom he betrayed with a kiss.

Yet, did not the Old Testament predict the betrayal by Judas? Peter thought so. In Acts 1:15-20, Peter points to Psalm 69:25 and Psalm 109:8 as predicting Judas's sin. He states that "the Scripture had to be fulfilled concerning Judas" (v. 16). His fate was foreknown and predicted before Judas was born.

Being both God and man, Christ was omniscient (John 2:24). He knew and predicted that Judas would betray Him "from the beginning" (John 6:64). Lest someone try to avoid this truth, John gives us an infallible interpretation of verse 64 in verse 71.

Luke also tells us that Judas's betrayal of Christ was not only foreknown and predicted by both the Old Testament and Christ, but also had "been determined" (Luke 22:22).

Just because the sin of Judas had been foreknown, foretold, and determined by God did not mean that Judas did not do what he *wanted* to do. God did not force Judas to do anything against his will. Judas was a thief and a liar from the beginning (John 12:6). After stating that his betrayal "had been determined," Jesus adds, "but woe to that man through whom He is betrayed" (Luke 22:22)!

Since Christ clearly stated that the actions of Judas were predetermined and that Judas was responsible at the same time, then we who are His disciples have no other choice than to accept both truths as well. Since He put the two truths together, let us leave them together.

> The *predetermined* plan and foreknowledge of God (Acts 2:23, emphasis mine).

Not only does this passage speak of God's "plan" and "foreknowledge," but it also states that God's plan was "predetermined," i.e., determined *before* the event happened.

In the context Peter is speaking of Christ's death. His death was not only "determined" but predetermined. Yet, at the same time, the men who murdered our Lord are held fully accountable for what they did because they did what they wanted to do. They were not coerced or forced to crucify Christ against their own wills. Divine predestination and human responsibility are seen together.

> And He made from one every nation of mankind to live on all the face of the earth, having *determined* their *appointed* times, and the boundaries of their habitation (Acts 17:26, emphasis mine).

The God of Scripture did not make man and then walk off uninterested in his future. He not only created mankind but also "determined" when and where man would live and die.

It is either one way or the other. No middle ground is possible. Either Paul is right and God "determined" the times and habitations of all men, or Paul is a liar and God did not determine anything. The unity of mankind finds its basis in Creation just as the diversity of mankind finds its basis in God's Providence which determines man's future.

4. *God destines and predestines (Acts 4:28; Romans 8:29-30; 1 Corinthians 2:6-7; Ephesians 1:5, 11; 1 Thessalonians 5:9).* It is amazing to us that anyone should be confused as to whether or not God "determines" and "predestines" the future. The book of Genesis starts with the beginning of history and the book of Revelation tells us about the end of

history. The Bible is thus a book which covers the history of the Creation from beginning to end.

All space-time history is recorded *before* it is finished. The end is treated by the prophets as being just as certain as what has already passed. The Bible has no loose ends or surprise endings. The book of Revelation does not leave the conclusion of human history up to chance, chaos, or the Devil. God is the Alpha and the Omega, the Beginning and the End of history. History is a straight line, which has a beginning and an end ordained by its Creator.

If the Bible did not tell us about the end of history, it would be telling us only half the story. But it reveals all of history from beginning to end as unfolding according to the plan of God. This gives us the courage we need and the hope we enjoy that good will triumph over evil in the end.

God's act of "predestination" is rooted in eternity, for it took place "before the foundation of the world" (Ephesians 1:4).

5. *God ordains and fixes (2 Samuel 17:1-23; Psalm 139:13-16; Acts 17:22-34).* Does God "ordain" the future so that it is "fixed"? Or, is the future a crap game awaiting the "roll of the dice"? This question is not to be solved by how we feel about it or by what we think is reasonable. The Word of God is alone the final authority in all matters of faith and life.

Has God "fixed" history? Is it traveling toward a predetermined climax? Will there be a Day of Judgment? Will the righteous be vindicated and the wicked punished? Will justice be established? Will the resurrection take place?

While even the lowest demons know that the "time" of their torment has already been appointed (Matthew 8:29), some modern philosophers state that God has not appointed the future in any sense. The demons would be greatly relieved if this were true.

6. *God chooses and elects.* The Biblical doctrine of election is summarized in the following ten points.

- We are told that God chooses individuals such as Abraham (Nehemiah 9:7) or Rufus (Romans 16:13). Election is thus personal and individualistic.
- God also chooses groups of people such as *the nation of Israel* (Deuteronomy 7:6) or *the Church* (1 Peter 2:9). Election can thus be *corporal* as well as individualistic.

- People are "elect" because God chooses them (Mark 13:20). God does not elect us because we chose Him.

- The choice of God is not conditioned by anything in us but flows out of God's own will and love (Deuteronomy 7:7-8). It is *unconditional* in that sense. If it were based on something we did, it would not be of grace, argues Paul in Romans 11:5-6.

- While God can "choose" or "elect" someone unto service (John 15:16), there is also an election unto *salvation*. (Acts 13:48; 2 Thessalonians 2:13).

- God's election is based on His *grace* and is not merited by works (Romans 11:5-6).

- God's choice took place *before* the world was created (Ephesians 1:4; 2 Thessalonians 2:13), i.e., "from all eternity" (2 Timothy 1:9).

- Those who are chosen or ordained unto eternal life will *believe* (Acts 13:48).

- The Scripture frequently speaks of "the elect," "His elect," "the chosen ones," or "chosen." (Matthew 24:24, 31; Luke 18:7; Colossians 3:12; 1 Thessalonians 1:4; 2 Timothy 2:10; 1 Peter 1:1; etc.)

- Election has as its *goal* our adoption into God's family (Ephesians 1:4) and our glorification (Romans 8:28-30).

Conclusion

The linguistic and hermeneutical burden of those who teach that God neither knows nor ordains the future is tremendous. All the Biblical terminology is against them. When they open the Bible such words as *order, direct, set up, determine, decree, destine, predestine, predetermine, ordain, fix, choose,* and *elect,* leap off the page and assault them. Such words as *foresee* and *foreknow* terrify them.

If the Biblical authors did not believe in such things as "predestination," why did they speak of them with approval? Are we to believe they used the very words that meant the opposite of what they taught?

Philosophers will have a hard time convincing the average reader of the Bible that the words of Scripture mean the exact opposite of what they mean in everyday life. If *predetermine* does not mean "to determine beforehand," then what does it mean? Whatever it means, it *can't* mean "indeterminate" or "nondeterminate!"

An additional burden is difficult for these philosophers to carry. Not only is the Biblical terminology against them, but also they don't have any passages where God is explicitly said to be ignorant of the future or where the future is said to based on chance.

Where does the Bible use the word *chance* or the phrase *free will* in the philosopher's sense? Nowhere. If such a "free will" were foundational to Biblical thought, why doesn't even *one* passage set it forth as a doctrine?

Modern processians do not even bother to examine Scripture as we have done. Since the Bible is not *authoritative* to them, why should they bother? They pride themselves on not "proof-texting." Indeed, since they have no texts to prove their position, what else can they do?

CONCLUSION

T here is but one eternal triune God, existing in three persons: Father, Son, and Holy Spirit, who is infinite in all His attributes. He is everywhere present in the totality of His immutable person, being, perfection, power, knowledge, sovereignty, and glory. The earth is the Lord's and the fullness thereof, and they who live on it should bow before Him.

God's exalted nature cannot be compared or reduced to the finite gods of the heathen. They are mere idols, the works of men's hands or minds. They are no Gods at all, seeing they are limited in being, power, and knowledge. They are only creatures of space and time and cannot be the Creator of all things.

The Lord Jehovah sits on His throne and laughs at the puny attempts of men to make gods in their own limited and marred image. They are cracked cisterns that carry no water. They are trees without fruit and clouds without rain. Those who are deceived by them are not wise.

Who but the LORD of all the earth, all-knowing and all-powerful, is worthy of our wonder, awe, and praise? Who among the gods is like Him? He knows, He decrees, and He ordains the future destiny of men and angels. He is the master Potter and we are the clay.

Thus we worship and bow down before the Father of eternity. We lie prostrate in the dust before the God of the Prophets, Apostles, and the Fathers. We submit the eternal welfare of our immortal souls to Him who is the sovereign King of kings and Lord of lords. He alone is our God and the only God we will ever worship. To Him alone be all the glory!

END NOTES

CHAPTER 1: THE GATHERING STORM

1. Duane Magnani, *The Heavenly Weatherman: A Look at a god Who Doesn't Know All Things—The God of The Jehovah's Witnesses* (Clayton, Calif: Witness, Inc., 1987).
2. Harold Lindsell, *The Battle For The Bible* (Grand Rapids, Mich.: Zondervan, 1976).
3. David R. Griffin, *A Process Christology* (Philadelphia: Westminster, 1973), p. 143.
4. The ethical problem of such thinkers who now openly admit what they have been secretly teaching is hinted at by Clark Pinnock in David Basinger and Randall Basinger, ed., *Predestination and Free Will* (Downers Grove, Ill.: Inter Varsity, 1986), p. 157, n. 28. We cannot help wondering how many covert processians are now teaching in evangelical institutions. We agree with Pinnock that they should become "courageous" and openly identify themselves. To remain in institutions that have orthodox doctrinal standards and to teach against those standards is sheer hypocrisy.
5. Clark, Pinnock, "God Limits His Knowledge," in *Predestination Free Will*, ed. by Daivd Basinger and Randall Basinger,(Downers Grove, Ill: Inter Varsity Press, 1986), p. 151.
6. Pinnock states, "I agree with David Griffin's position" (ibid., p. 151, n. 13). "I am in complete agreement with Alex Steuer" (p. 153, n. 18). "I agree with Nelson Pike" (p. 157, n. 27). In addition to his essay in ibid., see Clark Pinnock, "The Need for a Scriptural and Therefore a NeoClassical Theism," in *Perspectives On Evangelical Theology* (Grand Rapids, Mich.: Baker, 1979), pp. 37-42; idem, *A Case For Faith* (Minneapolis: Bethany House, 1988); idem, "Between Classical and Process Theology", in Ronald Nash, ed., *Process Theology* (Grand Rapids, Mich.: Baker, 1987), pp. 313-27.
7. Michael Peterson, "Orthodox Christianity, Wesleyanism, and Process Theology," *Wesleyan Theological Journal*, 15 (Fall, 1980): 47-49.
8. Stephen Davis, *Logic and the Nature of God* (Grand Rapids, Mich.: Eerdmans, 1983).
9. *The Writings of James Arminius*, 3 vols. (Grand Rapids, Mich.: Baker Book House, 1956) III:477-84.
10. For documentation, see the Chapters 22 and 25 below.
11. For detailed documentation of YWAM's involvement with "moral government" teaching, see Alan W. Gomes, *Lead Us Not Into Deception* (La Mirada, Calif.: Telion).

12. Howard R. Elseth, *Did God Know? A Study of the Nature of God* (St. Paul, Minn.: Calvary United Church, 1977).

13. Gordon C. Olson, *The Truth Shall Make You Free* (Franklin Park, Ill.: Bible Research Fellowship, 1980); and idem, "The Foreknowledge of God," unpublished paper, 1941.

14. Richard Rice, *God's Foreknowledge and Man's Free Will* (Minneapolis, Minn.: Bethany House, 1985).

15. Gomes, Alan, ibid., p. 112.

16. Pinnock in *Predestination and Free Will*, p. 157, n. 28.

17. Gomes give an excellent chart in Chapter 5 that gathers documentation from the papers, tapes, books, and training manuals of Elseth, Olson, etc. We have also relied on the documentation set forth by Walter Martin, the Passantinos, and our own contacts within YWAM.

18. Dave Hunt and T. S. McMahon, *The Seduction of Christianity*, (Eugene, Ore.: Harvest House, 1987), p. 83. See also, Constance Gumbey, *The Hidden Dangers of the Rainbow* (Shreveport, La.: Huntingdon House, 1983), pp. 141ff.

CHAPTER 3: THE GODS OF THE PEOPLE

1. Gene Wolfe, *Soldier of the Mist* (New York: TOR Books, 1986).

2. For an example of Mariolatry see: James Alberione, *Glories and Virtues of Mary* (Boston: The Daughters of St. Paul, 1982).

3. Robert A. Morey, *How to Answer a Mormon* (Minneapolis, Minn.: Bethany House, 1983).

4. Dave Hunt and T. McMahon, *The Seduction Of Christianity* (Eugene, Ore.: Harvest House, 1985).

CHAPTER 4: THE GODS OF THE PHILOSOPHERS

1. Eduard Zeller, *Outlines Of Greek Philosophy* (New York: Meridian Books, 1967), pp. 18-19.

2. Ibid., p. 20.

3. Ibid.

4. Ibid.

CHAPTER 5: THE ORIGIN OF THE FINITE GOD

1. Donald A. Carson, *Divine Sovereignty and Human Responsibility* (Atlanta: John Knox Press, 1981), p. 99.

2. Ibid., p. 102.

3. Ibid., p. 100.

4. Kenneth Scott Latourette, *A History of Christianity* (New York: Harper & Row, 1953), p. 793.

5. Ibid., p. 795.

6. Ibid.

7. *The New Schaff-Herzog Encyclopedia of Religious Knowledge* (New York: Funk & Wagnalls Co., 1911), 10:491.

8. Ibid.

9. *Moral Discourses of Epictetus*, ed. by Thomas Gould (New York: Washington Square Press, 1964), p. 7.

10. Ibid., p. 233.

11. Ibid.

12. John McClintock and James Strong, eds., *Cyclopedia of Biblical, Theological, and Ecclesiastical Literature* (Grand Rapids, Mich.: Baker Book House, [1867-87] 1981), 9:844.
13. John Owen, *Vindiciae Evangelicae; or the Mystery of the Gospel Vindicated and Socinianism Examined,* in Owen, *Works,* 16 vols. (London: Banner of Truth Trust, [1850] 1966) 12:85.
14. Ibid., p. 86. Emphasis added.

CHAPTER 6: THE FINITE GOD OF SECULAR PHILOSOPHY

1. Robert A. Morey, *The New Atheism and the Erosion of Freedom* (Minneapolis, Minn.: Bethany House, 1986), p. 78.
2. Edwin A. Burtt, ed., *The English Philosophers from Bacon To Mill* (New York: Modern Library, n.d.), p. 741.
3. Ibid., pp. 744-45.
4. Ibid., p. 752.
5. John Stuart Mill, *Three Essays On Religion* (New York: Greenword Press, 1969), pp. 130-31.
6. Ibid., pp. 182-83.
7. William James, *The Will To Believe* (New York: Dowen Pub., Inc., n.d.), p. 180.
8. Ibid.
9. Ibid., p. 181.
10. Ibid., p. 181, n. 1.
11. William James, *Essays in Radical Empiricism and a Pluralistic Universe* (Gloucester, Mass.: Peter Smith, 1967), pp. 28-29.
12. Ibid., pp. 29-30.
13. Ibid., p. 30.
14. Ibid., p. 111.
15. Ibid., p. 311.
16. Ibid., pp. 310-11.
17. Ibid., p. 318.
18. Ibid., p. 305.
19. Ibid.
20. John Fiske, *The Idea of God as Affected by Modern Knowledge* (New York: Houghton, Mifflin and Co., 1886), p. xx.
21. Henri Bergson, *Creative Evolution* (New York: Modern Library, 1944), p. 230.
22. Ibid., p. 239.
23. Robert S. Ehrlich, *20th Century Philosophers* (New York: Monarch Modern Library, 1944), p. 230.
24. Samuel Alexander, *Space-time and Deity* (London: Macmillan and Co., 1927), 2:364.
25. Ibid., pp. 364-65.
26. Ibid., p. 365.
27. Andrew Seth Pringle-Pattison, *The Idea of God in the Light of Recent Philosophy* (London: The Clarendon Press, 1917), p. 407.
28. Ibid.,p. 299ff.
29. Ibid., p. 385.
30. Francis H. Bradley, *Collected Essays* (New York: Books For Libraries Press, 1968), 2:472.
31. Edgar Sheffield Brightman, *The Problem of God* (New York: Abingdon Press, 1930), pp. 100ff.
32. Ibid., p. 124. See also pp. 113, 125.

33. As quoted in Cornelius Van Til, "Boston Personalism" (Chestnut Hill, Pa.: Westminster Theological Seminary, 1956), pp. 26-27.
34. Ibid., p. 41.
35. Ibid.
36. Ibid., p. 42.
37. Edgar Sheffield Brightman, A Philosophy of Religion (New York: Prentice Hall, 1940), p. 191.
38. Ibid., p. 307.
39. Ibid., p. 314.
40. Ibid., p. 321.
41. Ibid., p. 318.
42. Ibid.
43. Ibid., pp. 318-19.
44. Ibid., p. 309.
45. Ibid., p. 286.
46. Ibid., p. 327.
47. Ibid., p. 289.
48. Ibid., p. 288.
49. Ibid., p. 287.
50. Ibid., pp. 290-91.
51. Ibid., p. 291.
52. Ibid., pp. 299, 301.
53. Ibid., p. 314.
54. Ibid., p. 327.
55. Ibid., p. 340.
56. H. G. Wells, God: the Invisible King (New York: Macmillan Co., 1917), p. ix.
57. Ibid., p. xi.
58. Ibid., pp. xviii-xix.
59. Ibid., p. 5.
60. Ibid., pp. 6-7.
61. Ibid., p. 13.
62. Ibid., p. 14.
63. Ibid., p. 15.
64. Ibid., pp. 18-19.
65. Ibid., p. 61.
66. Ibid., pp. 157ff.
67. Alfred North Whitehead, Dialogues of Alfred North Whitehead (Boston: Little, Brown, & Co., 1954), p. 30.
68. Ibid., pp. 182-83.
69. Ibid., p. 60.
70. Ibid., p. 175.
71. Ibid., p. 189.
72. Ibid., p. 277.
73. Ibid., p. 174.
74. Ibid., pp. 59-60.
75. Ibid., p. 61.
76. Ibid., pp. 198-99.
77. Ibid., p. 92.
78. Ibid., pp. 370-71.
79. Alfred North Whitehead, Process and Reality (New York: Macmillan Pub. Co., 1978), p. 95.
80. Ibid.

81. Ibid., pp. 344-55.
82. Ibid., pp. 348-49.

CHAPTER 7: THE FINITE GOD OF EVANGELICAL PROCESSIANISM

1. Anthony Kenny, *The God Of The Philosophers* (Oxford: Clarendon Press, 1979), p. 121.
2. Ibid.
3. Ibid.
4. Ibid.
5. Robert A. Morey, *The New Atheism and the Erosion of Freedom* (Minneapolis, Minn.: Bethany House, 1986), pp. 152-6.
6. Kenny, p. 51.
7. Ibid.
7. Ibid.
9. Axel D. Steuer and James W. McClenden, Jr., ed., *Is God GOD?* (Nashville: Abingdon, 1981), p. 94.
10. Ibid., p. 99.
11. Ibid., p. 104.
12. Ibid., p. 103.
13. Ibid., p. 104.
14. Ibid., p. 99.
15. Ibid., p. 99.
16. Ibid., p. 101.
17. Ibid., p. 101.
18. Ibid.
19. Carsten Johnsen, *Day of Destiny: The Mystery of the Seventh Day*, (Loma Linda, Calif.: The Untold Story Publishers, 1982), pp. 130-53.
20. Richard Rice, *The Openness of God* (Nashville: Review and Herald, 1979), p. 17.
21. Ibid., p. 28.
22. Ibid., p. 37.
23. Ibid., pp. 8-9.
24. Ibid., p. 8.
25. Ibid.
26. Ibid., p. 28.
27. Ibid.
28. Ibid.
29. Ibid., pp. 15-16.
30. Ibid., p. 28.
31. Ibid.
32. Ibid., pp. 8ff.
33. Ibid., p. 29.
34. Ibid., pp. 36-37.
35. Ibid.
36. Richard Rice, *God's Foreknowledge and Man's Free Will* (Minneapolis, Minn.: Bethany House, 1985).
37. Stephen T. Davis, *Logic and The Nature of God* (Grand Rapids, Mich.: Eerdmans, 1983), pp. 15-16. The first edition was published by Macmillan.
38. Ibid., p. 76.
39. Ibid., p. 19.

40. Ibid., p. 16.
41. Ibid., p. 25.
42. Stephen T. Davis, *The Debate About the Bible: Inerrancy Versus Infallibility* (Philadelphia: Westminster Press, 1977).
43. Davis, *Logic and the Nature of God*, p. 2.
44. Ibid.
45. Ibid.
46. Ibid., p. 24.
47. Ibid.
48. Ibid., p. 76.
49. Ibid., p. 86.
50. Ibid., pp. 93-94.
51. Ibid., p. 96.
52. Ibid.
53. Ibid., p. 88.
54. Rex A. Koivisto, "Clark Pinnock and Inerrancy: A Change in Truth Theory?" *Journal of the Evangelical Theological Society* 24(1981):151.
55. Henry W. Holloman, Review of *The Scripture Principle*, by Clark H. Pinnock *Journal of the Evangelical Theological Society* 29(1986):95.
56. Ibid., Citation from Pinnock, *The Scripture Principle* (San Franscisco: Harper, 1984), p. 77.
57. Ibid., pp. 96-97.
58. Clark H. Pinnock, *A Case for Faith* (Minneapolis, Minn.: Bethany House, 1988), pp. 109-10.
59. Ibid., p. 110.
60. See Pinnock's comments on the book cover of William Fudge, *The Fire That Consumes*, (Verdict Pub., 1982). Fudge rejects the biblical view of a conscious afterlife and eternal punishment and favors a concept of soul-sleep and annihilationism that is held by Jehovah's Witnesses and the Adventists. A full refutation of his views can be found in Robert A. Morey, *Death and The Afterlife*, (Minneapolis, Minn.: Bethany House, 1984).
61. David Basinger and Randall Basinger eds., *Predestination and Free Will* (Downers Grove, Ill.: Inter Varsity Press), p. 150.
62. Ibid., p. 149.
63. Ibid., p. 143.
64. Ibid., p. 144.
65. Ibid.
66. Ibid., p. 96.
67. Ibid., p. 97.
68. Ibid., pp. 97-98.
69. Ibid., p. 138.
70. Ibid., p. 150.
71. Ibid., p. 151.
72. Ibid., p. 157.
73. Ibid., p. 147.
74. J. Gresham Machen, *Christianity and Liberalism* (Grand Rapids, Mich.: Eerdmans, 1974), pp. 141ff.

CHAPTER 8: RELIGION, REASON, AND REVELATION

1. See B.B. Warfield, "On the Emotional Life of Our Lord," in Warfield, *The Person and Work of Christ* (Philadelphia: Presbyterian and Reformed, 1950), pp. 93-145.

CHAPTER 12: THE INCOMPREHENSIBILITY OF GOD

1. Stephen Davis, *Logic And The Nature Of God* (Grand Rapids, Mich.: Eerdmans, 1983), p. 19.
2. Ibid.
3. Ibid., p. 4.
4. Ibid., p. 16.

CHAPTER 16: INVISIBLE AND INCORPOREAL

1. David Basinger and Randall Basinger, eds., *Predestination and Free Will* (Downers Grove, Ill.: Inter Varsity Press, 1986), pp. 154-55.

CHAPTER 17: PERSONAL AND INFINITE

1. H. H. Leupold, *Exposition of the Psalms* (Grand Rapids, Mich.: Baker Book House, [1959] 1969), pp. 989-90.
2. Franz Delitzsch, *Biblical Commentary on the Psalms*, 3 vols., trans. Francis Bolton (Grand Rapids, Mich.: Eerdmans, n.d.) 3:400.
3. Carl Bernhard Moll, *The Psalms*, trans. with additions J. Fred. McCurdy; in John Peter Lange, ed., *Commentary on the Holy Scriptures*, Eng. ed. Philip Schaff, 24 vols. bound in 12 (Grand Rapids, Mich.: Zondervan [1872] 1976), vol. 9 (bound in vol. 5), pp. 671f.

CHAPTER 18: THE PERFECTION OF GOD

1. Franz Delitzsch, *Biblical Commentary on the Book of Job*, 2 vols., trans. Francis Bolton (Grand Rapids, Mich.: Eerdmans, n.d.) 2:301.

CHAPTER 19: THE ETERNITY OF GOD

1. Stephen T. Davis, *Logic and the Nature of God* (Grand Rapids, Mich.: Eerdmans, 1983), p. 11.
2. Ibid., p. 16.
3. Ibid., p. 11.
4. Ibid., p. 23.
5. Ibid., p. 22.
6. Ibid., p. 23.
7. Ibid., p. 24.

CHAPTER 20: THE IMMUTABILITY OF GOD

1. In David Basinger and Randall Basinger, ed., *Predestination and Free Will* (Downers Grove, Ill.: Inter Varsity Press, 1986), p. 155.
2. Ibid., p. 96.
3. Ibid., p. 154.

4. C. F. Keil and F. Delitzsch, *Biblical Commentary on the Pentateuch*, 3 vols., trans. James Martin (Grand Rapids, Mich.: Eerdmans, rep. 1968) 3:467.

5. Clark Pinnock, *Perspectives in Evangelical Theology* (n.p., n.d.), p. 40.

6. Charles H. Spurgeon, *The Treasury Of David*, 7 vols. (various editions), vol. 4 (1884), p. 426.

7. Cited in Ibid., p. 272.

8. Carl Bernhard Moll, *The Psalms*, trans. with additions J. Fred. McCurdy; in John Peter Lange, ed., *Commentary on the Holy Scriptures*, Eng. ed. Philip Schaff, 24 vols. bound in 12 (Grand Rapids, Mich.: Zondervan [1872] 1976), vol. 9 (bound in vol. 5), pp. 521f.

9. Joseph Addison Alexander, *The Psalms, Translated and Explained* (Grand Rapids, Mich.: Baker Book House, [1873] 1975), p. 413.

10. Franz Delitzsch, *Biblical Commentary On The Psalms*, 22 ed., trans. Franu's Bolton, 3 vols. (Grand Rapids, Mich.: Eerdmans, rep. 1968) 3:117.

11. Matthew Henry, *Commentary On The Whole Bible* (various editions [1710]), comments on Psalm 102:23-28.

12. Ibid., comments on Malachi 3:1-6.

13. Albert Barnes, *Notes On the Old Testament* (Grand Rapids, Mich.: Baker Book House, rep. 1960), vol. 16, p. 490.

14. C. F. Keil, *Biblical Commentary on the Twelve Minor Prophets*, trans. James Martin, 2 vols. (Grand Rapids, Mich.: Eerdmans, rep. 1969) 2:462.

15. Thomas Moore, *Haggai And Malachi*, (London: Banner Of Truth, [1856] 1960), p. 157.

16. Joseph Mayor, *The Epistle Of James* (Grand Rapids, Mich.: Zondervan [1892]) p. 61.

CHAPTER 21: THE OMNIPRESENCE OF GOD

1. David Basinger and Randall Basinger, eds., *Predestination and Free Will* (Downers Grove, Ill.: Inter Varsity Press, 1986), p. 152.

CHAPTER 22: THE OMNISCIENCE OF GOD

1. *The Works Of Jonathan Edwards*, 2 vols. (Edinburgh: The Banner of Truth Trust, 1974), 1:30.

2. *The Complete Works of Augustus Toplady* (Harrisonburg, Va.: Sprinkle Pub., 1988), p. 756.

3. Gotthard V. Lechler, *The Acts of the Apostles*, trans. with additions Charles F. Schaeffer; in John Peter Lange, ed., *Commentary on the Holy Scriptures*, Eng. ed. Peter Schaff, 24 vols. bound in 12 (Grand Rapids, Mich.: Zondervan [1866] 1976), vol. 18 (bound in vol. 9), pp. 280-81.

4. J. A. Alexander, *Commentary on the Acts of the Apostles* (Grand Rapids, Mich.: Zondervan, 1956), pp. 545-46.

5. R. C. H. Lenski, *The Acts of the Apostles* (Minneapolis, Minn.: Augsburg Pub. House, [1934] 1961), pp. 611-12.

6. Heinrich A. W. Meyer, *Critical and Exegetical Handbook to the Acts of the Apostles*, 4th. ed., trans. Paton J. Gloag, rev. William P. Dickson. *Meyer's Commentary on the New Testament 4.* (Winona Lake, Ind.: Alpha Publications [1884] 1979), p. 288.

CHAPTER 24: THE TESTIMONY OF THE CHURCH FATHERS

1. J. B. Lightfoot, trans. and ed., *The Apostolic Fathers: Clement, Ignatius, and Polycarp*, 2 parts in 5 vols. (Grand Rapids, Mich.: Baker Book House, [1889] 1981), part 1, vol. 2, p. 170.
2. Ibid., part 2, vol. 2, p. 572.
3. Ibid, p. 343.
4. Ibid., part 2, vol. 3, p. 87.
5. Ibid., part 2, vol. 1, p. 181.
6. The Patristic references to Greek philosophy are as follows: ANF 1: 28, 196-98, 272, 273-78, 331, 399, 401, 415; ANF 2: 75-76, 95-97, 111, 132; ANF 4: 50, 51, 130, 246, 272, 309.

CHAPTER 25: THE TESTIMONY OF THE CREEDS OF THE CHURCH

1. Philip Schaff, *The Creeds of Christendom*, 6th ed., 3 vols. (Grand Rapids, Mich.: Baker Book House, [1931] 1983) 1:21; 2:52, Emphasis mine.
2. Ibid., 1:27, Emphasis mine.
3. Ibid., 1:27-28. Emphasis mine.
4. Ibid., 2:62. Emphasis mine.
5. Ibid., 2:66-70. Emphasis mine.
6. Ibid., p. 71.

CHAPTER 26: THE TESTIMONY OF EVANGELICAL THEOLOGY

1. Timothy Dwight, *Theology Explained and Defended* (New York: Harper & Brothers, 1849), vol. 1, pp. 136-39.
2. Charles W. Hodge, "Dr. Tennant on the Divine Omnipotence and the Conception of a Finite God," *Princeton Theological Review* 18 (1920):337-42.
3. William Hallock Johnson, "Is God Almighty?," *Princeton Theological Review* 20 (1922):562-83, and idem, *Princeton Theological Review* 21 (1923):521-40.
4. Clarence Bouma, "Finitistic and Pragmatic Theology," *Princeton Theological Review* 22 (1924):447-64.
5. David S. Clark, "Theology and Evolution," *Princeton Theological Review* 23 (1925):193-212.
6. Carl F. H. Henry, ed.,*Christian Faith and Modern Theology* (New York: Channel Press, 1964), pp. 67ff.
7. Carl F. H. Henry, *God, Revelation, and Authority* (Waco, Tex.: Word, 1982) vol. 5.
8. Gordon H. Clark, *Religion, Reason, and Revelation* (Nutley, N.J.: The Craig Press, 1961), pp. 198-99.
9. Royce Gordon Gruenler, *The Inexhaustible God* (Grand Rapids, Mich.: Baker Book House, 1983)x.
10. Ibid., p. 15.
11. Ibid., p. 7.
12. Ibid., p. 31.
13. Ibid., p. 105.
14. Ibid., pp. 38-44.
15. Ronald Nash, *The Concept of God* (Grand Rapids, Mich.: Zondervan, 1983), p. 24.
16. Ibid., p. 31.

17. Ibid., p. 31-32.
18. Ibid., p. 31.
19. Ibid., p. 36.

CHAPTER 27: THE TESTIMONY OF SCRIPTURE

1. H. Roy Elseth, *Did God Know? A Study of the Nature of God* (St. Paul, Minn.: Calvary United Church, 1977), p. 109.

SELECT BIBLIOGRAPHY

Achtemeir, Elizabeth. *The Feminine Crisis in the Christian Faith.* New York: Abingdon Press, 1965.

Adler, Mortimer J. *How to Think About God.* New York: Macmillan Pub. Co., 1980.

Alexander, Samuel. *Space, Time, and Deity.* London: Macmillan and Co., 1927.

Archer, Gleason L. *Encyclopedia Of Bible Difficulties.* Grand Rapids, Mich.: Zondervan Pub., 1982.

Archer, William. *God and Mr. Wells.* New York: Alfred A. Knopf, 1917.

Baker's Dictionary of Theology. Edited by Everett F. Harrison. Grand Rapids, Mich.: Baker Book House, 1960.

Baker, Rannie Belle. *The Concept of a Limited God.* Washington, D.C.: Shenandoah Pub. House, 1934.

Basinger, David, and Randall Basinger, eds. *Predestination and Freewill.* Downers Grove, Ill.: Inter Varsity Press, 1986.

Bavinck, Herman. *The Doctrine of God.* Edinburgh: Banner of Truth Trust, 1977.

Berkhof, Louis. *Systematic Theology.* London: Banner of Truth Trust, 1966.

Beunke, Donna A. *Religious Issues in Nineteenth-century Feminism.* Troy, N.Y.: The Whitston Pub. Co., 1982.

Bloesch, Donald G. *Is The Bible Sexist?* Westchester, Ill.: Crossway Books, 1982.

Binns, Leonard Elliott. *Mr. Wells's Invisible King.* London: S.P.C.K., 1919.

Boyce, James. *Abstract of Systematic Theology.* Christian Gospel Foundation, n.d.

Bradley, Francis Herbert. *Collected Essays.* New York: Books For Libraries Press, 1968.

Brightman, Edgar Sheffield. *A Philosophy of Religion.* New York: Prentice Hall, Inc., 1940.

_____. *The Problem of God.* Nashville: Abingdon Press, 1930.

_____. *Creative Evolution.* New York: The Modern Library, 1944.

Bergson, Henri. *The Two Sources of Morality and Religion.* New York: Doubleday & Co., 1954.

Bulfinch, Thomas. *Myths of Greece and Rome.* New York: Penguin Books, 1981.

Carmody, Denise Lardner. *Feminism and Christianity.* Nashville: Abingdon Press, 1982.

Carson, Donald A. *Divine Sovereignty and Human Responsibility.* Atlanta: John Knox Press, 1981.

Charnock, Stephen. *The Existence and Attributes of God.* Sovereign Grace Book Club, 1958.

Clark, Gordon H. *John Dewey.* Philadelphia: Presbyterian & Reformed Pub. Co., 1960.

_____. *Religion, Reason, and Revelation.* Nutley, N.J.: The Craig Press.

_____. *William James.* Philadelphia: Presbyterian & Reformed Pub. Co., 1963.

Copleston, Frederick. *Contemporary Philosophy.* Westminster, Md.: The Newman Press, 1966.

Cranford, Alexander H. *The Religion of H. G. Wells and Other Essays*. London: T. Fisher Unwin, 1909.

Cunningham, William. *Historical Theology*. London: Banner of Truth Trust, 1969.

Dabney, Robert L. *Lectures in Systematic Theology*. Grand Rapids, Mich.: Zondervan Pub., 1972.

Dagg, J. L. *Manual of Theology and Church Order*. Harrisonburg, Va.: Gano Books, 1982.

Danby, Herbert, ed. *The Mishnah*. Oxford: Oxford University Press, 1983.

Davis, Stephen T. *Logic and the Nature of God*. Grand Rapids, Mich.: Eerdmans, 1983.

Edwards, Jonathan. *The Works of Jonathan Edwards*. Edinburgh: Banner of Truth Trust, 1974.

Elseth, H. Roy. *Did God Know?* St. Paul, Minn.: Calvary United Church, 1977.

Epictetus. *Moral Discourses*. Thomas Gould, ed. New York: Washington Square Press, 1964.

Farrer, Austin. *Finite and Infinite*. London: Dacye Press, 1943.

Fiske, John. *The Idea of God as Affected by Modern Knowledge*. New York: Houghton, Mifflin, and Co., 1886.

Freeman, David H. *Tillich*. Philadelphia: Presbyterian & Reformed Pub. Co., 1962.

Gomes, Alan. *Lead Us Not Into Temptation*. La Mirada, Calif.: Telion, 1986.

Grant, Robert M. *The Early Christian Doctrine of God*. Charlottesville, Va.: University of Virginia Press, 1966.

Griffin, David Ray. *God, Power, and Evil: A Process Theodicy*. Philadelphia: Westminster Press, 1976.

Gruenler, Royce Gordon. *The Inexhaustible God: Biblical Faith and the Challenge of Process Theism*. Grand Rapids, Mich.: Baker Book House, 1983.

Gumbey, Constance, *The Hidden Dangers of the Rainbow*. Shreveport, La.: Huntingdon House, 1983.

Gunton, Colin E. *Becoming and Being*. Oxford: Oxford University Press, 1978.

Hack, Roy Kenneth. *God in Greek Philososphy to the Time of Socrates*. Princeton, N.J.: Princeton University Press, 1966.

Hartshorne, Charles, and William L. Reese. *Philosophers Speak of God*. Chicago: University of Chicago Press, 1953.

Henry, Carl F. H. *Christian Faith and Modern Theology*. New York: Channel Press, 1964.

——————————, *God, Revelation, and Authority*. Waco: Word, Inc., 1976.

Hodge, Charles. Systematic Theology. London: James Clarke & Co., 1960.

Harsberger, Caroline Thomas. *Gods and Heroes: A Quick Guide to the Occupations, Associations, and Experiences of the Greek and Roman Gods and Heroes*. Troy, N.Y.: The Whitson Pub. Co., 1977.

Jaeger, William. *The Theology of the Early Greek Philosophers*. Oxford: Oxford University Press, 1947.

James, William. *The Will to Believe*. New York: Dover Pub., n.d.

——————————. *Essays in Radical Empiricism and a Pluralistic Universe*. Gloucester, Mass.: Peter Smith, 1967.

Johnson, Carlsten. *Day of Destiny*. Loma Linda, Calif.: The Untold Story Pub., 1982.

Kenny, Anthony. *The God of the Philosophers*. Oxford: Clarendon Press, 1979.

Latourette, Kenneth Scott. *A History of Christianity*. New York: Harper & Row, 1953.

Lightfoot, J. B. *The Apostolic Fathers*. Grand Rapids, Mich.: Baker Book House, 1981.

Machen, J. Gresham. *Christianity and Liberalism*. Grand Rapids, Mich.: Eerdmans, 1974.

Marsh, John. *The Fulness of Time*. London: Nisbet & Co., 1952.

Mill, John Stuart. *Three Essays on Religion*. New York: Greenwood Press, Pub., 1969.

Murray, John Courtney. *The Problem of God*. New Haven, Conn.: Yale University Press, 1964.

Nash, Ronald H. *The Concept of God*. Grand Rapids, Mich.: Zondervan Pub., 1983.

Ogletree, Thomas W. *The Death of God Controversy*. Nashville: Abingdon Press, 1966.

Olson, Carl, ed. *The Book of the Goddess Past and Present*. New York: Crossroads, 1983.

Olson, Gordon C. *Sharing Your Faith*. Chicago: Bible Research Fellowship, 1976.

On Process Theology. Grand Rapids, Mich.: Baker Book House, 1988.

Owen, John. *The Works of John Owen*. London: Banner of Truth Trust, 1966.

Pike, Nelson. *God and Timelessness*. New York: Schocken Books, 1970.

Pink, Arthur W. *The Attributes of God*. Grand Rapids, Mich.: Baker Book House, n.d.

Prestige, G. L. *God in Patristic Thought*. London: S.P.C.K., 1959.

Pringle-Pattison, A. Seth. *The Idea of God in the Light of Present Philosophy*. London: Clarendon Press, 1917.

Rice, Richard. *The Openness of God*. Nashville: Review & Herald Pub., 1979.

_____. *God's Foreknowledge and Man's Free Will*. Minneapolis, Minn.: Bethany House, 1985.

Schaeffer, Francis. *How Should We Then Live?* Old Tappan, N.J.: Fleming Revell Co., 1976.

Schaff, Philip. *The Creeds of Christendom*. Grand Rapids, Mich.: Baker Book House, 1983.

Sproul, R. C. *Chosen By God*. Wheaton, Ill.: Tyndale House Pub., 1986.

Steuer, Axel D., and McClendon, James William, Jr., eds. *Is God GOD?* Nashville: Abingdon Press, 1981.

Storms, C. Samuel. *The Grandeur of God*. Grand Rapids, Mich.: Baker Book House, 1984.

Strong, Augustus H. *Systematic Theology*. Valley Forge, Pa.: Judson Press, 1976.

Swinburne, Richard. *The Existence of God*. Oxford: Clarendon Press, 1979.

The History of the Christian Church. Grand Rapids, Mich.: Wm. B. Eerdmans, 1972.

The Truth Shall Make You Free. Chicago: Bible Research Fellowship, 1980.

Thomas, J. M. Lloyd. *The Veiled Being: A Comment on Mr. H. G. Wells' "God the Invisible King"*. Birmingham: Cornish Brothers, Ltd., 1917.

Wells, H. G. God The Invisible King. New York: Macmillan & Co., 1917.

Whitehead, Alfred North. *Dialogues of Alfred North Whitehead*. Boston: Little, Brown, & Co., 1954.

_____. *Process and Reality*. New York: Macmillan Pub., 1978.

Wolfson, Harry Austryn. *The Philosophy of the Church Fathers*. Cambridge, Mass.: Harvard University Press, 1904.

Zeller, Eduard. *Outlines of the History of Greek Philosophy*. New York: Meridian Books, 1967.

Order these informative and challenging books by Dr. Robert A. Morey

Christian Apologetics

The New Atheism and the Erosion of Freedom $6.95

A solid refutation of all the arguments used by atheists, sceptics and free thinkers against the existence of God, the inspiration of the Bible and the historicity of Jesus Christ.

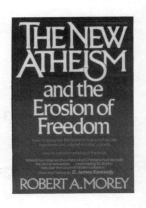

The Christian Handbook for Defending the Faith $2.95

A survey of the Christian world view and how it applies to history, art, ethics, psychology and marriage.

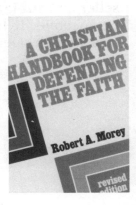

Battle of the Gods $9.95

A comprehensive and unassailable statement of the changelessness, wisdom and sovereignty of God. A definitive rebuttal of the "god as finite" view.

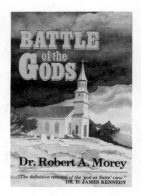

The Cults and Occult

Horoscopes and the Christian
$2.95

The number one worldwide best seller on astrology from a Christian perspective. It has been translated into French, German and Italian.

Reincarnation and Christianity $2.95

The classic refutation of the arguments used by reincarnationists. The first Christian book ever written against reincarnation.

How to Answer a Mormon $4.95

A practical step-by-step method for answering Mormons. It contains the documents from Mormon sources which prove that Joseph Smith was a false prophet and the Book of Mormon is a fraud.

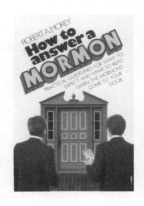

The Cults and Occult (continued)

How to Answer a Jehovah's Witness
$4.95

A practical step-by-step method for answering Jehovah's Witnesses. It proves that the Watchtower Society is a false prophet.

Hell, Death and the Grave

Death and the After Life
$12.95

The most significant work on the subject of death in a century. It defends the Christian position that man has an immortal soul. It documents from Scripture and Rabbinic literature that Jesus and the apostles believed in the eternal conscious torment of the wicked. It contains the most detailed refutation ever written of universalism, annihilationism, conditionalism, soul-sleep and the occults.

Christian View of War

When Is It Right to Fight?
$6.95

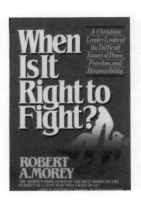

The most thorough refutation ever written of pacifism. It upholds the Christian's right to defend himself, his family and his country.

The Christian Life

Worship Is All of Life $5.95

The only book of its kind. It explores private worship, family worship and public worship. It views all of life as worship.

Write to:

CROWN PUBLICATIONS, INC.
P.O. Box 688
Southbridge, MA 01550
508-248-3994

See next page for order form.